Through it all, Love

A stem cell transplant journey

By Dan Hartman

Through it all, Love Copyright © 2016 by Dan Hartman.

All rights reserved. Printed in the United States of America. No part of this book may be used or reproduced in any manner whatsoever without written permission except in the case of brief quotations em- bodied in critical articles or reviews.

For information contact; dan.hartman@att.net

Front cover design by Motomi Naito. Cover photos by Sachiko Eubanks

First Edition: 2/2016

10 9 8 7 6 5 4 3 2 1

For Laury,

I have loved you since I first saw you and I will love you until my eyes close in final sleep.

Contents

- INTRODUCTION 3
- SECTION 1 – PRE-TRANSPLANT 5
- CHAPTER ONE 7
  - MARCH 7
- CHAPTER TWO 26
  - APRIL 26
- CHAPTER THREE 52
  - MAY 52
- CHAPTER FOUR 82
  - JUNE 82
- SECTION 2 – THE TRANSPLANT 86
- CHAPTER FIVE 87
  - IN THE HOSPITAL 87
- SECTION 3 – HOME HEALING 122
- CHAPTER SIX 123
  - JULY 123
- CHAPTER SEVEN 156
  - AUGUST 156
- CHAPTER EIGHT 189
  - SEPTEMBER 189
- CHAPTER NINE 219
  - OCTOBER 219
- CHAPTER TEN 245
  - NOVEMBER 245
- CHAPTER ELEVEN 270

| DECEMBER | 270 |

CHAPTER TWELVE **291**
    JANUARY 291

CHAPTER THIRTEEN **315**
    FEBRUARY 315

CHAPTER FOURTEEN **333**
    MARCH 333

CHAPTER FIFTEEN **355**
    APRIL 355

CHAPTER SIXTEEN **372**
    MAY 372

CHAPTER SEVENTEEN **386**
    JUNE 386

CHAPTER EIGHTEEN **398**
    THE FINAL POST 398

EPILOGUE **400**

ABOUT THE AUTHOR **402**

The Practice of Walking

"There is no road, the road is made by walking." - Antoni Machado

My transplant walk began on June 4, 2014, with my husband, Dan, by my side. As with so many of life's journeys, this one did not have a road map or any signs to follow; our steps created my road. We took each day one single step at a time. We knew and felt that the rhythm of our lives was changing emotionally, spiritually, as well as physically. We were also changing as a couple.

I was not in charge, but was rather invited to be a participant in the mystery of healing. While I was not always overly willing to participate, I did consent to the healing process as prayer and meditation whispered a quiet "yes". This past year has been the most alienating and connecting year of my life, which proved to be a true paradox of living in the present moment. A deep sense of being surrounded by love in a community of Saints grew around me. However, at times, when fear knocked, I felt that I, alone, was there to open the door to usher it in.

This road has not been a linear path. Many times there were detours, U-turns, and speed bumps along the way. While this journey was something I prepared for, I found the most difficult thing was to consent to give some control of my life away. While control is a quality of being human, Richard Rohr says, "In letting go of your powerlessness, you do not lose yourself, but fall into your foundational and grounded self. This is your true self or divine self in God."

Life this year meant living many days breath to breath, and taking things slowly and carefully by placing one foot step by step in front of the other. My intention was to stay connected to my inner self and to find the love that was all around me. We still walk this road without maps, signs or rules, yet our direction remains: healing! With the help of the wonderful doctors, nurses, technicians, friends and family, I will continue to heal. Love is my guide.

Laureen Hartman

Gift of Hospitality

A Prayer for Graft Versus Host Disease

Come Holy One into the fallow soil of my bones where we can be one.

The light of dawn wakens me to receive, to be the loving one of hospitality.

Come, enter, do not be shy, we are one.

Creating our own season, rhythm, and life together.

Like the waters dripping into a stream we are one.

Like the vast universe of our creator we are one.

Laureen Hartman

INTRODUCTION

"There is no love which does not become help." – Paul Tillich

I am normally a very private person. The thought of sharing so much of our lives on the web, through a Caring Bridge web site, had never occurred to me. I look at my Facebook page, but almost never post anything, a quiet observer of life. My wife, Laury, and I visited other Caring Bridge sites of friends and decided that we would create a site for Laury when she went in for her bone marrow transplant. We had no idea how these posts would take on a life of their own, and how much they would mean to our healing.

Laury was diagnosed with Essential Thrombocythemia (ET) in 1996. She lived with ET until 2008 when it morphed into Myelofibrosis. We knew then that at some point in the future Laury would need a bone marrow transplant. In the summer of 2013, Laury's spleen began to grow, and by February of 2014 she was in preparation for the transplant.

As part of the transplant preparation, Laury underwent three rounds of chemo therapy to shrink her spleen. The chemo treatments took us to the University of Chicago Medical Center every day for two weeks, after which we received two weeks off, only to begin the chemo again. When we would leave the clinic, Laury would start calling her parents, brother, sister, and our daughters. The calling list grew longer and longer, so Laury and I decided the best way to communicate with our loved ones was to start a Caring Bridge site. The list of loved ones grew as more people asked if they could be part of the community.

This book is a collection of my daily posts to our Caring Bridge site. I have copied the entries here pretty much as they were posted. I have tried to limit the editing or make corrections. These were written during happy and difficult times, but always from my heart. Laury wanted me to convey what we were going through and to capture our feelings. The use of quotes to start each post was Laury's idea. Sometimes finding the right quote was the hardest part of writing the post. I used the web to find the quotes, so I apologize for any that have been misquoted.

The two way communication of the Caring Bridge site brought us many healing and uplifting comments and gave us strength to travel on this journey. I have decided not to include the comments we received from friends and family. These comments were freely given and I want our community to feel they are safe to say whatever they want.

I hope these writings help others find the love all around them as they travel on a similar journey.

The book is broken into three sections. Section 1 contains the posts from the months before Laury's transplant. Section 2 is made up of the posts I wrote while Laury and I were in the hospital for her transplant. Section 3 is the largest section and contains the posts from the healing time after the transplant.

Section 1 – Pre-transplant

Laury and I knew things were changing. After seeing him for several years, Dr. Baron transitioned us to the transplant specialist Dr. Odenike in the anticipation of a bone marrow transplant. When we met with Dr. Odenike, she began to lay out the plan for the transplant. Laury and I thought that Dr. Odenike would talk about finding a donor and Laury's admittance to the hospital for the start of chemo in preparation for the transplant. I read widely about the process, and Laury and I viewed videos of survivors talking about their experiences.

What we had not expected was the amount of time it takes to find the donor and prepare for the actual transplant. In February, Dr. Odenike was talking about the end of May or early June as the most likely time for the actual transplant. Dr. Odenike's timeframe surprised both Laury and me. I was concerned that Laury might not live that long. The last blood tests showed Laury had gone into acute Leukemia.

Dr. Odenike talked with us about using the time before the transplant to better prepare Laury. Laury's spleen had grown quite large by this time. Laury commented that she looked six months pregnant. Dr. Odenike explained that she wanted Laury to undergo chemotherapy to reduce the size of her spleen. The doctors were concerned about the transplant's success if Laury underwent it with such a large spleen because the spleen would consume all of the new stem cells before they had a chance to engraft.

Laury and I had an appointment with Dr. Odenike on Thursday, February 27th 2014. At this appointment, Dr. Odenike told us that Laury would be starting chemotherapy to reduce her spleen. Laury asked when we would start and Dr. Odenike replied, "Monday."

Laury asked about her return to teaching, to which Dr. Odenike replied no. A return to teaching was out of the question because the chemo was going to reduce her blood counts and her ability to fight infections. A high school was no place to jeopardize one's immune system. On the drive home Laury cried and called her co-teacher and department chair to inform them that she would not be coming back to work. It was a long weekend with Laury reconciling the need to move quickly on her health care and not being able to say good-bye to her friends and students. On Monday, we started the chemo treatments. What follows are my journal entries for those months of pre-transplant chemo treatments.

CHAPTER ONE

March

Monday, 3/3/2014 - Waiting

"Whatever we are waiting for -- peace of mind, contentment, grace, the inner awareness of simple abundance -- it will surely come to us, but only when we are ready to receive it with an open and grateful heart." - Sarah Ban Breathnach

Today we began the waiting. Laury and I headed down to U of C today for her first chemotherapy treatment. On paper, and when the treatments were described to us, it sounded like a really big deal - which it is. I guess what we were not totally prepared for was the not so big deal of waiting around. We have gotten used to visits to U of C being an all-day affair, so I am not sure why we thought that going down for just a shot would be any different. First we met with the head nurse and Laury signed a release form - again. Then it was over to the labs for a blood draw, then back to the infusion clinic for the treatment. All of which took about an hour. Then we were shown into the infusion clinic and proceeded to wait another hour for the shot.
The process goes something like this: we go over all of the paperwork, including medications, vital signs and an explanation of what this chemo drug is, and how it works, and what the possible side effects are. Then Laury is given a pill to combat nausea - but not before we are told all of the possible side effects of this pill. Then we wait for the pharmacy to mix the shot, then the shot is given and we can leave - all of which takes about one and a half hours.

So far things are going well. Laury has no side effects and the discomfort of the shot wore off quickly, so now we wait. And we do it all over again tomorrow....
Love to everyone.

Tuesday, 3/4/2014 – Perspective

"See me, feel me, touch me, heal me"- The Who

Day two went pretty much as Day one, except Laury discovered that if the nurses inject the chemo quickly it doesn't hurt as much.

I do want to share an observation from our trips to U of C. We have been going to U of C since 1996, when Laury was first diagnosed with ET. At first it was once a year, or every six months, depending on how she was doing. Once the ET transformed into Myelofibrosis we began going more often. I would often see people with masks on and others in wheel chairs who knew the staff by name, and the staff would welcome them by name, as well.

I wondered if we would ever be in the same situation. Now here we are. As we walked in yesterday, we met Dr. Baron who has been Laury's doctor since the beginning. We went to the infusion desk and the woman recognized Laury from the day before. We saw the nurse who treated Laury the first day and he greeted us by name.

The entire experience brought to mind the words from the rock opera Tommy by the Who – "see me, feel me, touch me, heal me." You have to go through all of these steps - you have to be seen by someone and recognized for who you are. Then the healer needs to feel you - see you as a unique individual. The nurse yesterday had never heard of Myelofibrosis and printed out some materials to read so she could better understand what was going on with Laury. You have to be touched in some way to make a connection, either while being given treatment or just talking with the patient next to you who might be undergoing the same treatment. Only after all of those things happen healing can take place.

All our Love.

Wednesday 3/5/2014 – Being Fed

"Imagine no hunger. ..." - John Lennon

Today was a speed record - in and out in forty-five minutes.

When Laury and I go to U of C, we always stop and get a chocolate chip cookie for the drive home. Since we are now going there so often, we thought it best to change our choice of snacks. Now when we leave the hospital, Laury and I have a tangerine and some graham crackers. As we are driving along Lake Shore Drive heading toward the city, Laury peels the tangerine and feeds me pieces. Laury's feeding me in the car goes way back to our first road trips together. Not wanting to stop until we got to our destination, she would feed me as I drove.

But on the drive home tonight, it occurred to me that Laury feeds me in other ways. Anyone who knows me knows that I hate traffic and I am not the most patient driver. There is one exception to this rule, when Laury is sitting next to me. I am not in a hurry to get anywhere. I am content to be with her, no matter the traffic.

If that's not being fed, then I don't know what is.

All our Love.

Thursday, 3/6/2014 – So Far, So Good

"I usually know almost exactly how I feel. The problem is, I just can't tell anyone." – Meg Cabot, Princess In Love

I wanted to set the record straight on something. It came up today in a conversation with a friend of Laury's. "I heard you were so sick. You don't look sick." Laury is sick. She has a very serious disease, however, right now she doesn't look sick. She still has a lot of energy and feels great. It throws people. I am not sure what they expect, and there certainly may come a time when Laury does look more sick, but for now she is healthy and happy. Our goal is to keep her that way as long as possible and then bring her back to this after the bone marrow transplant.

We are taking it one day at a time. Today was a good day, even with the wait at U of C and the crazy traffic on the way home.

All our Love.

Friday, 3/7/2014 – Home Again

"Experience: the most brutal of teachers. But you learn, my God do you learn." – C. S. Lewis

Today ended week one of Laury's first round of chemo therapy. So far Laury has had no side effects from the chemo; although she has some side effects of the anti-nausea meds. We have learned a lot this week. We know that the traffic going into the city is much lighter and faster than we thought, and it only takes about forty-five minutes to get to Chicago. We learned that coming back from Chicago takes one and a half hours pretty much every time. We learned new phrases like "Chemo Check!" - which is what the nurse calls out before she can give Laury her shot. Each time her injection must be checked by another nurse, including showing the details to Laury to make sure everything is correct.

We (mainly Laury) learned the names of several people - including the always-smiling lady behind the counter with the amazing grey hair.

We learned to lean on each other when the other is tired - yes I was tired this week, too. We learned that we can still sit down and have a nice dinner together and be thankful for the day.

All and all, a good week.

Back to it on Monday.

All our Love.

Monday, 3/10/2014 – Missing in Action – also known as 15 tubes

"It is impossible to go through life without trust." - Graham Greene

Laury and I started our second week of chemo therapy today. We drove down to Chicago on a beautiful, almost-60-degree day. The first thing we noticed when we turned on to Lake Shore Drive was the ice that had been solid, as far out as we could see, was totally gone. The lake was a deep mesmerizing blue and very calm for a windy day.

Laury checked in and we went over to the lab for her blood draw. When we arrived at the lab, there were no other patients waiting, so Laury was taken in right away. Usually blood draws are simple in-and-out procedures - even using the small needle (Laury asks them to use a small needle to prevent damaging her veins. The smaller needle makes the blood flow slower) Laury is never back in the room more than five minutes. I sat back and settled in for what I thought would be a short wait. After about fifteen minutes, I began to get worried. Was she alright, were they having problems, what was going on? At twenty minutes the receptionist closed her station and turned out the lights. I wondered if they had taken her out the back door. I wondered if she was still there. At twenty-five minutes three nurses left with their coats on - clearly done for the day. I began to wonder what the heck was going on. There I sat in semi-darkness thinking, "Should I go back there and see what is going on?" At thirty minutes another young lady came over to the area and asked me if I was waiting for a patient. I said I was, but I was beginning to think I missed her. The young lady replied that there was only one way out, so I couldn't have missed her. My foot started tapping a little harder, and I kept telling myself everything was OK. Then, after a few more minutes, Laury came out smiling. I was very relieved, but also very curious - what had taken so long? Laury explained that instead of the usual four or five tubes of blood they took fifteen! I was surprised that Laury was smiling and able to walk! When I asked her how she felt, she replied, "I feel sorry for the nurse- she had to stay late to get all my blood".

That's Laury. Just been through thirty minutes of getting blood drawn, only to worry that the nurse would be late for dinner. God I love this woman.

All our Love.

Tuesday, 3/11/2014 – Slow Down

"The Divine Spirit does not reside in any except the joyful heart" - The Talmud

Today was a good day. We had the usual light traffic down to U of C, got a close in parking spot and a short wait to be taken back for Laury's treatment. We left feeling good at the record time for in and out. Even the elevator came quickly. Laury and I stepped on to the elevator, and I saw an elderly woman standing near the door looking at me. I held the door and asked her if she was going down. The woman replied "We are, but my husband is really slow." Just then her husband came into view, shuffling along at his own pace. Her husband wore a mask like many of the patients and as he stepped on to the elevator he said "Yes, I am the only slow person in the hospital". We all laughed at the irony of what he had said. Laury then mentioned the forecast for snow tonight. The man's wife replied "Oh, I hope we get home in time!" We told her the snow was predicted for later tonight so they should be fine. The man then spoke tapping his chest, "It will be a spring snow, not a winter snow, and you will know the difference in your heart."

Laury and I were glad we held the elevator.

All our Love.

Wednesday, 3/12/2014 – Chocolate Chip Cookie Day

"Sometimes it's the journey that teaches you a lot about your destination" - Drake

Today was full. We had to get to U of C early because Laury had a CT scan. The CT scan is part of the testing that Laury is going through to assess her overall health in preparation for the bone marrow transplant. We found out after we arrived at the hospital that she had also been scheduled for a chest x-ray. The CT scan area is in the lower level of the medical center - kind of dark and not as nice as the rest of the facility. The waiting room had a TV playing one of those afternoon Jerry Springer type shows with people taking lie-detector tests to see if they cheated on each other. No one was watching the show and we asked if it could be turned off but the receptionist didn't know how to turn the TV off - you couldn't reach it from the floor.

After the CT scan and x-ray Laury and I went up to the infusion area on the 6th floor. There, while we were waiting, we also had an appointment with the transplant social worker. His name is Marc and he was there to do an evaluation of Laury. He, like most of the others we have met so far, was surprised and pleased with the planning and attitude of Laury. It does make me wonder how many people approach something as huge as a bone marrow transplant with no idea of what is going on or what they are getting into. We assumed that Laury "passed" the evaluation with flying colors.

As we were leaving, Laury wanted a Chocolate Chip cookie instead of our usual tangerine and crackers. I said she had earned it and we both got one for the road.

On the way home they had the ramp onto I55 off of Lake Shore Drive closed and the traffic was backed up and we had to take a detour of a couple of miles in stop and go traffic. Once Laury and I were able to get on to I55 there was very little traffic coming home. It reminded me of what we are going through - a detour in our lives and when we are through it the rewards will be great.

All our Love.

Thursday, 3/13/2014 – Gap in time

"Time is the longest distance between two places" - Tennessee Williams

Today was quick, no additional tests, no lab work, no doctor appointments. We were driving home and Laury said to me "If the traffic lightens up we might be able to make yoga." I looked at the clock in the car and said "No, it is really four-thirty not three-thirty - we still haven't figured out how to change the clock." The new Mini has served us well these last two weeks driving back and forth to Chicago. But with any new technology comes the task of learning how it works. Laury and I both figured there had to be an easy way to change the time without having to reset the computer, upload new software, or go to the dealership. The problem was we didn't know it. The funny thing was neither of us thought much about the time unless we were in the car.

I managed to figure out the correct sequence of buttons to push to make the 1 hour forward adjustment for daylight savings time. It made the drive home longer because we lost an hour on the clock. It got me thinking about the time we have spent the last two weeks. I don't believe time is ever wasted. Yesterday I talked about the journey we are on being like a detour. Most detours take time away from us, however, this one is giving it back. All Laury and I are doing on this detour is spending time to gain more time. Laury will have more time as a result of this. More time with me, family, friends, and kids.

That makes this time very well spent.

All our Love.

Friday, 3/14/2014 – On the right path

"Over every mountain there is a path, although it may not be seen from the valley." - Theodore Roethke

Yesterday was a big day. Laury had her final shot in this round of chemo therapy. We also met with Dr. Ferris out here in Naperville. She is an oncologist that we will be seeing if Laury needs a transfusion. Dr. Ferris knows Dr. Baron and was very happy to be on Team Laury and help in any way she can. This means that for the next month all of the regular blood tests can be done here locally, thus saving us a trip to Chicago.

Laury also made a big batch of shortbread cookies for all of the nurses in the infusion center to say thank you for their good care over the past two weeks. She also made a batch for Dr. Odenike.

We met with Dr. Odenike and she was very pleased with Laury's progress so far. In fact Dr. Odenike said she couldn't be more pleased at how things are going. Laury's spleen is visibly smaller and her blasts have decreased significantly. In addition to those signs there is another marker that Dr. Odenike told us about that she has been watching. It is called LDH (nothing to do with cholesterol). It shows blood activity - I am not sure of all the science behind it. However, when Dr. Odenike saw Laury in 2009, her LDH was 535 - about twice the normal range - but not bad for someone with Myelofibrosis. In February of this year the LDH number had increased to 2,300- a clear indication that the disease had taken off. Yesterday Laury's LDH number was 735 - heading in the right direction.

So we now begin the month off period. Laury's blood numbers are likely to continue to drop and if they get too low she will need a transfusion, but for now we will be checking her blood on Mondays and Thursdays to see how things are going.

It seemed only fitting that yesterday when testing Laury's blood oxygen, she scored 100%! She had been telling the nurses that she was frustrated that every day Laury would get 98 or 99% and she was going to get 100% before this round was over. Small things make the journey special.

Laury has a couple more tests before the insurance approval will be granted for the bone marrow transplant. These tests are scheduled for the week of March 27th. Once they are done the hospital will start contacting donors and beginning the final preparations for Laury's transplant.

It appears we are on the right path.

All our Love.

Tuesday, 3/18/2014 – Beginning the waiting

"When you've seen beyond yourself, then you may find, peace of mind is waiting there." - George Harrison

It seemed strange not to post anything last night. Going up to the computer after dinner to write about our day has become part of my routine, something that in a strange way is very comforting. Yesterday Laury and I began the month of waiting between chemo treatments. I went back to the office after working from home, and Laury went back to an empty house. We both did things that we needed to do, Laury getting her eyes checked and a pedicure (I know how necessary those are!), and running a few errands, signaling a change from her going to work. Laury and I went to yoga last night and were greeted by much support and happiness to see us. It is a great community.

I am not sure how often I should post during this waiting period, I will certainly want to keep everyone informed of Laury's progress, but I also miss writing these messages. I think most of all I miss the replies and the "hearts" that show how much all of you are supporting us.

Laury and I really have found strength and peace of mind in all of you.

All our Love.

Thursday, 3/20/2014 – Honest Fatigue

"Never apologize for showing feeling. When you do so, you apologize for the Truth." - Benjamin Disraeli

Laury had her blood work done this morning and her numbers are holding good. The biggest thing Laury is dealing with right now is fatigue. Laury began to feel the fatigue on Wednesday, but thought it might have been from working with her friend Robin on Tuesday building a couple of containers. As we walked into the Cancer Center here in Naperville this morning I asked Laury if she wanted to take the stairs instead of the elevator to the second floor. She replied with an emphatic "No", saying she was too tired for the stairs. Laury also said that she felt like I had dragged her across the parking lot to get into the building. When Laury and I walk together I always let her set the pace. Since I am a foot taller than Laury I tend to walk faster than her, especially when we are downtown. So I was surprised to hear her say that it felt like I dragged her. I asked her how she was feeling and Laury said "I am very tired today. This is a new language for me, my body is telling me something but I am not sure what it wants." I again told Laury that she needs to be honest with herself and with me on how she feels. As I was saying it a small voice said to me, "Did you hear what you just said?"

People have been very kind in asking me how I am doing though all of this. I generally reply "I am doing fine." This for the most part is true.

However, over the last week I have been very tired, chalking it up to the events of the previous two weeks. But when I was honest with myself I knew it was more than that. This afternoon I went to my doctor and he confirmed what I suspected, I have a sinus infection.

When I thought about why I hadn't been able to tell Laury that I thought I had a sinus infection it was because I wanted to be strong and not burden her with anything so small. But I realize that for us to get through this together Laury and I have to be honest with each other and that means sometimes not being able to be the strong one.

Strength appears to have more to do with knowing yourself than in fooling yourself.

All our Love.

Friday, 3/21/2014 – Others

"We'll be Friends Forever, won't we, Pooh?' asked Piglet. Even longer,' Pooh answered." - A.A. Milne, Winnie-The-Pooh

Today Laury and I were both tired and were in a competition on who could consume more Tylenol. We didn't go out for a walk on this beautiful day. Laury did talk to friends and heard about recent weddings and travels.

It is hard sometimes to let people know that we still care about what is going on in their lives. Laury has said to me many times "It can't be all about me." Laury and I have friends who are facing issues in their lives like surgery, cancer, breakups. We want to be there for them and still be their friend.

Recently we added a door at the top of the stairs to keep the cats on the second floor when Laury comes home from her transplant. We have removed items from the house like plants that Laury will not be able to have around. We have cleaned, updated and changed things all in preparation. But it doesn't mean that our lives are all about this upcoming transplant.

Laury and I want to hear about your lives and your joys and concerns; this is what makes us friends. Laury is my best friend but it wouldn't be much of a friendship if she never asked about me.

Remember we are there for you too.

All our Love.

Monday, 3/24/2014 – Eating Right

"We should look for someone to eat and drink with before looking for something to eat and drink..." - Epicurus

Monday started off with a trip to the Cancer Center to have Laury's blood checked. The numbers continue to look good; her red blood numbers actually went up a little. Laury's white cells are dropping and getting close to where we will have to be more careful about her catching something and not having enough white cells to fight it off, but the doctors are pleased and Laury still feels pretty good.

My sister, Kim, called me on Saturday to tell me that she was going to be a grandmother again. It is great news and we wish Bryan and Julie the best. It reminded me of what Laury has been saying lately when asked by the nurses how she is eating. Laury replies "Like I am pregnant!" What Laury means is that she is eating well with no loss of appetite. But what it really means it that Laury is eating things she hasn't allowed herself to eat since she was last pregnant. You all know how healthy an eater Laury is. She will not allow anything to go into her body that is not healthy (with the possible exception of wine), as Laury says she gave up bread when she turned 40.

So you can imagine my surprise when last Thursday while driving home from her blood test Laury said she was in the mood for a Reuben sandwich. I can't tell you the last time we had sauerkraut in the house. But off to the store I went to get the fixings for the sandwich. It has been kind of fun being able to cook some "new" old things. Fried potatoes and onions, rice, braised beef ribs - things that are so good but that you can't justify the fat or calories.

But most of all it has been fun sitting down and watching Laury enjoy the food. There is nothing like cooking for someone who enjoys your cooking.

All our Love.

Wednesday, 3/26/2014 – Rookie Caregiver

"If you find it in your heart to care for somebody else, you will have succeeded" - Maya Angelou

I am new to the caregiver role. Most of the time I am "Mr. Fix-it". "Dad, the computer is not working"; "Honey, can you fix the sink?" are directives I am comfortable with. Laury has always been the natural caregiver in our family. At the first sign of vomit - I would run from the room with tears in my eyes and fear that I would soon be joining the chorus of retching. If I can't fix it I am not sure what to do.

Laury has been having night sweats again and my natural reaction is to want to fix them. I know I can't but it didn't stop me from looking on the web for moisture wicking sheets and pajamas. I was close to hitting the "Buy" button when I remembered something I read about care giving and I decided to talk to Laury first to see what she wanted to do.

Since this role is new to me I have done some research on being a caregiver. There are many great articles and books available that mostly give very good common sense advice. One piece of advice I read has stuck with me but I need to be reminded of it often.

"Do only those things your loved one can't do." - **Caregiving Basics, The Leukemia & Lymphoma Society**. It sounds simple but can be very hard to enact. This weekend I was not feeling great and the floors needed vacuuming. Laury said she was in the mood to do it and she did. The entire time Laury was vacuuming I felt I should be doing it and somehow I was failing as a caregiver. Yesterday, Laury had an appointment with her therapist and wanted to have lunch with her parents. Laury has been very tired lately and I wasn't sure if she should drive. I was at work in Oak Brook but it would have only taken me a few minutes to come home and drive her. Laury said she felt good enough to drive herself. Again that feeling of not being there for her came over me.

When I got home I could tell that going by herself had been good for Laury and she had been fine. I asked Laury if she ever gets tired of me asking her how she feels. She said, "I guess not, because I don't remember you asking me that much."

I know there are things that Laury can't do and there might be other things that come up as we go along this journey, but for now I need to let her do the things she can still do.

So, last night as I was making dinner, Laury was sitting at the bar and asked me if there was anything she could do to help. I said smiling, "You can sit there and look pretty". Laury smiled back and gave me a look that melted my heart. I hope that is something she never stops being able to do.

All our Love.

Friday, 3/28/2014 – Eleven Dollar Visit

"Everybody gets so much information all day long that they lose their common sense." - Gertrude Stein

When Laury and I go to the U of C we park in a large parking structure adjacent to the Center for Advanced Medicine. We usually find a spot near or at the top of the structure and have a bit of a walk to get to the clinic. On most days the parking costs us $6. Some days when we are there a long time, waiting, testing, waiting, testing and waiting, the parking bill goes up to $11. Yesterday was an eleven dollar visit.

Laury had two more tests for the insurance company to approve her transplant. The first was a Pulmonary Function test. We arrived right at one and a few minutes later a loud voice yelled for Laury to come back. About thirty minutes later Laury came out with a sense of urgency to get away from this area as fast as possible. I asked her as I quickly gathered my things, "How was it?" Laury replied, "That was the worst test I have ever taken!" I asked her why that was, and she said that she had been placed in a big plastic bubble-like room and asked to breath in and out through a large tube. The worst part Laury said was the woman kept yelling at her to breathe in more or breathe out more. The woman claimed she needed to do this to encourage the person being tested to do their best. Laury said all it did was piss her off and make her want to get out of there as fast as possible.

We then went to the next test. This was some kind of nuclear blood test! While sitting in the waiting area one of the elevator alarm bells started to go off. It was very loud and annoying, but the staff appeared not to be able to hear it. It went on for at least fifteen minutes before it was stopped. Laury was then taken back for her test that the technician said would take at least ninety minutes. After about twenty minutes the technician came out and asked me if I wanted to join Laury while she waited in the back. I said I did and was taken back to the small room in which Laury was waiting. Laury told me that the technician had taken a small amount of her blood and they were going to make it radioactive and then put it back in Laury to take pictures of how the blood is flowing in her body. Pretty cool!

Laury asked the technician how long the radioactivity would last and she said probably a couple of days. The technician said it was no big deal but Laury might set off an alarm at the airport. We laughed and said we were going to stop at Midway Airport on our way home and try it. Once they had "marked" her blood they were ready to put it back into Laury and take the pictures. The technician showed me where I could wait and Laury went to use the rest room. I waited but no Laury or technician, so I went back to the room where we had been. On the way there I passed the rest room and there was Laury and the technician working on Laury's bleeding arm. Laury looked at me and smiled, "I am bleeding", she said, "But I am fine." The blood was coming from where they had placed the IV that the technician had just removed.

After some clean up, Laury had her pictures taken and off to the visit with Dr. Odenike. The wait for Dr. Odenike was not long and she came in and began to ask Laury about how she has been doing. As a result of the conversation, Dr. Odenike wants Laury to begin the second round of chemotherapy next week and not two weeks from now, as originally planned. The reason for this is that they usually give the patient four weeks for their body to recover from the chemo. Laury's body had recovered already and the disease had shown signs of coming back.

We start the next round on Monday afternoon. It is another 10 days of shots. While waiting to see Dr. Odenike, a woman was wheeled up to the receptionist counter by a younger woman. The younger woman told the receptionist the woman's name and the name of the doctor she was ther to see. The receptionist asked the woman her name and her birth date. The woman gave her name and her birthday of April 14th. The receptionist asked what year she was born and the woman replied, "I am 100 years old". The younger woman said to her, "Yes I know that but what year were you born?" The older woman answered in a tone that suggested she also rolled her eyes, "1914". The younger woman replied, "Oh my lord, where is my head?" I chuckled, but also realized that I had not been able to do the mental math either. It had been a long day.

All our Love.

CHAPTER TWO

April

Tuesday, 4/1/2014 – Out of Balance

"We can be sure that the greatest hope for maintaining equilibrium in the face of any situation rests within ourselves." - Francis J. Braceland

Yesterday Laury began her second round of chemotherapy. It wasn't a bad day, but it wasn't a good day, either. Laury said she felt cheated out of her two weeks more of rest. I wasn't sure what I was feeling. Laury and I certainly did not have the positive energy we had going into the previous round. I am sure this is going to happen from time to time where we just don't feel like going through this.

Laury and I believe that to be healthy you have to address the mind, body, and spirit. Yesterday we were tending to the body, but not the mind and spirit. It is hard sometimes to recognize what is wrong - but you can feel it. It is not that Laury and I both were down in the dumps, as it was a beautiful day, the traffic was light, the lake looked amazing, and we were together. Yet, all of these things felt like they were taking things away from us instead of feeding us.

When Laury and I got home I decided to go to the late yoga class. Yoga has taught me how to listen to my body, spirit and mind and to bring those into balance. The class helped a lot, and I felt much better afterward.

Today is a new day and Laury and I will head back down to the city this afternoon. I am looking forward to our time together in the car and to facing this new day with greater balance.

All our Love.

Wednesday, 4/2/2014 – Better Day

"Sometimes your joy is the source of your smile, but sometimes your smile can be the source of your joy." - Thich Nhat Hanh

Today was a better day. Thank you all for your uplifting words and prayers. Laury and I had a sunny day to drive down to the city and on the way home we stopped at a park and took in the beauty of the lake. We reached another milestone today, as well. Laury needs to begin wearing a mask in certain situations to protect her from infections. Laury's red blood numbers continue to be good but her white cells are so low that the nurses told her today to start using the mask.

Laury's reaction to this news was "I am going to say this. I don't want to wear a mask." I said, "I know, but you also said you don't want to get an infection or wind up in the hospital." Laury replied to me, "I didn't say I wouldn't wear one, I just said I didn't want to wear one." Silly me. As we were leaving the clinic Laury, with her mask on, asked me how she looked and I replied, "You look cute and your new glasses really work well with the mask!"

We stopped at the restrooms before leaving the building and Laury said. "I am going to look at myself in the mirror and see how cute I really am with this mask on."

I waited and Laury came out with a huge grin that no mask could contain and said, "I really do look cute in this!"

Yes it was a better day.

All our Love.

Wednesday, 4/2/2014 – Unmasked

"Never miss an opportunity to make others happy, even if you have to leave them alone in order to do it." -Author Unknown

I have to tell you all something about me: I hate needles. I can't watch when I have a blood test. I close my eyes when someone is given a shot on TV. I most certainly close my eyes every day sitting next to Laury when she gets her shot. Sometimes the nurse will notice my closed eyes and Laury will say "He doesn't like shots". The nurse will sometimes say something like "He isn't the one getting the shot!"

It is hard for me to watch Laury go through all of this, including the shots. I want to fix it, to take her place, to wish it away. But I can't. I sometimes try too hard to make it right and I make Laury angry. Today, I did it again. As I mentioned yesterday, the nurses told Laury she should be wearing a mask when she is in the clinic. When we arrived Laury put on her mask as we walked to the infusion center. While sitting there in the uncrowded space Laury took her mask off. I didn't like Laury having it off and when they called her back to take her vital signs I said to Laury as she walked away, "Wear your mask". I knew as soon as I said it that it was not going to turn out the way I had hoped. Laury came back after her vitals and was not happy with me. She finally said, "You can't be telling me what to do. I have to do this on my terms otherwise I will feel over managed."

Laury is right, and I am sorry for trying to tell her what to do. She is managing this beautifully and I need to celebrate that more and not try to tell her what to do.

I do love and trust Laury with all my heart. She has done everything she is supposed to do and continues to amaze the doctors and me. Now I just need to remember that "caregiver" does not mean "controller".

All our Love.

Thursday, 4/3/2014 – Good News

"How beautiful upon the mountains are the feet of the messenger who brings good news" - Isaiah 52:7 (edited)

Today was a good day, even though it was cold and rainy. Laury and I arrived at the U of C without problems and found a close-in parking spot. Laury has been having some pain in her tongue caused by her white blood counts being so low. Our nurse Kim came over to get all of the information from Laury regarding medications, how she is feeling, whether or not she has gone to the bathroom normally, etc., and Laury mentioned that her tongue was hurting. Laury told our nurse yesterday as well, and Dora (our nurse from yesterday), said to wash her mouth with a mixture of salt, baking soda and water. Today we asked if someone could look at Laury's tongue to make sure it was not something more serious.

A few minutes later Lisa, Dr. Odenike's nurse, came into the area where we were sitting. Lisa looked at Laury's tongue and said that it was not an infection and that Laury could rinse using the same directions Dora had given us. Lisa did mention that there is a prescription that they could give Laury, but it numbs the mouth and makes everything taste funny. Laury decided to wait to see if it got worse and said we would decide tomorrow on the prescription. Lisa then asked how Laury was feeling and went on to explain that Dr. Odenike had decided not to increase the dose of the chemo this week. Laury and I had asked about it the previous day because I noticed that the dose was still the same, even though Dr. Odenike had told us at our last meeting she was going to increase it.

Lisa then said, "Did anyone tell you that one of the donors in the bone marrow database is a perfect match for you?" Laury was stunned, she got tears in her eyes and said, "No, but I have been praying for that person for five years." This is great news! The perfect match makes the odds of a good outcome of the transplant much higher.

Once we have the insurance approval they will contact the donor and see if they are still willing to donate and begin working out the schedule for the transplant.

I know that I am the perfect match for Laury, but it is nice to know that there is someone out there with a perfect match for her bone marrow.

All our Love.

Friday, 4/4/2014 – Good Eats

"Life itself is the proper binge." - Julia Child

Laury and I ended the week on a good note. Laury's energy was very good today. She cleaned the refrigerator and did wash and felt great. Laury's blood numbers look good, her red blood count continues to rise and this is probably the reason for her energy. Her tongue felt a lot better today. Laury and I stopped yesterday and got baking soda to go with the salt for her mouth wash. It made a huge difference and Laury felt much better.

We also had delicious mac and cheese for dinner. Now that might not seem like such a big deal but Laury claims (and I believe her) that the last time she had mac and cheese was when she was 10. I asked Laury on the way home what she wanted for dinner and Laury said, "Something soft and cheesy, like mac and cheese." I almost ran into the car in front of me because I was staring at her in amazement. "Like real mac and cheese?" I asked. Laury said, "Yeah that really sounds good to me. Plus, my weight is a little down and I don't want to eat anything crunchy because of my tongue".

Making this even more of a miracle is that Laury actually made the cheese sauce. Every year for Thanksgiving Laury makes cheesy onions, that cheese sauce was the basis for the mac and cheese.

The week started out difficult and got better as it went on. All of you helped us along this week. It is hard to complain about life when you get to have mac and cheese for dinner.

All our Love.

Saturday, 4/5/2104 – The road ahead

"It is good to have an end to journey toward; but it is the journey that matters, in the end." - Ernest Hemingway

Our daughter, Keri, thought it would be a good idea to clarify what the next steps are for Laury and the transplant. I know earlier in the week I mentioned that Laury has a perfect match in the donor database. This doesn't mean that we will be doing the transplant next week. The process takes its own time and Laury and I are for the most part along for the ride.

Once Laury has insurance approval, which we should have shortly, the hospital will start contacting the donors in the database. The hospital will contact multiple donors to see if they are still willing to donate, and if they are the donors will be asked to send in blood samples. These samples are then tested again to see if they are a match for Laury. Once a match is found then they will contact the donor to schedule the treatment to harvest their stem cells.

The donor's schedule really determines ours at this point. The donor has to go into the clinic for a series of shots over two weeks to force the stem cells out of their marrow into the blood stream. Once the shots take effect the donor comes in and their blood is removed and filtered (out of one arm into the other) and the stem cells are collected and stored. At the same time this is happening Laury will go into the hospital and begin the chemo to kill her bone marrow. This chemo takes about a week, and then she has a day off to rest, and then is given the new stem cells in a transfusion.

The most likely schedule for all of this is anyone's guess at this point. Laury and I think that insurance approval will probably come this week and most likely the transplant will be near the end of May or early June. Most people who have gone through the transplant celebrate the transplant date as a new birthday. If the transplant happens at the end of May then Laury could get the stem cells on my birthday or if early June our daughters' birthday (they both have the same birthday). Either way, it will be a celebration of new life.

All our Love.

Monday, 4/7/2014 – Connections

"What matters in relationship isn't how you see each other, but whether you see each other." - Eric Michael Leventhal

Today was a good day. Laury's energy is good, she feels and looks great.

Laury and I started the second week of this round of chemotherapy, with a very long wait. The infusion waiting area was packed when we arrived and it was clear they were running behind. But the wait afforded us some time to sit quietly with each other and to take in the people around us. I ran into a good friend at the grocery store this weekend and I was telling her how before when we use to go to U of C Laury and I felt like we were visitors, not really part of something. The visits with the doctors were good, but it was like going to an event and leaving, not really being part of the cast of characters. I told her that now after being in the clinic for several weeks Laury and I feel more part of what is going on there.

You start to see the same people, not just the staff, but the other patients, as well. During our very first visit to the infusion center we had a young couple next to us, and Laury and I started chatting (mostly Laury started chatting- you know her). The young woman has breast cancer and is going through chemo. She and her husband are there every Monday and we have seen them most Mondays, including today. We saw her first with hair then with it cropped close, then shaved. She has remained a smiling beautiful woman throughout it all.

There are others Laury and I have seen, including the man with the big nose and his very old mother whom he yells at in some language I don't understand. I even saw Cardinal George sitting across from me at the lab.

It is hard not to see these people and wonder about their story. You know that they all won't turn out good, but that doesn't keep you from wanting to know the story, anyway.

I know that I am being changed by this experience. I am not sure how, but I know it is for the better.

All our Love.

Tuesday, 4/8/2014 – Normal Life

"To live is so startling it leaves little time for anything else." - Emily Dickinson

I asked Laury at dinner what I should write about tonight, and she replied, "I don't know. It was just a normal day". I thought to myself, "Since when is going to U of C and getting chemo a "normal" day?" Laury and I had an easy drive there and back, which is not normal. We got in and out of the infusion center is less than thirty minutes- not normal.

So how come today was a normal day? I think it was because we drove down and back in silence, neither of us feeling the need to talk, to fill the space, but to just be together. Laury and I sat in the waiting area, my hand on her knee and hers behind my neck gently rubbing, not saying a word, content to just be together.

Laury and I came home and made a nice dinner and ate and the only words exchanged were the "Yum", and "This is so good" of appreciation. I love being with Laury, no matter where we are and what we are doing. Normal is to feel that way. I guess today was a very normal day, after all.

All our Love.

Thursday, 4/10/2014 – The right amount of fear

"Ultimately we know deeply that the other side of every fear is freedom." - Marilyn Ferguson

What a beautiful spring day yesterday was. Laury and I drove down and back to the clinic with the sun roof open, enjoying the fresh air. Again, yesterday, Laury and I were in and out of the infusion center in less than thirty minutes. We arrived home in time for us to go to yoga. Last night's practice was restorative and we figured that there wouldn't be too many people attending, so it would be good and safe for Laury. (Thank you Marinda. Even though my hamstrings were cursing you last night, they are singing your praises this morning!)

Managing Laury's fear of getting sick versus her need for people interaction and yoga is a challenge.

Fear is a strange thing. Too much fear and we cease to be alive. With the right amount of fear we are able to do wonderful and fun things, or sometimes even simple things. Not enough fear and we can do really stupid things, like telling Laury to wear her mask at the wrong time.

Laury said to me yesterday that she is no longer living in fear of her transplant. She welcomes it as the next step on the journey to healing. Laury asked me if I had seen a change in her since the fear has left, and I said that I had seen it, in both her and me. Laury said that she had lived the last five years in fear of the transplant and its effects on her. I must admit that I lived in fear that she would wait too long to agree to the transplant and would be too sick for it to work. We both had trouble voicing our fears to each other. I asked Laury why she thought she no longer fears the transplant. Laury replied that through yoga, therapy, reading, prayer, friends, and family she has learned to face it.

What Laury is facing is not without risk, and therefore should be faced with a certain amount of fear. But now Laury feels she is facing it with the right amount of fear. With that fear she will accomplish wonderful things.

All our Love.

Thursday, 4/10/2014 – The real deal

"Nothing ever becomes real 'til it is experienced." - John Keats

Our daughter, Lyndsay, went with us today to the U of C. She wanted to meet Dr. Odenike and see where Laury has been getting her chemotherapy. The days we have an appointment with Dr. Odenike are long, but today was even longer. We arrived at two and left the clinic at six. I asked Lyndsay to share her experience with all of you and she agreed to write something up for me over the next day or so. I will post it as soon as Lyndsay sends it to me.

The wait felt longer today with Lyndsay there. Maybe because I knew Lyndsay was not used to it and wanted to spare her the discomfort of long hours in crowded waiting areas. Laury kept apologizing for the wait as if it was her fault, but the reality is that this is how it goes sometimes.

Our meeting with Dr. Odenike went well, and she was pleased with Laury's continued health and spirit. Dr. Odenike does want Laury to do another round of chemo, starting in two weeks. Tomorrow is our last day on this round and then Laury will get two weeks off and then start another two week round. At the end of that round Laury and I hope we will be ready for the transplant.

It was good to have Lyndsay there with us today, to see where her mom goes and to meet the people we have talked about for so many years. It also reminded me that this is all new to Lyndsay and to others and that seeing it for the first time is an experience.

All our Love.

Friday, 4/11/2014 - Tired tonight

"I'm sleepy, exhausted, and tired. I must be in love." - Jarod Kintz

Laury and I ended this round of chemo today. The drive down was great, another sun-roof-open day. This has been a long week, and even though we had two days of fairly quick visits, I am still tired tonight. Laury and I stopped on the way home to meet our good friends, Robin and Mark, for dinner. It was great that Laury's white counts are up enough that she can go out, and as long as she is careful, meet and eat at a restaurant.

I sometimes think that Laury and I both charge each other up for the week and when it is done, so are we. (Although Laury seems to be a lot less tired than I am right now!) We hope to do some yard work together tomorrow - mostly Laury telling me what she wants done and me doing it, but it will be good to have the weekend and not have to start up again on Monday.

Next week Laury and I will watch for any signs of her numbers dropping, but we are not expecting that since we have been through this before. I will keep you all up to date on the events of our journey - I say "our" meaning all of ours - you all included.

Thanks again for your support and love.

All our Love.

Saturday, 4/12/2014 – A few simple steps

"Don't walk in front of me; I may not follow. Don't walk behind me; I may not lead. Just walk beside me and be my friend." - Albert Camus

Yesterday, in addition to the chemotherapy shot, Laury met with a group from the Transplant center to complete some cognitive tests. The Transplant center likes to do a baseline for some simple tests so they can compare the results before the transplant to certain times after the transplant. The tests were pretty simple: they timed Laury getting up out of her seat and walking three meters; she had to repeat a statement, guess the time, then recite the months of the year backwards. After Laury recited the months, they asked her to say the statement again. As you can imagine, Laury did really well.

The group then tested Laury's grip strength. I was thankful I was not the one being tested - especially yesterday. These were simple tests, but it did make wonder if there is going to come a time when these things will be hard for Laury to accomplish. There may be times when taking a few steps will be difficult because of the weakness caused by the transplant. But even if this happens, I know Laury will still have the same positive and healthy attitude as she does now. Laury said she was going to practice the tests and memorize the statement so that the next time she takes the test she will get it perfect.

Laury and I worked out in the yard today and we both wore masks. Laury wore gloves over rubber gloves. She asked me, "Aren't you proud of me? I am being a good patient, and you were afraid I was not going to be a good patient!" I said I was because she can be so stubborn and feisty. Laury said, "That feistiness is what makes me a good patient!"

Laury is right - it is her spiritedness that carries me and makes me know that everything will turn out great.

All our Love.

Monday, 4/14/2014 – Another routine

"The true secret of happiness lies in taking a genuine interest in all the details of daily life." - **William Morris**

Laury and I went back to our new routine today, that is to say the routine of not having a routine. I went back to the office and wondered how Laury was doing at home. She was at home wondering how I was doing at work. We so appreciate the time we have spent together.

Laury and I were able to both go to yoga tonight. It was a great class and I couldn't help thinking the practice was put together just for us. Another part of our routine has become Laury showing off her shrinking spleen. I hear it every morning, "Honey, look!" as Laury stands sideways to show me how flat her stomach is. For those of you who don't know, the spleen is a softball sized organ that sits up under your ribcage on your left side under the heart. The spleen's purpose in life is to filter your blood. Except in rare case like Laury's when the bone marrow can no longer make enough blood cells, the spleen tries to make up the difference. The problem is that the spleen is not very good at making blood, so it grows bigger to make more blood. In Laury's case her spleen has grown so large that at times it makes her look six months pregnant, or worse, as she says "fat".

So the fact that the chemo is shrinking Laury's spleen is a good thing both medically, and emotionally. It is the most concrete example of things getting better.

So if Laury pulls up her shirt and shows you her spleen, smile and say, "That's nice" and know that it really is nice.

All our Love.

Tuesday, 4/15/2014 – Real Money

"Teach us to give and not to count the cost." - Saint Ignatius

One of the topics I have not discussed is the cost of Laury's care. Laury and I are blessed with very good health insurance and we both have decent jobs. But make no mistake the monetary cost of this journey is high. The average cost for a bone marrow transplant is one and a half million dollars. Each of Laury's chemo shots is twenty five hundred dollars. We have begun to see some of these bills even after insurance paid their part to be scary. You put your head down and say - "Whatever it costs we will do this".

I know that there is no price that I am not willing to pay to make Laury well again. What I don't like is when Laury sees the bills, and how much it hurts her that we have to pay it for her. I can say, "We can't afford a vacation, or a new car, or new clothes" but I can't say, "We can't afford you." If I could we probably wouldn't have had kids! - Just kidding.

I know managing these costs is another part of this journey we are on. Just like most of this journey, we are in new territory, but Laury and I can approach this the same way we have met everything so far: together and in love.

We will get through this and then count up the cost. Until then I will not be afraid to open a bill or face any other aspect of Laury's healing.

All our Love.

Wednesday, 4/16/2014 – Blood Ties

"The bond that links your true family is not one of blood, but of respect and joy in each other's life." - Richard Bach

Laury and I went to the clinic in Naperville today to get her blood checked. The red numbers are still pretty good - but Laury's hemoglobin is below 9, so she is feeling a little tired. Her white counts are now down to mask-wearing range, but she is nowhere near transfusion levels.

I stopped and looked at the number of visits, hearts and comments that we have had on this site so far. It is incredible how many of you come every day and share. All of us are tied together by Laury's blood. We are family, each caring for the other by checking and sharing. Today at the clinic there was an older man with his wife and two daughters. The nurse said to him, "I see you have your entourage with you." I wanted to say to her, "You can't see them but we have dozens in our entourage!" Each of you comes with us everywhere we go on this journey.

It has been said that it takes a village to raise a child - this proves that it takes a community to heal each other.

All our Love.

Thursday, 4/17/2014 – "Yes, I did it!"

"Accomplishments will prove to be a journey, not a destination." - Dwight D. Eisenhower

Laury and I went to yoga tonight, even though Laury's white counts are not great and her sore tongue is back. We both decided that it was worth the try, and the benefits would outweigh the risks. But going to yoga in a mask is different than doing a yoga practice wearing a mask. With some encouragement from Marinda, Laury wore her mask for the entire class. When we left the class, on the way to the car, Laury said, "Yes I did it!" This is a huge accomplishment, worthy of some great praise, but it is also a simple step along this journey. Each time Laury faces something new at first it seems like it will be a big deal and a great effort. But, as she meets these challenges Laury accomplishes another milestone. Laury and I may not go back to yoga until her numbers come back up, but we now know that Laury can practice in a mask if she wants to.

I am humbled by Laury's spirit and drive, and I am warmed by her love.

All our Love.

Saturday, 4/19/2014 – Twists and Turns

"The road of life twists and turns and no two directions are ever the same. Yet our lessons come from the journey, not the destination." - Don Williams Jr.

Today Laury and I went to the city to get our hair cut. Megan, our stylist had asked us to come about thirty minutes early so she could teach Laury how to do head wraps for when she loses her hair. When we got there Megan had several scarfs of hers that she had picked out and a few that Jamie, the owner, had purchased for Laury. Megan set up Laury's phone to video tape the lesson so Laury could watch it later if she forgot how to do one of the styles.

After showing Laury how to twist and turn the scarf into the first style, Laury tried it and when she was done she began to cry and said to

Megan, "I don't want to be bald." Laury came over to me and asked me how she looked. I told her she looked great and would be able to look great no matter what. We hugged and Laury went back to learn a few more styles. Once she tried a couple of other styles she liked, she felt better and said to Megan, "It's only f**king hair! I can do this." Megan laughed and said, "Yes you can."

We are overwhelmed with Megan's generosity for taking the time and giving Laury so many beautiful scarfs.

The twists and turns of the scarf are like the twists and turns of this journey we are on. Sometimes we turn a corner and things don't look good and we cry, then the next corner brings joy. I guess the important thing to do is to keep moving forward and to be grateful for the love that travels with us.

All our Love.

Monday, 4/21/2014 – The eyes have it

"Love knows not distance; it hath no continent; its eyes are for the stars." - Gilbert Parker

First, let me apologize to Magen for spelling her name wrong. No excuse! I had her card right in front of me. Second, we went for blood work today and Laury's numbers are looking good. Laury's hemoglobin is up (still under 9) and her platelets came back up, too. Her white counts are very low, but we saw this last time, and the second Monday after the last chemo treatment is when they bottomed out. Laury feels and looks great, and we are going to yoga tonight, with a mask.

We have a new phrase Laury has been using lately, "Hug me with your eyes." She got it from her father who says it comes from a long ago movie. The reason Laury is using this phrase is because her white blood counts are very low again and she has to limit her contact with other people for fear of infection. Laury is a hugger, she has taught me to become a hugger, and anyone who knows Laury long enough will become a hugger. For Laury not to be able to hug and say, "Hi" or "Thank you!" is really hard. She can't stop hugging, not now, not ever. It simply is part of who she is.

To learn to hug others with her eyes is something new on this journey. But rather than save up all the hugs you all so richly deserve, hug Laury with your eyes, and let her hug you with her eyes. That way the connection is maintained and the love knows no boundaries.

All our Love.

Tuesday, 4/22/2014 – Cleaning the garden

"Gardens are not made by singing 'Oh, how beautiful!' and sitting in the shade." - Rudyard Kipling

Today Craig came with his crew and cleaned out all of our gardens. It is a passage of spring, one that leads to new growth. The leaves that protected the flowers now have to be removed to allow the new plants to get sunshine and grow. It reminded me of the analogy of a bone marrow transplant that Dr. Bishop gave Laury. Dr. Bishop is the head of the transplant department at U of C. He told Laury that her bone marrow is like her gardens. Right now her garden/marrow is full of rocks and weeds that are preventing the flowers from growing. The chemo at the beginning of the transplant process (called conditioning) is to kill all the weeds. Then we plant new seeds in the form of stem cells and help them grow. Once the stem cells start to grow and get strong, the rocks begin to dissolve and disappear. Laury is left with a beautiful healthy garden of bone marrow.

As I watched Craig's crew, it also reminded me that the cleaning and prep work is a lot of work and is not easy. But just as the gardens will thank Craig for his work, Laury's bone marrow will thank her for all her work.

And as a result, we will all get to enjoy the beauty of Laury and her gardens.

All our Love.

Thursday, 4/24/2014 – Off by a whisker

"I love cats because I enjoy my home; and little by little, they become its visible soul." - Jean Cocteau

Laury and I went to U of C today to meet with Dr. Odenike. We also met Paula, the transplant nurse. Paula came in to introduce herself and give us a copy of the latest stem cell transplant binder from U of C. We had met Paula six years ago when we thought Laury was going to need a transplant. She had given us a tour of transplant ward in the old hospital. There is a new hospital now and a new ward on the top floor with views of the lake and city. Laury and I have not seen it yet, but we will.

The meeting with Dr. Odenike went pretty much as usual; waiting an hour and a half for her to come into the examining room. Laury's numbers are good so we will be starting chemo again next week. We did get a few things cleared up. For example, I had misunderstood how to read Laury's white blood counts. Her neutrophils are at .08, I thought that the nurse said that Laury should wear a mask when her neutrophils were at .05. I was off by a little bit. We were told that Laury should wear a mask when her neutrophils are less than .5. I was only off by a factor of ten.

One of the downsides of her low white counts is that we will have to move the cats to upstairs. We have put a door at the top of the stairs to keep them up there and they will have two nice bedrooms to claim as their own. But it still saddens Laury and me not to have the cats down with us and in our laps whenever we sit still. They are part of the family and we will miss the constant interaction.

Laury mentioned this afternoon on the way to the city that she is trying to get used to the limitations of this journey. Being separated from the cats is another one to put on the list. It makes Laury and me sad even though we know it is not forever.

All our Love.

Friday, 4/25/2014 – I feel it too

"It's a fool who plays it cool by making his world a little colder" - Paul McCartney, Hey Jude

Laury spent most of today with her friend, Robin. She said it was like a vacation, a break from everything. It was a beautiful day here and I worked from home. I have an office upstairs, so I spent my time with two confused and not entirely happy cats that are now restricted to this space. They stayed close, and I could tell the cats wanted to know what they did to be banished. Not all of the changes we have to make can be explained in such a way as to satisfy the person (or in this case, cat) it affects.

As Laury and my daughters know, the above line from Hey Jude is my all-time favorite rock lyric. It speaks to me the importance of taking the good with the bad, not turning away from all that is around us. If you want to live a full life you have to be willing to see and feel the pain and disappointments of those around you. Today I felt the pain of the cats. I also felt my own pain. These changes have been hard for all of us. I miss a future that doesn't include a bone marrow transplant, and I look forward to a future when it is in our past. But here and now we can't close our eyes to how much this is affecting all of you, both good and bad.

I know I can't promise that it will all be good, but I can promise that we will all be in this together and that we will feel each other's' pains and joys.

All our Love.

Saturday, 4/26/2014 – Change places

"Look at situations from all angles, and you will become more open." - Dalai Lama

Today was a sunny cool spring day. The type of day all gardeners wait an entire winter for. To finally be able to get into the garden, pick weeds, prune bushes, move plants, it is what gardeners live for. Laury is a gardener, but today was not a good day for her. Because of her white blood counts Laury is not able to dig in the garden, or even touch the plants.

I spent most of the morning pruning the bushes, picking up sticks, and generally cleaning up around the garden. Laury sat inside or on the patio and watched. She would occasionally come out and talk with me or tell me how to do something she wanted done. But Laury was unable to keep her hands off the plants and so would go back inside. Later in the afternoon Laury said even if she had wanted to come out and help she was too tired.

This is a real role reversal for us. Usually I am the one watching Laury spend an entire day in the garden with what appears to be unlimited energy. Today Laury said she envied my energy and was grateful for all I did. The timing on this situation is terrible. In the winter Laury would be content to stay inside and read, but in spring it is hell not to be in her gardens.

We know it is temporary, and the gardens will still look great, but to not be able to do something you love so much and to have waited all winter to do it again doesn't make that knowledge any easier to take.

All our Love.

Monday, 4/28/2014 – Sunday

"Too often we underestimate the power of a touch, a smile, a kind word, a listening ear, and honest compliment, or the smallest act of caring, all of which have the potential to turn a life around." - Leo Buscaglia

Sunday was a better day. Laury and I got up and went to yoga which always helps. I know many of you expressed concern about how Laury was feeling on Friday and Saturday. They were difficult days. I don't want to hide the fact that there are times when this disease catches us off guard. It can still disrupt and upset our lives, and even though Laury and I have plans in place and have talked about everything, there are times when it just stares us in the face. It can't be overcome without your help. And once again, that is what you all did, came through with your positive thoughts and kind words.

Laury and I can't do this without you. Today we start back with the chemo.

There is some comfort in the routine of seeing the nurses and doctors again. We will carry all of you there with us, knowing you all care. Thank you.

All our Love.

Tuesday, 4/29/2014

Sorry for the short update. Laury was admitted to U of C hospital because of a fever. I will provide more details shortly. She is resting and doing ok.

Tuesday, 4/29/2014 – What a night

"How ridiculous and how strange to be surprised at anything which happens in life" - Marcus Aurelius

I am sorry for the short post this morning. I was operating on three hours of sleep and a Kindle with low battery and no keyboard. "The night did not turn out as planned", is a bit of an understatement. We started this first week of round three as we usually do, in the car on our way to Chicago. Laury's tongue had been sore all weekend and she had been very quiet. I assumed it was from the pain that talking caused her tongue. We had Laury's blood draw and then went to the infusion center. There they took her vitals and everything looked normal. Laury received her shot and we headed home. On the way home Laury asked me to turn up the heat in the car. This was my first clue that she was not feeling well. For the last several months Laury has been a little heater and I have been sitting in the car freezing as she asked me to keep turning down the temp. By the time we got home I could tell Laury was really not feeling well.

Laury lay down on the couch and I took her temperature. Laury said, "I don't have a temperature", and I watched the thermometer reach 100.2 and said, "Yes you do, and we are going to the ER." Laury didn't want to go to the ER so we compromised and went to the convenient care. The nurse who saw us told us that Laury should be at the ER and not the convenient care center. After taking Laury's vitals, the nurse left and the doctor came in. She immediately said, "You need to be going to the ER."

After talking with Dr. Odenike Laury and I headed back to the U of C. We were expected at the ER and got through triage quickly and were taken back to a room. The nurse in the room said he was surprised at how fast things were going. He said they already had a room for Laury, and after she was checked out by the ER doctor they would be transferring her upstairs to the new hospital. It was about 8:00 pm. We finally made it into the room at 3:15am. It took me asking if they could take all of the stuff off of Laury so we could go home to get them to find out what was taking so long and get the room ready.

Laury is still running a fairly high temperature, and they have taken several cultures, but the doctor told us that in about 50% of the times they don't find any reason for the fever. They are treating Laury with several antibiotics and anti-fungal medicines. She feels pretty crappy but still is in good spirits. Laury has read all of your comments and texts and they make her feel better.

Laury will probably be here a few days, and they have put off any more chemo until her blood numbers start to come back up. It was a night of surprises: we were surprised at how quickly the fever became serious, how long it took to get a room, how nice this room is, and how quickly and with so much caring you all have reacted.

All our Love.

Wednesday, 4/30/2014 – Sleep Interrupts

"I want to go to sleep in my time machine and wake up eight hours in the future." - Jarod Kintz, This Book Is Not For Sale

Anyone who has been in a hospital knows it is the worst place to get a good night's sleep. For Laury here at U of C it was no different. The staff woke Laury about every hour to check her temperature and give her medication and fluids. Laury can fall asleep in about ten seconds, so she didn't seem to mind too much. I, on the other hand, would fall back to sleep shortly before they came back in again.

The Attending Doctor stopped by this morning. He said that the blood culture that was positive yesterday came back positive again from the culture they took last night. The doctor says that it confirms that Laury has a bacterial infection. The doctor told us that they still don't know the source of the infection, but the good news is they have been giving her the correct antibacterial meds all along. Laury is still running a fever, it spiked a couple of times last night and they gave her additional meds besides the Tylenol to help bring it down. Laury's last temperature was only slightly above 100, so we are heading the right direction. Laury looks better today and ate a little bit of eggs for breakfast. She got out of bed to walk around a bit so those are good signs. I will post more later if we hear any more from the doctors.

I read Laury all of your comments and well wishes and they made her cry and smile. It means a lot to both of us that you are all with us.

All our Love.

CHAPTER THREE

May

Thursday, 5/1/2014 — New day

"I feel so grateful to discover that each new day brings me the opportunity to watch the sunrise and fall in love with you again." - Steve Maraboli, Unapologetically You

Today is already a better day. Laury is feeling better, her fever is being held down and she was able to get a good night's sleep. The doctor was in this morning with more information. They identified the bacteria as one commonly found in our mouths. I didn't give this to her! The doctors are continuing the treatments and so far none of the cultures taken since the first night have turned positive. Laury's blood numbers are still really low and because they have taken so much blood from her, Laury will be getting a transfusion later today. This should help her feel a lot better. Laury and I were able to get into the shower and wash her hair. Laury is sitting up next to me on the couch waiting for it to dry so it doesn't go flat - her words. Amazing how much a hot shower can help you feel better.

Still no word on when Laury can go home. I will let you all know when I hear something on that front.

The days have run together and we were both surprised to hear that today is May Day. Hopefully things keep going in the right direction and Laury will be home soon.

Thanks again for all your kind and uplifting words and prayers.

All our Love.

Friday, 5/2/2014 — A Laugh

"The first time her laughter unfurled its wings in the wind, we knew that the world would never be the same" - Brian Andreas

Yesterday Laury continued to improve. Laury's fever stayed down all day, she was able to get up and walk around more and to talk with her parents, and Keri and Lyndsay. We met the Infectious Diseases doctors (two women - yeah) yesterday afternoon. The doctors said that Laury will need to continue the antibiotics for at least another week. The drugs are given intravenously but will not require Laury to be in the hospital. The doctors also ordered an echo cardiogram to make sure the bacteria had not attacked her heart. They said they were very confident it hadn't, but they wanted to make sure. Laury and I have not heard the results yet, but it was cool to watch the screen and see all of my baby's heart valves in action.

Laury received a unit of blood late in the day. She was feeling well enough at that point that I ordered a pizza for delivery and when the pizza arrived we sat together and watched TV and the blood slowly dripping from the IV pump. Sounds gross, but the pizza was some of the best Laury and I have ever had and the blood was making Laury feel so much better. The night nurse came in at seven and introduced herself and said the doctors are talking about letting Laury go home today. We both know better than to get too excited. Hospitals are like airlines - a small delay can mean eight hours.

Last night Laury and I both slept great, me with a full tummy of pizza, and

Laury with some pizza and a full tank of blood. At 2:00 am they came in to give Laury her one of her antibiotics and check her vitals. Laury got up to go to the bathroom and change her gown (her night sweats are back). I asked Laury if she needed any help and she said no, but I got up after a few minutes because I could see she was still trying to get the new gown on. As I helped Laury get the gown on we noticed that she had her IV line tangled around the sleeve and after we fixed that she had to do a couple of turns to unwind from the line. Laury laughed and said, "I guess I did need help!", and there it was; the thing that had been missing for the last week, even before we came to the hospital. Laury had not laughed over the weekend. That should have been my first clue on how bad she was feeling. The laugh made me feel so good. I love Laury's laugh and more importantly last night, I loved that it meant that she was back. We hope to have much more to laugh about today.

All our Love.

Friday, 5/2/2014 – Not today

"Learn from yesterday, live for today, hope for tomorrow." - Albert Einstein

The doctor stopped by a little while ago and passed on the news that we are not going home until tomorrow. The lab results on the bacteria are still not done so the doctor can't prescribe the final round of antibiotics. Laury and I hope the tests will be done today so we can be released early tomorrow.

Laury is disappointed but not surprised. We are going to find some fun food for delivery tonight and try to get a good night sleep and head home tomorrow.

All our Love.

Saturday, 5/3/2014 – Home soon – we hope

"How often have I lain beneath rain on a strange roof, thinking of home?" - William Faulkner

When the doctors came by on their rounds yesterday Laury asked them if we could now kiss. Laury and I hadn't been kissing because of not knowing where the bacteria came from. The doctor smiled and said we could but that it might be difficult with the sore tongue. Laury did her Madeline Kahn imitation from Young Frankenstein and said, "No tongues!" One of the medical students said, "I just watched that movie last night!" The doctors all laughed and one even blushed.

Last night we ordered Thai food from Snail Thai - thanks Becky! The food was delicious and Laury and I ate while watching TV. Once you shift from being here and getting Laury well to going home mode, time slows down. Laury and I couldn't wait for the doctor to come in this morning. The doctor arrived and gave us the good news that the final lab result is in and now we know what antibiotic Laury will be on for the next week or so. It is a once-a-day intravenous, so Laury will still need home health care but it won't be too bad. Laury got her pick line put in yesterday, and even though it was a little painful, it has already saved her arm veins from being poked three more times for blood samples. The doctor said they will be doing their rounds between eight-thirty and ten-thirty and then will prepare Laury's discharge papers.

It looks like a beautiful day out there and we look forward to being home. This has been a sometimes scary, educational, and filled with love, stay.

Laury and I have learned a lot about life in the hospital here and we know now more of what to expect when Laury comes back for her transplant.

The other thing Laury and I learned is that no matter where we are we are still together. Sitting watching TV, reading your replies, or just sitting quietly together waiting to be released from the hospital, life is good.

All our Love.

Saturday, 5/3/2014 – We are home

Just a short post - we are home - ready for a hot shower, clean clothes and a nap.

More later.

All our Love.

Sunday, 5/4/2014 – Gratitude

"If the only prayer you said was thank you, that would be enough." - Meister Eckhart

It is great to be home. Laury and I both slept well, even though we both admit to having very strange dreams. I guess our brains are still trying to process all that went on last week. Laury and I learned a lot about how things operate in the hospital. The room was set up well for me to get some work done and not disturb Laury. We don't know if when Laury goes in for her transplant if we will have such a large room. The room was "L" shaped and the couch that I slept on was away from the bed side and my snoring didn't wake Laury.

I think the biggest thing Laury and I learned last week was that gratitude goes a long way in a hospital. Laury would thank her nurse assistants for their kind care - most were surprised at this and admitted that most patients are not very nice when they are woken to get their vital signs taken. I would hear the technicians come in every four hours and say, "Miss Hart, I am so sorry to wake you but I need to get your vitals." Laury would tell them it was OK and not to be sorry and they were so sweet to wake her so nicely.

Laury would thank the doctors for their good care, and the doctors would thank her for being a good patient. The doctors and nurses would say they were sorry that Laury had to be in the hospital. Laury would say she was grateful that she was in such a good place.

Every day I would read Laury your comments and she would cry, and smile and say thank you to you all. All of this gratitude is not required, but it makes the days brighter. The nurses all seemed to like talking with Laury and the doctors all smiled when they came into the room.

It made Laury and I both realize that the simple act of saying thank you is very important to everyone's healing.

Thank you all again for your words of encouragement, love and gratitude.

All our Love.

Monday, 5/5/2014 – Nurse Dan

"The most essential prerequisite to understanding is to be able to admit when you don't understand something" - Richard Saul Wurman, Information Anxiety 2

Yesterday, the Home Care nurse came to give Laury her intravenous antibiotic. I say "give" but the nurse was really here to teach me how to give it to Laury. When the nurse arrived she asked Laury if she had anyone to give her the treatment, and Laury replied, "You, home care nursing." The nurse answered, "No, I am here to teach someone how to do it." I then said, "Well I guess that would be me. But I must tell you I really don't like needles." The nurse said then it was my lucky day because the procedure did not involve any needles. "Whew."

I learned how to push the air out of the saline syringe without letting the cap get contaminated. I learned how to clean the cap on the Picc line and how to flush the line before and after the antibiotic syringe. The hardest part was the antibiotic syringe has to go in slow, three to five minutes slow, so Laury and I set up a timer and I watched it as I would push a little at a time.

When I was done (it all takes about 5 minutes) Laury said, "Doctor Dan!" The nurse replied, "Everyone wants to be the doctor, nobody wants to be the nurse." Laury said, "You are right, Nurse Dan, even though I like the alliteration of Doctor Dan better."

Laury and I head back down to U of C today for a doctor visit and to start the chemo treatments again. It feels a little like Deja Vu all over again.

All our Love.

Monday, 5/5/2014 – Another step in the process

"A process cannot be understood by stopping it. Understanding must move with the flow of the process, must join it and flow with it." - Frank Herbert

Laury and I went down to U of C today for a meeting with Dr. Odenike and we thought the start of another week of chemo. I carried with us today's dose of intravenous antibiotic that I was supposed to give to Laury at noon. I was not able to get the Picc line flushed and I called the nurse and decided just to bring it with us so the nurse could show me what I was doing wrong. Turns out I was not doing anything wrong, but the position that Laury was sitting in at home was cutting off the line in her shoulder. The nurse had Laury lie back and when she did the Picc line worked fine. Laury and I sat in the infusion area and I gave her the antibiotic. The nurse was also able to take Laury's blood through the Picc line, saving her veins for a few more days.

Laury and I met with Dr. Odenike and the first thing she said was we had finally received insurance approval for the transplant. This is great news, but it also felt a little anti-climactic. What this means is the hospital can start contacting donors and scheduling the actual transplant. Dr. Odenike said that she is requesting that the hospital move as quickly as possible to get everything done. Even with this additional effort it will most likely be six weeks before Laury gets the transplant. The other news Dr. Odenike gave us is that she wants Laury to wait another week to finish her antibiotics before starting the chemo again. We all agreed that last week was rough and Laury needed some more time to heal before hitting her again with the chemo.

It was hard for Laury and me today to get back into the waiting mode. We have gotten used to having to wait for so long that we now know why they are called patients. But today was different, maybe since Laury and I had just left the hospital on Saturday and we were not ready to go through it again so soon. Whatever it was, Laury and I both felt it and it made the waiting harder today than usual. Laury and I know we have a lot of waiting ahead of us and we also know that our patience will come back. You cannot be in a hurry to go through this. I guess it is just like life.

All our Love.

Tuesday, 5/6/2014 – Speaking their language

"Meow" means "woof" in cat." - George Carlin

Reading some of the latest post, I noticed that Laury and I have begun to learn a new language. New words have entered our vocabulary, such as, "Picc line", "vitals", and "blood counts". Laury and I have learned that to effectively communicate with the doctors you have to learn to speak their language. For example, last week when Laury was in the hospital, her calf muscles were really sore. She kept mentioning it to the doctors and they said it was normal. The doctors gave Laury extra potassium and said her legs would get better when she was feeling better. When we met with Dr. Odenike yesterday, Laury mentioned the problems she had with her legs. Dr. Odenike said that it was not uncommon for the legs to feel weak when you run a fever. Laury tried to explain to her that her legs had not felt weak but were cramped. Dr. Odenike said, "Oh we could have done something more about that like getting physical therapy to visit to work your muscles." It seems that Laury and I were not using the right words to describe the problem.

When Laury and I met with the infusion nurse yesterday and I was explaining to her that I couldn't get the line to flush, she asked me how hard I was pushing. I said pretty hard and the nurse said, "You have to push a little hard to get it started, but if you are using all your strength, then that is too much." That made it much clearer: push hard but stop short of using both hands and feet. The nurse also showed me how I could pull back on the saline syringe if pushing didn't work at first. The nurse who came on Sunday told me never to do that. When I mentioned that to the infusion nurse, she said, "You can do it if you are careful, but remember I am a professional," I think that means "Don't do this at home."

With this new language we hope to communicate better with Laury's caregivers. If however, Laury and I ever get to the point that you can't understand what we are saying, just remind us that we are mere mortals and this new language is only for professionals.

All our Love.

Thursday, 5/8/2014 – Thoughts

"You should listen to even the smallest voice, someday it could be the one that makes a difference." - Crystal Marcos

Yesterday evening Laury and I were walking the gardens and seeing the plants pop. The ground looked pretty dry so I hooked up the sprinkler system we installed last year and watered the front garden. As we walked around to check each sprinkler head to make sure it was working and hitting the things that needed water, Laury said to me, "Did you insist that we install this system because you knew we were going to need it this summer?" I said that I noticed that it had become harder for Laury to drag the hoses around to do the watering and yes I knew that there would come a time when we would need the system. But I didn't know it would be this summer. Laury replied, "Thank you for the system and thank you for not telling me why."

Sharing your thoughts are important, knowing when to share them is priceless.

All our Love.

Friday, 5/9/2014 – Small plans

"Have patience with everything that remains unsolved in your heart. ...live in the question." - Rainer Marie Rilke, Letters To a Young Poet

This week was for Laury to heal fully from last week. Laury and I did some planning for the transplant based on what we learned from our hospital stay. Laury ordered some walking shoes and some lounging clothes for both her and me. I also ordered her a couple of Picc line covers, so I didn't have to cut up any more of my socks. Laury learned how to order a movie from Amazon to our Kindle, and I looked at a bunch of cheap books for the Kindle.

Today the home care nurse stopped by and changed the dressing on Laury's Picc line. Laury's soreness has finally gone away, although she would still like to punch the woman who put the line in. The nurse says the bruising is normal, but it didn't change Laury's feelings about the woman.

Next week we head back down to U of C. We meet with Dr. Odenike on Monday, and if she approves we will start the chemo again. Laury is feeling and looking good. I think the week in the hospital took more out of her mentally and emotionally than we thought. Her spirit is still strong, but it was tested.

Laury and I spent a lot of time this week talking about the future, what we can expect when we get to the transplant, and what it is going to be like when she comes home. Laury and I also talked about vacations and family visits, knowing those are much further off. But it was good to be able to think about things that we will do once the transplant is behind us.

Our plans are good, but Laury and I also know that they are small and easily changed. Change is the only thing we can plan for with certainty.

All our Love.

Saturday, 5/10/2014 – Together

"Alone we can do so little, together we can do so much." - Helen Keller

Today was a beautiful day, sunny not too warm and Laury was itching to get in her gardens. Laury and I talked about what we wanted to do today and how we could get things done. I went up to ACE Hardware to get some things for the hoses and gardens, and Laury stayed home. When I returned home Laury was sitting in the chair on our deck and was looking very forlorn. I asked her what was the matter and Laury said, her voice cracking, "I don't know what to do." I asked her what she meant, and Laury said that there is so much that she sees the gardens need but she doesn't know what she can or can't do. I hate to see Laury this way, so discouraged. I asked her what she wanted to get done. Laury and I looked at all of the things and started working together. Laury did things that she could do, with her mask and gloves on, and I did things that she couldn't. Together we got a lot done. The patio is set up, the lawn is cut, one of the fountains is working, and all of the dead plants in the pots are taken care of.

Laury and I accomplished more than either one of us thought we would.

We make a great team, just like all of you. Sometimes it takes working together to get more done than each of us could accomplish on our own. I know it was sure a lot more fun having Laury at my side today.

All our Love.

Monday, 5/12/2014 – Fish and Champagne

"Let us celebrate the occasion with wine and sweet words." - Plautus

The fish I had planned for dinner, but the Champagne was not planned. Tonight we celebrated the news from Dr. Odenike that they have located and contacted a donor and additional testing confirms he is a perfect match. Dr. Odenike has requested that the donor be available for "harvesting" the second week of June. This means that Laury would go in the first week of June to begin the transplant process. Dr. Odenike said she had not heard back from the donor yet on the dates, but was pretty confident that it will work out.

Laury and I greeted this news with a numbed reaction. Laury said she thought she would jump up and down when the news came through - I think Lyndsay is doing that for her tonight with her friends. The news made us both quiet. This has always been our prayer that a donor would be found and that Laury would move forward with the transplant. Now that it is really happening, it is met with mixed feelings. Laury and I know that there is a lot more to be done and a lot more to go through before this is over and this is just one important step.

The plan as it now sits is that Laury will have another two week round of chemo and then a week off and then the transplant. Pray that the doctors keep making good decisions. Laury's body has recovered from the chemo and the fever, and her blood numbers are really good. However, Laury admits that maybe last week she was a little depressed. I don't know how she couldn't be; we did everything we were supposed to do and Laury still got very sick. But we have to remember that Laury and I (and all of you) are in training and the event now has a date. Having the date will intensify our efforts and focus our spirits.

But tonight we relax and celebrate. You all have gotten us this far, so enjoy part of our celebration tonight. Tomorrow the work continues.

All our Love.

Tuesday, 5/13/2014 – Really Real

"Life is not a problem to be solved, but a reality to be experienced." - Soren Kierkegaard

Laury and I were trying to figure out why we both felt so numb yesterday at the news of the donor and the tentative schedule. We both agreed it was because the transplant became real again. I think our minds have a built-in mechanism that only allows us to take in what we can handle at any given moment. Laury and I both have said on several occasions that we can't believe this is happening. Sometimes it doesn't feel real, the diagnosis, the chemo, the hospital visits, can Laury and I really be going through this?

Yesterday was a reality we couldn't ignore, this is really happening. There have been other times when I have felt this way: the day we got married, the day the girls were born, the day Keri got married. When I reflect, most of the times when Laury and I have felt this way it has been because we were overwhelmed with love and gratitude.

Laury and I have to face all of the emotions that the reality of the transplant brings with it, the fear, the excitement, the uncertainty. We also know the waiting has been tough, not knowing when the transplant would happen, me worried that Laury might get too sick. That is behind us now. Laury and I can plan and move into this with the confidence that we have the love and support of all of you.

All our Love.

Wednesday, 5/14/2014 – Light of mine

"She was bendable light: she shone around every corner of my day." - Jerry Spinelli, Stargirl

Today Laury and I went back to U of C for a chemo treatment. As we usually do, we played music on the way down and listened to a book on tape on the way back. We waited about an hour before Laury was taken back for her shot. Pretty much the usual state of affairs.

What made today different was that Laury's light was back. I could see the sparkle in her eyes again and the sense of determination and spirit that was dimmed over the past couple of weeks. I don't know if it was Laury going to yoga this morning, or talking with her brother on the phone, or just feeling better, but her spark was back. Laury's light is contagious. It lifts me and anyone around her who is willing to take notice. Laury said she still felt a little numb from the news yesterday, but she looked alive and wonderful.

I gain so much joy from Laury's presence. To have her next to me and feeling good and bright is wonderful. Laury constantly tells me I am her strength right now, but she is and always will be my light.

All our Love.

Thursday, 5/15/2014 – Stories

"After nourishment, shelter and companionship, stories are the thing we need most in the world." - Phillip Pullman

Laury and I watched a couple of YouTube videos on Robin Roberts' journey through a stem cell transplant. It was good for Laury to see more of the process and the recovery. The first thing Laury said to me after watching the videos was that she noticed all the plants in Robin's apartment. I said the plants were probably fake. We both recognize that these videos are good, but they are Robin's story and not necessarily ours.

Each of us has a story. Sometimes our stories cross or are similar but they are never exactly the same. Our nurse yesterday, whose name is Kim, told us about her friend who was going through a bone marrow transplant. Laury and I hadn't seen Kim for several weeks and when we saw her yesterday, Laury asked how her friend was doing. Kim lit up and said, "He is doing great! He went home already." It was good to hear his story, too.

Watching Robin's video, I couldn't help wonder if she had to make a list of things to take care of while in the hospital, like how are we going to do our laundry, how will we get our mail, where we can get take-out food. Did Robin have to leave a list of directions for the person staying in her house; a list containing things like, how much to feed the cats, how to work the TV and what the password to the Wi-Fi is? Probably not.

Laury and I have begun to think about these things and make lists. Yesterday we sat in the waiting room of the infusion center and looked over the list Laury had started for the person who will be staying in our house while we are gone. The list contained the obvious things like, what and when to feed the cats, when the trash is picked up, how to contact us, etc. It was funny trying to think of things this person might need to know about staying in our home. A few weeks ago the U of C hospital gave us a binder of information on the stem cell transplant process. It is well done and very well organized, containing everything you would want to know, but from the hospital's point of view. It didn't contain anything on how or where to get our dirty laundry done. Laury and I are hoping that someone will be able to answer this question - because neither of us has enough underwear to go a month.

Our story is and will be different from Robin's and Kim's friend. There will be similarities and we can learn from each other's' stories.

This is our story and I am honored that you all are letting us share it with you.

All our Love.

Thursday, 5/15/2014 – Wine

"Either give me more wine or leave me alone." - Rumi

Laury and I have started walking each night after dinner. We want to get into the habit, so when Laury goes into the hospital and comes home, walking will already be part of our routine. All of the reading we have done and what the doctors have told us, is that walking will be really good for Laury's recovery.

Laury bought a new pair of walking shoes and she said that they were the first shoes she has ever put on that she doesn't want to take off. The shoes are cute and comfortable, two prerequisites for walking shoes, I am told.

Laury and I usually head out and walk up the hill by our house, then around the four blocks and back home, three quarters of a mile. Not a long walk, but it gets us moving.

Tonight when I asked Laury if she wanted to go for our after dinner walk she replied, "No, I just want to drink wine." I couldn't argue with that so we stayed home. I guess the wine is a stronger routine then the walking.

All our Love.

Friday, 5/16/2014 – Ironic

"Love takes off masks that we fear we cannot live without and know we cannot live within." - James A. Baldwin

You all know that Laury needs to wear a mask when her white blood counts get low. This is for her protection against nasty things that can invade Laury's body when it can't properly defend itself. As you remember, getting Laury to wear the mask took time and patience, and I made a few mistakes along that path.

However, recently Laury has been sneezing and coughing after wearing her masks. We are not sure, but Laury might be having an allergic reaction to something in the masks. We do know that some masks contain latex and it could possibly be the latex that is causing the problem. The masks that I bought say latex free on the box, but we don't know about the other masks we have gotten from the clinic. There is irony in that the mask that is supposed to protect Laury might, in fact, be giving her these reactions. It also could be that it is a really bad allergy season and with her weakened immune system the allergies are just worse. We will need to get to the bottom of this mystery.

Laury and I are going to try using only the masks that say latex free to see if that makes a difference. If it doesn't, we will have to visit the doctor to find out what is going on. We both could laugh at the irony of the situation, but Laury is sneezing too much to find it funny.

All our Love.

Saturday, 5/17/2014 — Beauty

"A woman who cuts her hair is about to change her life." - Coco Chanel

Laury and I went down to Chicago this morning to get our hair cut. We go see Magen about every three weeks and Laury and I get a coffee and a cookie to eat while we wait. This morning we had to go early because someone had taken our usual nine o'clock appointment. Magen had agreed to come in early so we met her before anyone else, at seven fifteen in the morning.

Laury had decided earlier this week that she was going to get her hair cut really short. This is to prepare her for shaving her head before she goes into the hospital for the transplant. I told Laury that I would get my hair cut short, too. Laury was surprised and grateful at my gesture but said that she liked my hair and that I didn't need to get it cut that short. When we met with Magen, Laury told her to cut it short, and they began. I watched as they took off most of Laury's hair, and she began to get even more beautiful. The first thing you notice is her eyes, which have always been one of my favorite features. I kept hearing Laury telling Magen, "I can do this." Laury did and she looks great.

When it came my turn I told Magen to take it all off, shorter than Laury's. Part of the reason I did it was to be on the path with Laury, but part of it was I saw how good she looked and thought, "Hey, maybe it will improve my looks too."

When we were done Magen took a picture. We sent the picture in a text to Keri in England. She replied, "Mom looks cute, not a good look on Dad." Ouch! Oh well - it was worth a try.

All our Love.

Monday, 5/19/2014 – What's in a ml

"I have measured out my life with coffee spoons." - T. S. Eliot

Today Laury and I began our second week of Chemo. The traffic has been unusually heavy due to construction on another freeway pushing everyone over to the one we want to use. We have been enjoying books on tape and our time together, so it is not too bad.

Laury and I had the usual wait in the infusion center of about an hour. We were taken back to one of the chairs and met our nurse. The nurse asked Laury all of the usual questions about medicines and how she is feeling. We received a copy of Laury's blood results from last Friday and the numbers were really good. Laury's white blood counts are up enough that she doesn't need to wear the mask, we are hoping that a few days without the mask will heal her nose.

As I mentioned in a previous post, the nurse always calls for a chemo check before giving Laury her shot. Another nurse comes over to double check that everything is OK. Today, the nurse said to Laury, "It is 10mg in a 2ml solution." We have heard these numbers so many times that both

Laury and I said at the same time, "That is not right." The nurse looked at us, confused and I said, "It is supposed to be 10mg in a 1ml solution." The nurse said, "Really? I will go check with the pharmacy." After a few minutes the nurse came back and said we were correct, and the pharmacy had made a mistake and it was good that we caught it. One milliliter is a very small amount and we are not sure what the impact would have been if Laury would have gotten the wrong amount. The shot contained the same amount of chemo, just diluted more. The fact is Laury and I didn't want to find out the answer to that question.

Everyone says you have to be your own advocate when it comes to health care. Today proved that you have to pay attention to every detail.

This is a tough job, one I am grateful to be able to help Laury with.

All our Love.

Tuesday, 5/20/2014 – Little Things

"You need to let the little things that would ordinarily bore you suddenly thrill you." - Andy Warhol

Today was a series of little things. No great events or happenings that changed our lives forever. Laury and I went down to U of C for Laury's chemo, driving to and back in unusually heavy traffic.

There was a bunch of little things that made it a good day. We were together, and faced them as a couple, which makes the little things important. There was a young girl getting on to the elevator using crutches while holding and talking on her cell phone. All of us in the elevator were impressed with the girl's ability to maneuver and talk without falling over. The woman next to me said, "I think she got off on the wrong floor." Her husband said, "I thought you said she got off on the wrong foot!" We all saw the humor and the entire elevator chuckled.

When Laury and I got to the infusion center we were taken back very quickly, it was a little thing, but still nice. Sonya said to us, "You will need to stop at the desk on the way out and make appointments for the rest of the week. We don't have you on the books. Just tell them I said it was OK that we are over booked." We did as we were told and now have appointments for the rest of the week. I did not question why we were not in the books in the first place.

Our nurse today talked potted plants with Laury. The nurse talked about how she loves going to the nursery and picking out plants and arranging them into her large containers. I could see the joy in the nurse and Laury's eyes as they discussed the plants and their placement. The nurse asked for a chemo check and when the other nurse, named Nevada, came over, Helena looked at the shot and said, "Hang on, I will call you right back." and quickly walked away. The nurse came back a few minutes later with another shot. I said, "Got the right one this time?" She smiled and said, "Yup."

Our days are made up of these little things, and I can't help wondering how many more I miss. Time takes on a different personality while we are at U of C. You have time to look around, to notice things, to wonder about the people you see. I can't image going through this with our eyes closed, not noticing these things. It makes the waiting, the driving, the pain, somehow better. There is always something to notice, little thing that makes a difference in our time there. It would be nice to think we live that way all the time, noticing the little things. I am not sure we do.

All our Love.

Wednesday, 5/21/2014 – Balancing act

"Happiness is not a matter of intensity but of balance and order and rhythm and harmony." - Thomas Merton

Laury and I were talking today and we both realized that much of what we are doing right now is to try to keep our lives in balance. I am trying to balance care giving and working full time. Laury is trying to balance staying active and feeling good with being sick. Every day we have tradeoffs and decisions on how to maintain the balance in our lives. It doesn't take much to throw the balance off. The trick is not to get too far off balance so that it requires a great amount of effort to get it back.

Laury's recent stay in the hospital was a balance altering event. She and I have pretty much been able to regain the balance, but it has taken much work. Yoga teaches about balance, physical, mental and emotional. Yoga helps both Laury and me to regain and maintain our balance. Our spirits teach us to look around and welcome acts of balance from others. Today there were events that could have tipped us one way or the other. But when Laury and I focused on one event we were able to find another that balanced it out. Really bad traffic is balanced out with a good book on tape, a close in parking spot is balanced out by having to wait for the doctor to sign the lab order, getting a chemo shot is balanced out by the smiles and welcome greetings of the nurses.

The next month will present Laury and me with many opportunities to tip the balance off and we will need your help to get us back on center. I know now after all of your comments and well wishes that you all are up for it. Thanks.

All our Love.

Thursday, 5/22/2014 - Starting point

"I had as many doubts as anyone else. Standing on the starting line, we're all cowards." - Alberto Salazar

Laury and I met with Dr. Odenike today and we have a date - June 4th, Laury goes in to the hospital and on June 12 she will receive her new bone marrow. We now have a date, a starting point and Laury and I are both excited and nervous. We have known this was coming for years, and Laury and I have known for a couple of weeks that it was tentatively planned for the first week of June. But to have a date makes it real.

The plan for the next couple of weeks is as follows. Tomorrow we need to get blood work done out here in Naperville, Laury's white counts are low and her hemoglobin in near the point where Laury might need a transfusion. Laury and I will get her blood checked again on Tuesday in Naperville and then on Thursday we go back down for a visit with Dr. Odenike. On Wednesday, June 4th Laury and I will head down to U of C where the doctor will insert a Hiccman line into Laury and check her into the transplant ward. Laury will undergo seven days of chemo and then a day off and then the next day receives her stem cells.

Laury and I both feel like we ran a marathon today, winded, tired, but excited. We know this is another step on this journey, but it is a big one. But like a marathon Laury and I are in it together for the long haul. This race has just started.

All our Love.

Saturday, 5/24/2014 – A brother's love

"I sustain myself with the love of family." - Maya Angelou

Laury and I were granted a slight reprieve yesterday from our U of C visits. Dr. Odenike had decided that Laury did not need her final chemo treatment, so we did not have to go into the city. We did, however, have to get Laury's blood checked out here in Naperville. Laury's brother, Bobby is in from Dallas and Laury and I asked if he wanted to go with us. He did. We sat together and talked while waiting for Laury to be called back. We talked about nothing in particular, sometimes focusing on what Laury is going through and sometimes not.

Laury was called back and Bobby and I sat talking about stuff, none of which I can recall. When Laury came back out she was showing us her middle finger. The technician had taken the blood for Laury's CBC from her finger instead of her arm. Laury was elated that she did not have to get another needle in the vein. Bobby said, "Oh I thought you were just flipping us off." We laughed and then Bobby took a picture to remember the event.

Laury, Bobby and I waited for the triage nurse to call Laury back to go over the results and take her vitals. After about fifteen minutes Laury and I went back with the nurse. Laury's numbers are holding steady, her white counts were up a little as well as her hemoglobin and platelets. Laury will get her blood checked again on Tuesday.

After leaving the cancer center we stopped and got brats and a pulled pork sandwich from Kreger's and met Lyndsay at home to eat lunch outside. Bobby spent the rest of the afternoon with Laury and me sitting out on the patio and talking. As he was getting ready to leave, Bobby asked about our plans for tomorrow. He asked what are days are like and if his visit was interrupting anything. Laury replied, "You are not interrupting anything. This is pretty much what my days are like right now.

Do a little, rest a little." Hopefully, Bobby is coming over today and I can give him and Laury some time by themselves. I know how glad Laury is that he is here. Thanks for coming, Bobby.

All our Love.

Monday, 5/26/2014 – "I am happy"

"Now and then it's good to pause in our pursuit of happiness and just be happy." - Guillaume Apollinaire

This weekend has been an oasis; a time to pause and enjoy the weather and enjoy time with family. Yesterday Laury's parents, her brother, as well as Lyndsay came over for a picnic. We served the usual- brats with potato salad, and baked beans. We had time to talk and laugh and tell stories. Laury's upcoming transplant was a topic of conversation, but not the only one. The conversation brought us up to speed on each other's lives and we listened to old stories told again with love.

It is good to have these respites in our journey, to reconnect and be reminded of all the good things in our lives. After everyone left last night, Laury and I were standing in the driveway and Laury said to me, "I am happy."

A day cannot be asked to give more than that.

All our Love.

Tuesday, 5/27/2014 — Privacy versus community

"It was a train full of strangers, and they were all the same." - Cherie Priest, Dreadnought

Today Laury and I went to the infusion center here in Naperville to have her blood checked. Laury's numbers are still holding steady, so she did not require a transfusion today. The center is new and nicely appointed, full of light and bright, welcoming colors and furniture. It is quite a difference from the infusion center at U of C. Today was the first day Laury and I actually got to see the infusion rooms. The center was busy so they put us in one of the rooms to wait for the nurse to evaluate Laury's results.

At U of C there are always people in the waiting area, sometimes as many as twenty of us sitting in the area waiting for our turn. The waiting area at the infusion center out here never has more than two or three people sitting quietly. The "rooms" at U of C are more like recliners with the hospital curtains that can be pulled around them for some privacy. The rooms out here are new, more private with nice views of a courtyard.

Laury and I should like the experience of the local center better. But while sitting there today I said to Laury, "Why do we like the U of C center so much better?" I said I thought it was because there is a sense of community at U of C that we don't feel here. Not just with the staff but with the other patients, as well. It seems like the local infusion center has sacrificed community for privacy.

Anyone who has spent any time in a hospital knows that privacy is pretty much an illusion. There are times when privacy is important and single occupancy rooms are better than sharing a room. But other times it is healing to see and meet other people dealing with their afflictions alongside of you dealing with yours. There is community in sharing and being part of something bigger. I am afraid that the designers of the local infusion center missed that point.

All our Love.

Thursday, 5/29/2014 – Positive thoughts

"The energy of the mind is the essence of life." - Aristotle

Laury and I traveled down to see Dr. Odenike this afternoon. Laury's blood numbers are still pretty good but her white count is now really low, so we have to be especially careful over the next week to keep her from any infections. Before Dr. Odenike came in Laury and I were visited by Christine, a Fellow working in the department. We had met Christine back in February and she remembered Laury. Christine said how much better Laury looked than the last time she saw her.

I sometimes forget how sick Laury was back in February and that my biggest fear was that she would get too sick to have the transplant. It was good to hear Christine say how much Laury had improved since the last time they had talked.

Also, today I went with Laury to her therapist visit. Pat is a special person and has greatly helped Laury in dealing with this disease and the journey it has placed us on. Today Pat did an anointing and blessing for both Laury and me for the upcoming transplant. It was special and very moving.

Both of these events reminded us of the importance of positive thoughts and energy. Laury and I work at keeping a positive attitude, but also at keeping positive energy around us. Laury and I know the next few weeks and months are going to be hard, and we will need all of the positive energy you all can spare. Laury and I ask that you focus on sending positive images and thoughts. They are the stuff that lifts us and sets our direction.

All our Love.

Saturday, 5/31/2014 – Together

"She had no need to ask why he had come. She knew as certainly as if he had told her that he was here to be where she was." - Leo Tolstoy, Anna Karenina

Yesterday I went into the office and Laury was at home. For most working people this is the norm, but lately it has not been for us. I have been able to work from home and be with Laury. I had several meetings during the day that made going into the office necessary. Laury's sister, Cindy, who is in from Kansas City, and Laury's mom came over to spend some time with Laury. When I am away from Laury I do wonder how she is doing. I don't so much worry as just wonder, and try to picture her.

When I got home Laury told me all about the "lovely" visit they had and how much she enjoyed spending time with her sister and mom. Laury showed me all of the gifts her sister gave her to prepare for her hospital stay. Laury also said how good it felt to just be outside yesterday to enjoy the day, to take a walk and just be. Later after her sister and mom left, Laury's co-teacher, John, stopped by to visit and bring news and well wishes from her friends and students. Laury was energized and overwhelmed with the love and support from her school.

When I got home Lyndsay was there and we sat out on the patio and talked and ordered pizza. Lyndsay expressed her concerns about the upcoming transplant and how we will all get through it. Loving concerns.

We decided to come in the house when the mosquitoes came out and Lyndsay had to leave to go watch the Black Hawks game.

It was a good day for Laury, and I love coming home to see her so happy and excited by her day. This weekend we continue to prepare, pack, and contemplate, together. I want to be nowhere else.

All our Love.

CHAPTER FOUR

June

Sunday, 6/1/2014 – Lightheaded

"As we work to create light for others, we naturally light our own way." - Mary Anne Radmacher

Today was for creating light in our gardens, life and family. Laury has in our back gardens several large boxwoods that didn't survive the winter. Laury had been fretting about seeing these dead plants in her garden. I knew that it was going to be a big job to dig them out and since they were still green, thought they could wait to be removed. But the more I saw how much these dead things in Laury's garden bothered her, the more I knew I had to remove the bushes before we went into the hospital. The job was not as big as I thought and when they were removed, Laury said, "Now we have more light in that garden and room for growth, kind of a metaphor for me right now." That made so much sense, and I then knew why it was so important to have those bushes gone.

Laury's parents and sister came over for dinner to celebrate my birthday (it was yesterday). Before they arrived Lyndsay came by with her hair clippers to shave Laury's head. Before she began on Laury, Lyndsay said to Laury, "You can do me first." Laury shaved Lyndsay's head and then Lyndsay shaved Laury's head and then they both shaved mine. It was very freeing, letting more light into our heads and our lives together. It meant a lot to Laury to have Lyndsay shave her head and for me to agree to it, as well. Laury said when we were all done, "Now we are all lightheaded!"

Laury's sister brought a great dinner she had made of different salads and Laury's mom made a delicious cake. We sat around the coffee table in the living room and ate and talked and enjoyed our time together. The mood was light, uplifting and happy.

I learned there are many ways to feel lightheaded - letting more light in to allow for growth, letting go of things we thought were important to our egos, and sharing the love of others. It is good to go through this lightheaded.

All our Love.

Monday, 6/2/2014 – Next stop...

The events in our lives happen in a sequence in time, but in their significance to ourselves they find their own order: the continuous thread of revelation." - Eudora Welty

Laury and I heard from U of C today, and we have our schedule for Wednesday, June 4th. The day will begin at 9:00am with Lyndsay and Laury's sister Cindy arriving here at our house to drive us down to Chicago. We then will proceed to our usual lab on the 6th floor of the clinic for blood work. After the labs are complete Laury and I then go down to the new hospital to check in. After that Laury will get her Hiccman line placed and be admitted to her room. When those events will happen is anyone's guess. I am sure the hospital has a schedule but they either never share it with outsiders or they never follow it. Either way it will most likely be a long day and will involve lots of waiting.

I am taking tomorrow off to help finish the errands and packing. Laury is excited that we are getting things done and crossed off the list. Laury admits that shaving her head must have been heavy on her mind and since her hair is gone she is feeling a lot more energy. I have noticed it too. This morning when I met her in the kitchen (I got up early to work from home) I said to Laury, "Hi, my bald baby!" and she smiled and gave me a big hug.

I love seeing the excitement and energy that Laury has right now. We head into this journey with our eyes open, aware of the risks but more so aware of the rewards and the love that travels with us.

All our Love.

Tuesday, 6/3/2014 – It is time

"I felt like I was an arrow, pulled back and ready to be launched into something big." - A. B. Shepherd, Lifeboat

Today was mostly about the final preparations for our hospital stay. Laury and I managed to get everything into our suitcases, and all of them have wheels and don't outnumber the landing party. Every once in a while we both would find ourselves stopping and trying to figure out if what is happening is real. It wasn't necessarily a bad feeling, but it wasn't like the day before Christmas, either.

Tonight Laury and I sat out on the patio enjoying the blue sky and some deep dish pizza. We were quiet, and occasionally one would ask the other if we had forgotten anything. We told each other how much we love each other and how grateful we are to be going through this together.
Tomorrow is a big day, but every day from here on out is a big day, each will be taken as it comes.

Thank you all again for your support and words of love and encouragement.

All our Love.

Section 2 – The transplant

When the day finally came for Laury and me to move into the hospital for her transplant, I believed that we were both as ready as we could be. I never once thought as we left the house that I might not be bringing Laury back there some day. Laury and I had talked about what to do if she died but I was sure that she was not going to. Moving into a hospital room that you know is going to be your home for the next month is strange. The longest vacation Laury and I had ever taken was ten days. It was hard to even think about what to pack.

Our daughter Keri had asked all of the Caring Bridge family members to send Laury cards she could open while in the hospital. The cards were labeled "Laury the Brave" so Laury knew they were for her hospital stay. I opened one card each day and read it to Laury. These cards played an important role in Laury's getting through the stay.

What follows are my journal entries from the twenty eight days we spent in the hospital.

CHAPTER FIVE

In The Hospital

Wednesday, 6/04/2014 – We have arrived

"Arriving at one goal is the starting point to another." - John Dewey

Laury, her sister Cindy, Lyndsay and I left the house early this morning to tears and well wishes. The traffic was heavy, but we arrived pretty much on time. Laury and I left Cindy and Lyndsay with our stuff in the sky lobby and walked down to the lab for blood work shortly after we arrived. We then came back to the lobby and went to the admission office and the patient registration. Then we waited. Laury's procedure to place her main line was scheduled for noon. Laury was called down to the room at close to two. The placement went quick and while we were down there the nurse informed us that they had her room assigned and we could send Cindy and Lyndsay up to unpack. While Laury was undergoing her procedure I went back to the sky lobby to grab a sandwich. After about an hour I was called back down to be with Laury to wait before they took her to her room.

I called Lyndsay to see how the room was and she asked if I wanted the good news, and I said yes. Lyndsay informed us that we have an east and north view corner room! Incredible views of the city and the lake. It was what we had hoped for. Thanks for all the positive energy that pulled it off!

Laury and I are getting settled into the room, meeting all of the staff that will be supporting Laury. Cindy and Lyndsay left a little while ago taking leftover pizza with them. They did a beautiful job of setting up the room and making if feel like home. Thank you both so much.

Tomorrow at 4:00 am they start Laury on the chemo regiment and the multitude of other drugs that will invade her marrow for the next week to prepare it for the new stem cells.

Laury feels great and told everyone we met today that today was her admission day. Laury delivered the news like a small child announcing her birthday or the loss of a tooth. I was nervous this morning and seeing how well Laury was doing, I was able to gain so much strength from her. She continues to amaze me.

So far so good, and I will continue to keep you all up to date on how things progress.

All our Love.

Thursday, 6/05/2014 – Early birds

"I awoke this morning with devout thanksgiving for my friends, the old and the new." - Ralph Waldo Emerson

"Good Morning!" I heard the nurse say to Laury. I hit the button on my phone and it read 3:23am. I am sure it was morning somewhere but not here in Chicago. This is how the day began. The nurse woke Laury to give her some oral medications and to push a few new intravenous ones in preparation for her first chemo treatment. After getting everything in Laury she was supposed to get into her, the nurse said, "I will be back in about ten minutes with your chemo." At 4:00am the nurse came back in with a chemo bag and began to hook Laury up. The nurse called for the chemo check and once that was completed began the drip. After thirty minutes, Laury's first chemo treatment was complete.

We both went back to bed and slept until six when the technician woke Laury up to take her vitals. This is how the days are going to go for the next week. We have discovered that the mornings are most active time in a hospital. It seems like everything has to happen before 8:00 am.

Last night around nine the nurse came in to give Laury some electrolytes and to inform Laury that she needed a transfusion. Laury's hemoglobin was at 7.3 and the doctors wanted to raise it up before the chemo started. This meant that the usual 4 hours of type and cross match had to be cut down to about an hour to keep everything on schedule. The charge nurse actually went down to the blood bank to hand carry the blood back to make sure Laury got it on time. Of course all this new blood in Laury made her wide awake and after a few hours Laury asked for something to help her sleep. Laury finally got to sleep around midnight, just in time to be woken for her vitals to be taken and to take more blood. After taking about 8 vials of blood I said to the nurse, "It looks like you are taking back all the blood you gave Laury last night!" The nurse laughed and said that it did seem like that.

Laury and I took a fifteen minute walk together around the ward this afternoon and then took a long nap. Laury is feeling no ill effects from the chemo and has met with the spiritual director and the physical therapist. We are settling into our new routine and will take each day as it comes - starting at 3:30am.

All our Love.

Friday, 6/06/2014 – Soul food

"The only time to eat diet food is while you're waiting for the steak to cook." - Julia Child

Today started at 3:30 am again, but Laury got to sleep through most of it. Today is the first day of the second chemo - so for the next four days Laury will be getting two different chemo treatments. Laury is feeling great, however she is struggling a little with some side effects of the anti-nausea medicine. The doctors have also started anti-seizure meds and they are making Laury a little loopy. She has been repeating herself, and asking the same questions a lot. Laury asked me if she was embarrassing me - as if that were possible.

The food here leaves a lot to be desired. Laury and I are still trying different things from the hospital food service and some have been OK and others not so OK. The doctor told Laury this morning that she should eat what she likes because the chemo is knocking the nutrition out of the food so what Laury needs right now are calories.

Laury has been having a little trouble falling to sleep at night. The reason for this is most likely that her schedule is out of whack. Yesterday Laury took a three hour nap. The physical therapist came in to talk with Laury and she couldn't get her to wake up. Laury had her ear buds in and was sound asleep. The therapist shook Laury's hand and took the ear buds out and Laury still didn't wake up. I asked the therapist if Laury was breathing, she laughed and said yes, she had already checked. Laury remembers none of this and doesn't even remember meeting the therapist. Later in the evening Laury and I met the recreational therapist and found out some of the fun things she will help Laury with, such as jewelry making. The therapist also brought Laury a quilt that was made by volunteers. She said after meeting Laury she went back to her office and this one had Laury's name on it. It is beautiful, in yellows, purple and greens. Dr. Odenike stopped by on her way home to say "hi" and give

Laury a hug.

Laury is opening one "Laury the Brave" card a day. They are fantastic, and really touch her soul. Thank you.

We are getting into a routine of walking after breakfast, lunch and dinner. Laury was a little wobbly this morning but after a few laps around the horseshoe her legs woke up and we were fine. I found out that twelve times around the horseshoe is a mile.

Everyone that Laury meets she touches and blesses. Every morning when she receives her chemo she blesses it. This morning when she was asleep for the second treatment, I blessed it for her. I hope it worked.

Everyone here is kind and brings such joy and energy, just like all of you.

All our Love.

Saturday, 6/07/2014 – Together

"It was only a sunny smile, and little it cost in the giving, but like morning light it scattered the night and made the day worth living." - F. Scott Fitzgerald

The days have been going by fairly fast. Today was a little different; things slowed down a bit. Neither Laury nor I is yet bored, as there is always something to do or be done. If felt a little like a winter Sunday when all your chores are done and you can just relax and read a book or take it easy. Sometimes we don't know what to do with days like that. Laury rearranged some of her things, and did a little yoga and we walked a lot. Laury and I tried out the exercise room, treadmill and bike. We both agreed it was boring, but we still will use it to keep active.

Yesterday a volunteer named Terri came by and she spent two hours with Laury making jewelry. Terri gets her beads from the store where Lyndsay used to work in Wicker Park. Laury and Terri laughed and had fun making the prayer chain.

Today Laury met our nurse Melisa who is getting married in September, she and Laury spent time looking at Keri's wedding book and pictures of Melisa's wedding dress. Nice to hear them laugh and talk wedding. Laury can make a connection and smiles with anyone she meets.

Laury continues to tolerate the chemo really well. She seemed more clear headed today than yesterday. This morning Laury woke up with a little bit of a puffy face from the steroids they give her before each treatment. But the puffiness seems to have faded as the day went on and she looks fine now - beautiful as usual.

Our nurse, Pat said yesterday that we are so ahead of other patients because we are here together. She said that going through this alone can be really depressing and overwhelming. I am glad that I can be here with Laury and together we keep each other's spirits up and make each other laugh.

All our Love.

Sunday, 6/08/2014 – Birthdays

"To give somebody your time is the biggest gift you can give." - Franka Potente

Today was Keri's and Lyndsay's birthday they were born on the same day three years apart. Lyndsay came down with Kelly and Robin to visit. When Laury met Lyndsay at door Laury told Lyndsay she was sorry she was in the hospital for her birthday, and Lyndsay replied, "That's OK, it's not the first time you were in the hospital for my birthday."

We did a short Skype with Keri so we could wish her a happy birthday, too. So at least electronically we were all together for their birthday.

Last night and today was not a great day for Laury. The staff came in every hour last night to wake Laury for medications, vitals, etc. Then when Laury did finally get a chance to sleep she became very nauseous. This is the first time that the chemo has gotten to Laury and it may have been the lack of sleep more than anything. We talked with the doctor and he was going to change the schedule around so they don't have to wake Laury every hour. Laury not feeling good meant that the visit from Lyndsay, Kelly and Robin had to be cut short. It was great to see the friends come down and get a chance to see where Laury is and see our great views. Robin brought an incredible birthday pie and Laury managed to get a piece down. Laury felt bad that they had traveled all the way down here and then had to leave after so short a visit. The time they spent with us meant so much to Laury and me. Thank you.

The next birthday we celebrate will be on June 12th when Laury gets her stem cells.

All our Love.

Monday, 6/09/2014 – Another step

"Step with care and great tact, and remember that Life's a Great Balancing Act." - Dr. Seuss

This morning Laury received her last round of chemo. The nurses congratulated Laury and there was a feeling of accomplishment, of another step on this journey that had been taken. However, the good feelings were short lived. Again today Laury is having problems with nausea. The doctors are giving her several different drugs to help, but they mostly just make Laury tired. She has not been able to eat anything today and the doctor said that Laury should probably not try to eat. The chemo attacks fast growing cells and the lining of our stomachs are made up of mostly fast growing cells. The doctor explained that the entire stomach lining is being stripped away and it will regrow, but for now, it is unpleasant.

We found out that Laury will receive her stem cells on Thursday around ten thirty at night. The stem cells are being flown in from Germany and if the flight is delayed the doctors will wait until early Friday morning to do the transplant. The next two days are for Laury to recover from the chemo and to rest.

Laury is frustrated with not feeling well and not being able to walk around. Her smile is still there but it comes with more effort today.

All our Love.

Tuesday, 6/10/2014 – Let it be

"Courage doesn't always roar. Sometimes courage is the quiet voice at the end of the day saying, "I will try again tomorrow." - Mary Anne Radmacher

Today was a better day. Laury was still very nauseous this morning but did not vomit. The doctors are giving Laury three different medications for the nausea and they are working, but she is very sleepy. Laury was able to eat a little rice for dinner last night and this afternoon she ate half my tuna sandwich - after saying she wasn't hungry - I knew I should have ordered her something.

The day was good for sleeping and recovering. The clouds and rain made it OK for Laury to not feel bad about not getting up and doing something. We did go for a short walk, and watched a little TV. Laury is watching a movie right now; but as I look over she has her eyes closed.

Thank you all for your loving comments. I read them to Laury this morning and she cried for the love you all are showing her. Laury wants to get up and move around and have strength but is not able to right now. This is the time when I reminded Laury that she needs to receive, to let it be. She knows, but it is hard for her to not take charge.

We are hopefully on the upside however, the doctor did say that the day after Laury receives her stem cells she might be worn out. The doctor says she is doing great and everything looks good and he is very encouraged by her attitude and smile.

All our Love.

Wednesday, 6/11/2014 – Closeness

"Intimacy is not a happy medium. It is a way of being in which the tension between distance and closeness is dissolved and a new horizon appears." - Henri Nouwen

Laury is feeling a little better today. Last night she was able to sit and watch TV with me and eat a half of a sandwich and a bag of chips. Laury went to bed early and got a good night's sleep. The nausea is under control, but the meds are making her really sleepy. The doctor and nurses said that was OK and that sleep right now is very good for Laury. Today, so far, she has been able to shower and eat breakfast and eat an entire sandwich for lunch. After lunch Laury did a short Skype with Keri. She hopes to take a short walk after dinner tonight.

The doctors have started Laury on anti-rejection drugs in preparation for the stem cells tomorrow night. These drugs will run continuously until the cells are here. As I said earlier, the stem cells, which are coming from a German man, will arrive around ten thirty as long as the flight is not delayed.

Laury's head has been cold and I asked one of the nurses if there was a place I could get a hat. The nurse called the Recreational Therapist and she brought Laury a bunch of hats that are knitted by her mother. Laury and I both chose two and each put one on to watch TV. As we watched TV last night Laury sat next to me on the couch. Laury was getting too tired to sit up and having my arm around her was not comfortable, so she lay down next to me with her head in my lap. Laury fell asleep like that and I sat there for a while before waking her to go to bed. It was nice to be close. At night in bed I am aware of the distance between us right now, not just the distance between Laury's bed and mine, but the distance between healthy and sick, and patient and caregiver. That distance has gotten greater over the last couple of days, but as Laury improves it will get smaller and eventually it will be gone. Last night sitting on the couch, Laury's head in my lap and my hand on her newly-hatted head, there was no distance again, it was just us. It felt good and right.

All our Love.

Thursday, 6/12/2014 – Today

"Toto, I have a feeling we're not in Kansas anymore." - L. Frank Baum

Last night ended on a high note that has continued through to this morning. Laury is feeling much better. She has been able to get off the anti-nausea medication and that has cleared Laury's head and given her some strength back. Late in the afternoon a yoga instructor from Gilda's Club stopped by and took Laury through a deep breathing practice. It was amazing to see how much she improved after the series of exercises. Laury ate a big dinner, and we have discovered that sandwiches are the way to go here.

Today is going to be very busy, with a lot of people stopping by to check different things, in preparation for tonight's stem cells. Laury opened several of the "Laury the Brave" cards this morning and laughed and cried at their love and humor. I have been hearing Laury laughter again, especially when she looks at herself in her new hat.

Laury, with the help of some friends, has prepared a blessing that will be said tonight when her stem cells are going into her blood. The text of the blessing is below. If you get a chance please say it sometime today to send all of the positive energy we can muster. Once the stem cells are here the doctors will be checking Laury every hour and a nurse will be sitting with her most of the night. Lyndsay will be here as well as all of you.

Thank you again for all your support and encouragement and love. Today is the day the Lord has made, let us rejoice and be grateful!

All our Love.

Guardian of our soul, Sustainer of life,

We come with grateful and open hearts

And pray mercy upon this passage.

We thank you for life, as you have given Laury through her bone marrow that worked so hard to get her this far in life before it could no longer function.

It allowed Laury to marry, raise a family, teach, garden, and walk down the aisle for her daughter's wedding, as she asked it.

We ask your blessing on these cells

As they create new life in Laury.

They are the seeds the Gardener sows on the beautifully prepared earth.

But bearing so much more fruit and flower than we can imagine

Bearing 30, 60 or a hundredfold.

We imagine them being watered with endurance,

And life sustaining reception of their new home.

Make them one with Laury, one with creation, and one with all eternity.

Laury as you receive these cells and they engraft,

May you find within yourself reserves untapped:

Patience, endurance, strength and humor

As you continue to be carried through community with love and prayer

May you experience the Eternal One's wisdom and compassion flowing through

Your Doctor and nurses' hands, Dan's devotion, Families' love and Caring Bridge Communities' support.

And finally, Creator God, bless this body for how it serves Laury, how it carries her through life, how it houses her spirit.

All this, and the concerns in us too deep for words,

We pray as we live, trusting in You, our God, The Eternal One.

Amen.

Thursday, 6/12/2014 – Sowing seeds

"Love is the seed of all hope. It is the enticement to trust, to risk, to try, to go on." - Gloria Gaither

The stem cells went in at ten - and just completed. Laury is feeling great - they will be checking her vitals every hour for the next four hours. So far so good.

Thanks for all your prayers.

More tomorrow morning.

All our Love.

Friday, 6/13/2014 – New home

"Patience, he thought. So much of this was patience - waiting, and thinking and doing things right. So much of all this, so much of all living was patience and thinking." - Gary Paulsen, Hatchet

Everyone we asked said that when Laury finally gets the stem cells it would be anti-climactic. They were wrong. Last night was beautiful, amazing, prayerful, and loving. It was the perfect birthday party.

Laury had been feeling really good yesterday. All of the clouds from the anti-nausea medicine had cleared and Laury was herself again, excited and nervous for the day's events. Late in the morning the nurses gave Laury a unit of blood, and as she now says, it made Laury feel better than a glass of wine and a pedicure. Laury and I went for a walk while waiting for the blood and she said to me, "My legs are pretty shaky this morning". I replied that if my hemoglobin was 6.3 I would be unconscious. When the nurse came to hook up the blood Laury again mentioned to her shaky legs and the nurse said to Laury, "If I was at 6.3 I would be asleep". Not Laury, she wanted to walk on non-shaky legs.

Robin brought Lyndsay down in the late afternoon and we spent some time together laughing and crying. Then as we have done so many times here, we waited.

Our night nurse Jerry came in around nine and said that the cells were here and they were in the lab being tested and should be up to the room in about thirty minutes. Laury cried and clapped her hands. "This is what we have been waiting for for five years". Laury got back in bed and the nurses began hooking up a bunch more lines and bags of stuff. The nurse paged the chaplain and he came in and introduced himself. We went over with the chaplain what we wanted to do when the stem cells were going in. Then around nine thirty the doctor came in and did a final check of Laury. A few minutes later the lady with a small pink bag of life came into the room. Laury began to cry and we started our little party. Lyndsay rang the Tibetan bells and I read Psalm 65, the chaplain read the blessing and I then read a short reading from Barbra Brown Taylor, the chaplain finished with a prayer. It was short and beautiful.

Then we all stood around Laury and watched the pink liquid quickly drip into her. After about thirty minutes it was complete and the doctor left. Lyndsay went to bed and Laury and I sat together for a while. I posted the short journal entry and then tried to go to sleep.

Even though she did not get much sleep last night, Laury is feeling great this morning. She says she keeps picturing the cells falling on the beautiful tilled and prepared soil, finding a new home and beginning to grow. It will be about two weeks before we see if the new cells have taken, but I can't think a better home for them.

Thank you all again for your warm, uplifting and loving thoughts.

All our Love.

Friday, 6/13/2014 – Energy

"She was full of some strange energy that morning. Her every movement had purpose and life and she seemed to find satisfaction in every little thing." - Anna Godbersen, Envy

Yesterday Laury was like the little energizer bunny. She hadn't slept the night before and was up and about early. Lyndsay was still here and they went for a walk and to the exercise room. Laury felt great. Last night Lyndsay walked to a Thai restaurant and we had a nice meal together before she left to go home. Laury and Lyndsay laughed and joked all day. I needed a two hour nap, but not those two.

Laury climbed in bed last night around nine but still was not tired. Laury called to me around ten thirty and said her main line area was really hurting. I called the nurse and he paged the doctor. The doctor came in a looked at it and said that maybe Laury had a line infection. The doctor put Laury on another antibiotic and she got some pain medication. However, Laury was still not able to sleep. The nurse gave her more pain meds and something to help her sleep and Laury was able to sleep from around four to eight this morning.

The doctor came by on rounds this morning and looked at the line. She wants to watch it today but says that if it doesn't get better they will have to take the line out. That is not a huge deal but it would mean they would have to place a Picc line. Laury asked the doctor what might be causing the restlessness and the doctor said she didn't know. The doctor is going to give her something different tonight to help her sleep.

Today we are going to take it easy and hopefully the line will get better and Laury will be able to get some sleep.

All our Love.

Saturday, 6/14/2014 – Valley day

"Just cause you got the monkey off your back doesn't mean the circus has left town." - George Carlin

All of the doctors and nurses have told us that this journey will have peaks and valleys. Today was a valley day. Laury was not feeling well all day. The vomiting had returned and we were trying to get it under control. Every time Laury tried to get out of bed to sit in the chair or go to the bathroom she got sick. I felt really bad for her, and Laury just kept saying to me, "I'm sorry".

The doctors have put Laury back on the heavy hitting anti-nausea medications and they knock her out. This may be a good thing because Laury has not been able to sleep since getting her stem cells.

Today was a quiet day, reading, helping Laury out of bed and smiling and telling each other, "I love you."

Hopefully Laury will be able to get a good night's sleep and her stomach will calm down. Tomorrow we hope for a peak day.

All our Love.

Sunday, 6/15/2014 – Gifts

"May it be a light to you in dark places, when all other lights go out." - J. R.R. Tolkien, The Fellowship Of The Ring

Today Laury is feeling a little better. The anti-nausea medication is working but making her tired. Laury was able to eat breakfast and lunch and we took a short walk. Laury's spirits are up even if her eyes are a little heavy today. Right now it appears that we have to trade off being fully awake for not being nauseous. For now it is a good trade.

Every day since Laury and I have been here, no matter how Laury feels she has opened one of your "Laury the Brave" cards and read it. On a couple of mornings I had to choose which one to open and read the card to Laury, but she always smiled and cried at the love and concern it contained. These small tokens have and continue to mean so much to Laury that she asked me to thank you all again. The creativity, words, images and thoughts that are contained in each one moves Laury. She still feels somewhat unworthy of it.

Every day I also read Laury your comments on the journal post. These too have lifted her and me. Laury and I walk by many rooms here that have only the patient. I can't image what it would be like to go through this alone or even just Laury and me. Knowing you are all out there watching and waiting to see how she is doing and providing support is unbelievable. Laury and I are truly blessed to know all of you.

All our Love.

Monday, 6/16/2014 – My type

"There are only two ways to live your life. One is as though nothing is a

miracle. The other is as though everything is a miracle." - Albert Einstein

Laury continues to improve. Laury switched from the heavy hitting anti-nausea medication to one that doesn't make her so tired. Her blood numbers continue to drop as expected and so Laury received two transfusions today. One transfusion was for platelets and the other was for red blood cells. I asked the nurse what blood type they were giving her. The donor has a different blood type than Laury and when the stem cells take over, Laury's blood type will change from her current B-positive to the donor's A-positive. The nurse explained that they check and cross type the blood every three days to make sure what they are giving Laury is a match.

A couple of people have asked me about whether Laury's DNA will change or stay the same, as a result of the transplant. I asked the doctor and he explained to me how it works. Laury's blood will carry the DNA of the donor and the rest of her will have her original DNA. This means if Laury gets a DNA test from her blood, it will show her donor's DNA and will have his Y chromosome. If, however, Laury gets a test from a cheek swab, it will show her own original DNA. The doctor said that he has already seen two CSI episodes where the killer left the donor's DNA behind.

The doctor also said that because Laury's blood has the Y chromosome, it will be much easier to track how well her new bone marrow is doing. The doctors will be able to tell where the blood is coming from by examining the blood for which chromosome is most prevalent.

Isn't science cool? No matter Laury's blood type she will always be my type.

All our Love.

Tuesday, 6/17/2014 – Bottoms Up

"It has long been an axiom of mine that the little things are infinitely the most important." - Sir Arthur Conan Doyle

Laury is doing much better. Her energy is good, especially after receiving her second bag of red blood today. The nausea is under control and Laury was able to walk a couple of times today and have a good visit from her friend Kelly.

Laury is having some problems sleeping at night. We think it might be one of the medications but the doctors are stumped as to which one it might be. They are trying something new tonight, so we are hopeful.

As I have written about before, there are many little things that make our days special here. Laury and I were walking last night and a nurse stopped and said, "How are our love birds?" Laury replied, "You have heard about us!" The nurse said yes that we have gone viral on the floor. Hearing this made us laugh and feel good. Every day the nurses stop by to see how Laury is doing, even the ones that are not assigned to her. Last night Pat, one of our nurses from last week, stopped by to get some essential oils from Laury. Pat stayed for about ten minutes to talk about her life. I guess we made her feel safe and welcome.

One of the small things that has become a big thing here is that Laury's bottom has been itching. Laury and I talked about whether we should mention it but we both agreed it shows the level of concern and care she is getting here. The itching has been part of what is keeping Laury up at night and the nurses and doctors have been trying different things to help. All day long it seems there is a nurse or doctor stopping by to offer up some suggestion. I did notice they are all women, but even so, it is like the entire floor has made it their goal to get Laury's bum back in order.

These little things show their concern, and make the days go by faster and brighter. Kelly bringing clean clothes, the "Laury the Brave cards", short phone calls, and restorative yoga are all little things that made today special. Laury and I decided going into this that we would take it one day at a time. The little things fill the days and make us grateful.

All our Love.

Wednesday, 6/18/2014 – Shut Eye

"Also, I could finally sleep. And this was the real gift, because when you cannot sleep, you cannot get yourself out of the ditch--there's not a chance." - Elizabeth Gilbert. Eat, Pray, Love

The doctors finally arrived at a magical combination of drugs that allowed Laury to sleep through the night. She has not been able to sleep since she received the new cells. We first thought it was the excitement but after two days it was pretty obvious that something was causing Laury to not stay asleep. Last night Laury didn't even wake when the IV pump beeped - which meant I had to get up and call the nurse.

Laury is feeling really good. Her bum is still giving her problems but even that is improving. The doctors are all smiles when they meet Laury each morning and keep telling her how good she looks and how well she is doing. I have gone back to work this week, which means I am on the phone most of the day. Laury has been arranging the room and we now have a "cocktail area" - our chairs face the beautiful view of the city and Laury and I sit and drink our afternoon water and talk.

Laury received platelets and red blood again today. For some reason her numbers did not come up with yesterday's transfusions. The doctor is not worried. She says that this happens sometimes, and if necessary, they will keep giving Laury blood. The doctor is very confident that we will see the new marrow beginning to work in about a week. Yesterday, on our evening walk around the "U", I said to Laury that I woke up with this thought, "You no longer have Myelofibrosis". Laury stopped and looked at me and said, "I hadn't thought of that. That is difficult to take in." It is hard to remember life before Laury's diagnosis. The disease has been such a part of our lives that for Laury to no longer have it does feel weird. We asked the doctor this morning if Laury was in fact cured and she said yes, we just now need the new marrow to grow.

It is a dream come true.

All our Love.

Thursday, 6/19/2014 – Anniversary

"She taught me to love by loving me, and I learned—rather slowly; I wasn't too good a pupil, being set in my ways and lacking her natural talent. But I did learn. Learned that supreme happiness lies in wanting to keep another person safe and warm and happy, and being privileged to try." - Robert A. Heinlein, Time Enough For Love

"there must always be time enough for love." - Robert A. Heinlein, Time Enough For Love

Laury is bright and happy today. She continues to improve and the doctors are just waiting for the new marrow to grow.

Thirty two years ago today I married this wonderful woman named Laury. We have since spent this day in many different places and situations. Many times it was spent with our family in our favorite vacation spot in Michigan, other times home by ourselves. This will be the first time Laury and I have spent our anniversary in the hospital. There were times when we had plenty of money, other times none. But in all the places and situations Laury and I were happy to be together. The same is true of today. While we both would like to be somewhere else than the hospital, Laury and I both agree we are glad to be together.

Neither one of us could have guessed that we would be here today, on that first day thirty two years ago, but we knew we would be in love, and happy. Laury and I fully intend to be together and happy on our next anniversary, too.

All our Love.

Friday, 6/20/2104 – Weathering storms

"If you want to see the sunshine, you have to weather the storm" - Frank Lane

Last night Laury and I had a great dinner and visit with our friends Bob and Vicky. It was nice to sit and talk, almost like we were home. Thanks again for the good food and company.

One of the big fears Laury and I had going into the transplant was how sick would she get from the chemo. We certainly have seen some side effects of the chemo treatments, such as the nausea. Today we were talking with the doctor and she said that Laury is through the peak side effects phase of the chemo. It should be out of Laury's system and from now on the side effects will quickly disappear. This is good news. It means that Laury can slowly come off some of the anti-nausea medications. It is hard to believe that this part of the transplant is over. We are not done with possible complications but from now on if they come, they will not be part of the chemo treatments.

Laury has been spending her days meditating, reading, journal writing, exercising and doing yoga. I am on the phone with work most of the day, so I look over at Laury and see her happily going about her day. Every time Laury looks at me she smiles. Laury and I go for walks at a break in the morning and after dinner at night. We sit and talk after work, and watch a little TV before bed. We have our routine down and Laury and I are now just waiting for the marrow to grow.

Yesterday, Laury admitted that she was a little afraid that the stem cells were not going to take and grow. I asked Laury what she does when she transplants a plant in her garden. Laury replied, "I say a blessing". I asked her if when she goes to check on the plant a few days later if she expects it to be dead or doing well. Laury said that she expects it to be healthy and happy in its new home, because she knows she has done all she can do to make it so. I then asked Laury, "Why do you expect it to be any different with your stem cells?" She looked at me and said, "Thanks, I will need you to remind me of that at times".

Laury has done such a good job of preparing her body for this transplant, she weathered the storm of cleaning out the old bone marrow, and now we can expect the new marrow to grow like the new plants in her garden. It can't happen any other way.

All our Love.

Saturday, 6/21/2014 – Signs of spring

"Can words describe the fragrance of the very breath of spring?" - Neltje Blanchan

Every morning the technician comes in at five thirty and draws blood from Laury. Because the technician uses her central line Laury doesn't always wake up. The labs are run and available to the doctor when they make their rounds later in the morning. This morning was no different. When the doctor came in to see Laury he did all of his usual things, like checking her lungs and listening to her heart. When he asked Laury about her urine she said that it was getting clearer. The doctor replied that her very dark urine was because her antibodies had broken down some of the new blood cells that she had been given. The doctor went on to say that Laury's old antibodies are going away and will be replaced by the new ones produced by the new marrow. Hearing that Laury asked, "Does this mean the stem cells are engrafting?" The doctor replied, "Yes and we see a slight rise in your white blood counts, which means the marrow is beginning to produce white blood cells." The white cells are the first to be produced by the new marrow.

Laury asked the doctor if this was good news, and he said yes, this is very good news. The doctor said that we should start to see the white counts come up as the new marrow takes over. Right now it is too early to say for sure, but all the signs point to the new marrow growing and producing cells. The first signs of life on the new plant have appeared. We welcome this new spring!

All our Love.

Sunday, 6/22/2014 – Silence

"Let us be silent, that we may hear the whispers of the gods" - Ralph Waldo Emerson

Today was lived in silence. Yesterday afternoon Laury started developing mouth and throat sores. These sores were expected, as most people going through transplants get them. We had hoped that maybe Laury would escape them, but no. They are very painful and Laury is taking pain medication and special mouth washes to help. Laury was not able to eat dinner last night or anything today besides a milkshake and Boost. The doctors say that the sores will improve quickly once Laury's blood numbers begin to rise. I guess these sores are mostly caused by her low platelets.

The sores make it very hard for Laury to talk, so we spent last evening and today in silence. I have tried not to ask Laury anything that couldn't be answered with yes or no. She has been listening to meditation tapes and I have been reading. It is not often that we go through a day without talking to each other. We still communicate with gestures and smiles. Laury says she is still happy and I believe her.

Laury's white counts were up again today. The doctor says that it is proof that the new marrow is working. He said that in a little bit they will do a DNA test on the blood to confirm that it is coming from the new marrow.

The next few days will be spent quietly choosing our words carefully and making each one count. This is probably a good way to communicate all the time, now that I think about it.

All our Love.

Monday, 6/23/2014 – Comfort

"If I can see pain in your eyes then share with me your tears. If I can see joy in your eyes then share with me your smile." - Santosh Kalwar

I hate seeing Laury in so much pain. The mouth and throat sores have gotten bad and the pain is keeping Laury from talking and being able to eat or sleep. All of the medications the doctors tried yesterday and last night did not work. Today the nurse finally hooked Laury up to a pain medication pump where she can control the release of the medication. So far Laury thinks it might be working.

Laury still tells me she is happy and she still smiles at me when I am near. Our goal is to get the pain under control enough to allow Laury to eat. The doctor says that the sores will go away as her white blood counts come up.

Last night at three I heard Laury call the nurse again for pain medication. I walked to her bed and sat down facing her. I took Laury's head in my hand and asked her how her pain was. Laury replied that it was bad. I said I was sorry, and she said to me through a half open mouth, "It will be OK". I said that I didn't like seeing her in pain and Laury whispered back, "It won't last forever." The nurse then came in and gave her some more medication and Laury tried to go back to sleep. I went back to my bed and had trouble falling back to sleep. I laid there wondering, who is comforting who. I replayed our conversation and Laury gave me more comfort than I was able to give her. If it is possible, I love her even more.

All our Love.

Tuesday, 6/24/2014 – Long day

"You are at once both the quiet and the confusion of my heart; imagine my heartbeat when you are in this state." - Franz Kafka, Letters To Felice

Laury's throat is still very sore. The pain pump has helped but she is still having problems swallowing and talking. Laury was able to get some sleep last night and today and in general feels a little better. The doctor came in this afternoon and told Laury that she is running a fever. This may be caused by an infection or it may be the new white cells going into action. Either way the doctors are going to treat it as an infection. We had to take Laury down for a chest X-ray and the technicians took a bunch of blood for cultures. The doctors are not too concerned if it is an infection because they are already treating her with antibiotics and they are going to add a couple more to make sure. The doctor seems to think that it is most likely the new white cells but they want to play it safe. So do we.

Laury's hair is starting to fall out. She is actually very excited by this and has shown the nurses the hair on the pillow to prove it. A few days ago, on our walk Laury said, "I will be disappointed if my hair doesn't fall out". I said, "Really?" and she replied, "Yes, I want to experience it, I signed up for the complete package!" For now the hair that is missing is where her pillow hits her head - so Laury has a sort of reverse bald spot - missing around the sides and still full on top. She still is cute as hell.

The doctors are sad that Laury is having the throat pain, but they are confident that since the white counts are going up (they doubled since yesterday), that the throat should clear up in a day or two. It is still hard to see all the tubes and pumps and other stuff attached to Laury, but it is still her and she still smiles at me when I am on the phone and sends me the "I Love You", hand signal. It has been a few long nights and I am tired as I know Laury is, but we hope the worst is over. The doctor said her goal is to have us home before the Fourth of July.

All our Love.

Wednesday, 6/25/2014 – Active day

"You must learn to be still in the midst of activity and to be vibrantly alive in repose." - Indira Gandhi

Today it seemed our room was a hub of activity. I was on a conference call with work most of the day, but every time I looked over there was someone in our room. The nurse came in this morning and said that she was going to have another nurse helping her today. This was good news because with four pumps and six lines running into Laury something almost always needs checking.

Laury received platelets and two units of blood today. Her white counts are up again over yesterday, but her red counts and platelets were down. The doctor thinks Laury's spleen is taking up all the platelets and red blood cells given her by transfusion. The doctor said sometimes this happens but it is not a big deal - they will just keep giving Laury more blood, if necessary.

Laury's throat is slowly getting better. She wants to try eating something tonight- more like drinking something, because it is still really painful to swallow. But the fact Laury is asking for something means she is feeling better. The doctors are hopeful that Laury is over the worst and will begin to quickly feel better. Laury has been able to get some sleep off and on - in between all of the people coming in.

The yoga instructor from Gilda's Club stopped by again today. He took Laury through some deep breathing exercises which really helped. It is amazing how just being able to slow your breathing down makes you feel so much better.

Laury is still smiling and thanking everyone for their good care. She is frustrated that she can't talk more with the new nurses and get to know them better. Sometimes it is like Laury forgets her throat hurts because the urge to reach out to someone overtakes her. Me, I would be a grump by now and not want to talk or see anyone, but not Laury. What makes Laury sad right now is that she can't connect with others verbally, so she connects with smiles and gestures.

All our Love.

Thursday, 6/26/2014 – Breaking through the clouds

"Laughter is magic that dispenses clouds and creates sunshine in the soul." - Richelle E. Goodrich.

Today we saw the return of some sunshine, both outside and in Laury. Her throat is getting better and she is able to talk and with some difficulty, swallow. Laury has been able to drink some protein drinks and is going to try some broth for dinner. Most importantly Laury feels better, her brightness is back and we can see an end to the soreness.

Lyndsay and Laury's good friend Kelly came for a visit today. Lyndsay coming was a surprise and that brought smiles and tears. It was good to hear the three of them talking and laughing. The days are long without laughter. They sat Laury in a chair in the bathroom and Lyndsay used my beard trimmer to shave what was left of her hair. They also took Laury for a walk - the first one she has had since Monday. Laury kept getting the days mixed up, and is missing a day or two since being on the pain medication. Laury's confusion was cause for some good-natured laughter.

The doctor told us that Laury's white blood count is above 1 (1.1) and that is a major milestone. She said everything looks good for us being home before the 4th. The doctor said the only reason we wouldn't be able to go home is if Laury's throat hasn't completely cleared up. Laury said that the 4th works for her so she would make sure her throat cooperates.

I have read all of your comments to Laury over that last few days and they really have helped her. This episode was not fun to watch, or I am sure for Laury, to go through. But once again your thoughts and prayers got us through. Thank you all.

All our Love.

Friday, 6/27/2014 – Giving

"To look forward and not back, To look out and not in, and To lend a hand" - Edward Everett Hale

As I mentioned in yesterday's post, Laury has been mixing up her days this week. What concerned Laury most was that she had missed Terri, the volunteer, who comes on Friday to do jewelry. Last Friday Laury made a pair of Goddess earrings and today she was looking forward to making a pair of feather earrings. Today Laury's head is clear and she was very excited for Terri to show up, almost like it was Christmas. I wonder if the volunteers here know how much they improve the patient's stay and make our days brighter.

Laury was up and out of bed today. Her throat is much better. It is still difficult to swallow but she is able to get water and other fluids down now. Laury did manage to eat some of a peanut butter and chocolate smoothie for lunch. Once Laury is able to handle swallowing the biggest pills, the doctors will move all her medications to pills and this will be the last hurtle to going home. Laury's white numbers continue to grow; today they were at 1.4 over 1.1 yesterday. Laury did need to receive a unit of red blood but not platelets today. But as I said before, the doctors will let Laury go home even if she is transfusion dependent.

The nurses and doctors all commented on how good Laury is looking and are confident that we will soon be out of here and home. Laury does look good and happy again, smiling as she is once again doing her exercises and rearranging the furniture and cards in our room. I gain so much comfort and happiness seeing Laury and being with her. I hope I make her feel half as good as she makes me feel.

All our Love.

Saturday, 6/28/2014 – Its time

"The direction of a big act will warp history, but probably all acts will do the same thing in their degree, down to a stone stepped over in a path or a breath caught at the sight of a pretty girl or a finger nail nicked in the garden soil." - John Steinbeck, East of Eden

Laury was standing in our room waiting to talk to the doctor when Dr. Stock walked in. The doctor asked her if she wanted to sit down and Laury said, "No, I want to know what I have to do to go home. It's time." The doctor laughed and said, "I think you are doing it." Laury is able to swallow all her pills; she is eating soft foods, and has seriously set her mind on going home. Laury told the doctor that last night she was able to eat some egg salad and apple sauce and that she had swallowed all her pills this morning. The doctor was impressed at the change from yesterday Laury said to her, "I do what I am told, and you told me I had to be able to swallow my pills and eat before I can go home. Now can I get disconnected from all these IVs?"

The doctor and I laughed and I said, "This is Laury with 7.5 hemoglobin. Can you image what she is going to be like when it is back to the normal range?" The doctor said, "You are not going to be able to keep up with her."

Today the doctors have removed most of the IVs - Laury just has one more round of antibiotics that have to complete tonight and then she can be disconnected completely. Laury told the doctor she has a cleaning lady coming on Wednesday and should she have her come sooner. The doctor said, "Yes you might want the cleaning lady to come sooner."

Laury and I are ready to go home, to see the cats, smell fresh air, have a beer, and eat our own food. We will find out more tomorrow but we know now that there is no set date to leave. It will be when Laury and the doctors are ready.

All our Love.

Sunday, 6/29/2014 – Looking down

"The realities of life do not allow themselves to be forgotten." - Victor Hugo, Les Miserables

A few years ago, while on a mission trip to Costa Rica with Lyndsay, I went zip lining. I am terrified of heights and the fear of zip lining had been in the back of my head for the entire time I was there. The day arrived and our group went to this beautiful nature preserve and was given our gear and instructions. I knew that I had to go first, because if I didn't I would chicken out. I was strapped into the harness and hooked on the wire and off I went. I didn't look down, but straight ahead at the landing spot in the trees. I made it. It was exciting, and scary. I continued through each of the twelve runs. However, on one of the runs everyone was talking about how beautiful the view was and, how you could see the river below and the different trees and plants. I decided to take a quick look on my way across. The reality of being on a wire 100 feet above the ground terrified me and I never looked down again.

Yesterday afternoon while Laury and I were talking we both admitted that looking ahead to going home had upset us. Laury was feeling very anxious and began having fears that her cough might be a cold and would prevent her from going home. The more we talked the more we realized that Laury and I had looked down for a minute. This journey has been scary and difficult. Sometimes the only way we can get through it is by not looking ahead. We take each day as it comes and realize we only have to make it through today. When we start looking too far ahead it can get too scary to deal with.

Laury and I are excited to go home, but we know there is a lot more work to be done. Going home isn't the end of the journey and there are many more zip lines to cross. We will have to stay focused, and when it seems like we are up on that wire, Laury and I will remember to look to the landing spot and not to look down.

All our Love.

Sunday, 6/29/2014 – The breakup

"You must have brought the bad weather with you

The sky's the color of lead

All you've left me is a feather

On an unmade bed" - Tom Waits

Lucille was cut loose today. Lucille was Laury's IV pole. She and Laury had been connected since the first day we arrived here. Everywhere Laury went- to the bathroom, shower, a walk- Lucille went quietly along. The nurse removed the last bag of fluids and antibiotics from Laury and she was free from Lucille.

I was watching a concert on my computer and Laury came walking into my space and said, "See?" and I replied, "See what?" Laury laughed and said, "No Lucille." Lucille had become such a part of us that I didn't even notice she was gone. Lucille leaving was the last step before going home, and the doctor told us this morning we are going home tomorrow. It still has to be approved by the doctor tomorrow morning but there is no reason why he wouldn't say yes.

Lucille, like so many other things here, has served us well. I can't say that I will miss her, but for a while she was like family.

All our Love.

Monday, 6/30/2014 – Disappointment

"It was one of those times you feel a sense of loss, even though you didn't have something in the first place. I guess that's what disappointment is- a sense of loss for something you never had." - Deb Caletti, The Nature Of Jade

Laury and I just found out that Laury is not going home today. Laury's liver function numbers are not right. The doctors are re-testing to make sure it wasn't a bad test. They also want to give Laury an ultrasound of her liver to make sure everything is OK. It means we will be here at least another day. If her liver is having problems then we have to wait for it to start functioning normally again, and we don't know how long that would be.

Another step backward. We will let you know more as we find out more.

Thanks for all your healing prayers.

All our Love.

Tuesday, 7/1/2014 – Going home

"If you have good thoughts they will shine out of your face like sunbeams and you will always look lovely." - Roald Dahl

All of your good thoughts paid off. Laury's liver numbers are back down and we are going home! We are just waiting for final orders and to meet with the nurse-practitioner for all of our at-home instructions.

The ultrasound of Laury's liver yesterday, came back normal. It did show signs that maybe Laury had had a small kidney or gall stone. If she did, this would have caused the numbers to go up, and since a stone didn't show up on the ultrasound it meant that it had passed and things were flowing normally again.

Once we got over the disappointment of not going home, Laury and I had to deal with the uncertainty of what was going on in Laury's liver. The fact that everything is clear and the numbers are down means we can leave with a clear head and heart.

Thank you all so much for your prayers and well wishes yesterday. It was a difficult day and you once again carried us through.

All our Love.

Section 3 – Home healing

Everyone and everything we had read said that the home healing would be the hardest part of the transplant process. Not only are you traveling back to clinic several times a week but you are managing medications and symptoms on your own. Laury and I were just happy to be home and in our own bed- together. We both felt that the hardest part was behind us and Laury was feeling better every day and things would continue on a straight line. This was not to be. We now understand why we were told about how difficult this part of the healing is. Nothing could have fully prepared us for the losses, the ups and downs, the waiting, the joy and the sorrow that was to be our life for the next several months. Going through the transplant changed Laury and me- as people and as a couple. What follows are my journal entries from this long and sometimes difficult time.

CHAPTER SIX

July

Tuesday, 7/1/2014 – Grateful

"Thankfulness creates gratitude which generates contentment that causes peace." - Todd Stocker

Laury and I are home. The last IV was removed, the nurse gave us our instructions, we went over the medications and the cab called to say he was here. It was hard to believe when Laury and I walked outside that it had been a month since we smelled the Chicago air. We came home to a beautiful clean house, (thanks Kelly and Devon) that never looked so good. The cats were glad to see us and couldn't wait to tell us all about their adventures while we were away.

I finally had my beer, and made a light dinner of fish (nothing fried or on a bun) and we said a grateful grace before eating.

I doubt either one of us will make it to eight tonight, it has been a long day, and in fact, couple of days. Dr. Odenike called us this morning after she saw Laury's numbers and talked with the other doctors. The doctors all sounded as excited as we were. The nurses had given hugs and wished us well. Laury and I left with so much more than we came with.

Tomorrow we meet with the home care nurse and I learn how to attach an IV, (Laury is still on fluids and an anti-fungal), and any other things I will need to know to be the caregiver at home. But that is tomorrow. Tonight we look forward to crawling into bed - together, and having a good night's sleep.

All our Love.

Wednesday, 7/2/2014 – Fragile

"Deep roots are not reached by the frost." - J.R.R Tolkien

Laury is so happy to be home that almost everything today is making her cry. As a result, Laury is feeling fragile. She did not get a good night's sleep last night. Laury woke me at midnight to go to an open-all-night Walgreens to get her sleep aid prescription filled. Laury has had trouble sleeping since she received her stem cells. We think it is probably one of the medications that the doctors started to promote the cells grafting. Laury and I both had the unrealistic expectation that just being home would fix the problem.

The home-care nurse stopped by this morning and trained me on how to hook Laury up to her fluids and medications. Fortunately, the process is similar to what I had to learn when Laury had her Picc line. It is all about washing your hands and "when it doubt, throw it out". The fluids are hooked up to a portable pump and runs for about four hours. The anti-fungal medication is on a disposable pump that runs for about an hour. We put both pumps and the excess tubing into a shoulder bag, that Laury has named Violet.

We go back to clinic tomorrow afternoon. The doctor will check Laury's blood, and if necessary, she will get a transfusion. For now, I need to keep track of Laury's temp, blood pressure and overall health, and if anything changes we call the doctor.

I am back working from the upstairs study, which made the cats happy, and Laury has been sitting outside enjoying the day. She says that she can't think about the hospital stay right now, as she is overwhelmed by being home and what she has gone through. Laury needs a few days of rebuilding her inner strength. It is still there, and strong, but she needs some help finding it, but being home is the best place for it to happen.

Our journey continues.

All our Love.

Friday, 7/4/2014 – The flow

"Trust what you know; have faith in where you go; if there's no wind, row; or go with the flow." - Ed Parrish III

Yesterday was a day to go with the flow. It was our first day of clinic, back at U of C. Laury and I headed down at noon and got home around eight, and traveled a winding path along the way. Much of the visit was the same routine of checking in, going to the lab to draw blood, coming back and waiting for the doctor. We had been asked to come very early in case Laury needed a transfusion, so that we could get that done before meeting with the doctor. We waited for an hour and found out that Laury was to be given platelets. We left the doctor's waiting area and headed over to the infusion center. There Laury and I were met by many familiar faces that greeted us with warmth and smiles. Once we had our place in the infusion center some of the nurses stopped by to see how Laury was doing. The nurses said they had been tracking Laury's progress through other nurse friends and were very glad that things had gone so well.

After receiving the platelets, Dr. Odenike stopped by and walked us back to her office. There we talked about the medications Laury is taking and which ones to continue and which one to stop. I found out that Laury no longer needs to take the anti-fungal intravenously, which is good news because it made her itch. We also found out that the fluids we were given contained Potassium and it had caused Laury's Potassium numbers to be too high. Laury was given a prescription for a medicine to remove the excess Potassium from her system and a new prescription for fluids.

Laury and I stopped on the way home to pick up the prescription for the Potassium-remover medication. Our regular pharmacy, Oswald's, didn't have it, so they directed us to another one down the street. The pharmacist called the other pharmacy and they had the medicine but were closing, but agreed to stay open until we got there. It should have taken us five minutes to get there but with Rib Fest going on and street closings it took us almost fifteen minutes. The pharmacy was still open and I told them how grateful I was for their patience.

I think this is how things are going to be for a while. Good news mixed with bad, mostly moving in one direction but sometimes taking detours, but in general moving in the right direction.

All our Love

.

Friday, 7/4/2014 – Today

"Begin at once to live, and count each separate day as a separate life." - Seneca

Today is day twenty one. Laury and I were asked many times in the hospital by the nurses, "What day are you?" With bone marrow transplants the doctors count the day you received your bone marrow as day zero. They look for things to happen on certain days, like the first signs of the new white blood cells showing up around day ten; the red blood cells and platelets around day twenty one.

Laury and I decided not to count the days. We know things happen when they are supposed to and each person is unique. And if Laury's white cells turned up early and her red decided not to show by day twenty one we didn't want to worry. Laury and I decided that looking for something to happen only made us anxious and these things are out of our control. We want to enjoy each day and be grateful, not disappointed.

So today is not day twenty one, it is the Fourth of July, a beautiful day. Laury's parents came over and brought us lunch and we sat around the table and talked and were grateful to all be together again. Each day will bring something new, not just a bigger number. Laury and I do know that the next major milestone is day 100. I guess that is when the doctors consider the bone marrow transplant a success. I consider every day I have with Laury a success and I am not counting them, just living and loving her.

Happy Independence Day.

All our Love.

Saturday, 7/5/2014 – Chores

"For a minute, we're just two people wondering why things are the way they are." - Kathryn Stockett, The Help

Getting up early this morning to go to Chicago to get my hair cut was difficult, after listening to my neighbors shoot off fireworks until eleven thirty last night. I hooked Laury up to her IV and we sped off in the Mini at seven fifteen. Magen agreed to meet us there early, mainly because we didn't have an appointment but also to make Laury's visit easier. Laury is supposed to avoid crowded places and the Circle Salon on a Saturday morning can be very crowded. Laury got her head shaved of the little bits of remaining hair and her eyebrows colored. The coloring was to make them blend in better or something like that - not really my area of expertise.

I decided to keep my hair short and so I helped Magen improve her razor skills.

Laury slept most of the way down there and back. She says the car is great because it is the one place where she is able to get a "natural" sleep. Laury spent most of the day today out on the couch on the patio. Laury said she felt tired but not in a bad way, more like how you feel on a raining day, cozy. The itching is still bothering her at times and Laury doesn't always want to take the Benadryl, because it can make her sleepy.

I cleaned the house and did the grocery shopping and finished the laundry. There were times I would stop and see Laury's bald head from the back of the couch and I would wonder how she was doing. Laury and I have been side-by-side for so long that when I go to the store or spend a bunch of time inside away from Laury it feels weird. We are however, two people, and coming home means resuming our lives and chores. Laury's chore right now is to get stronger and grow bone marrow; mine is to do everything I can to support her. I still think her job is harder than mine.

All our Love.

Sunday, 7/6/2014 – Sunday

"Let us make one point, that we meet each other with a smile, when it is difficult to smile. Smile at each other, make time for each other in your family." - Mother Teresa

Today was quiet. Laury and I were able to finally sleep in, which was nice since the smoke detector in our bedroom malfunctioned at two thirty in the morning. After hooking Laury up to Violet we went outside, Laury sat on the patio and I weeded the back gardens and trimmed the rose bush. Laury has done a good job of training me as a gardener, I can no longer walk by a garden without seeing the weeds and wanting to stop and pick them. I don't really enjoy weeding, but it calls me, nonetheless.

I called my Mom on the phone today and we had a good talk. She asked me some very good questions about how Laury is doing. It made me think that if you all ever have a question please feel free to ask, I will do my best to answer it. Lyndsay joined us for dinner, which is always nice. She brought us up to speed on her life and happenings. Keri and Laury Skyped, and laughed and cried.

Today was almost a normal Sunday, one I hope we have many more of.

All our Love.

Monday, 7/7/2014 – A good plan

"Plans are an invitation to disappointment." - Derek Landy, Mortal Coil

Today did not go as planned, but then I am not sure why we thought it would. We had clinic today, so Laury and I left the house at noon. Our appointment with Dr. Odenike was not until four thirty but they once again had instructed us to come early in case Laury needed a transfusion. On paper it sounds like a good plan: get their early, check the blood and if need be have a transfusion all before meeting with the doctor. Unfortunately, it didn't go as planned. We arrived a little after one and Laury had her blood checked. We then waited until five to be told that Laury needed a transfusion. It was too late to have the transfusion at the transfusion center so we would have to go to the hospital. Laury and I decided to go home instead, arriving here around seven thirty.

We had previously set up a relationship with a local doctor to handle transfusions in Naperville, if necessary. Laury and I decided to wait until tomorrow and have the transfusion here.

These visits exhaust Laury. There is a lot of up and down emotionally, the waiting, the news, and the explanations. Today Laury's platelets were up, a good sign, but her hemoglobin was down to 6.5. Dr. Odenike explained that the red cells can be the last to appear, especially when there is a blood type mismatch between the donor and the patient. Dr. Odenike is not worried and told us we should not be worried if Laury requires transfusions for a while longer.

The itching Laury is experiencing is driving her crazy. We talked with Dr. Odenike about this and unfortunately, the medication that is most likely causing the itching cannot be replaced. Dr. Odenike prescribed a new antihistamine to help the itching but said Laury will just have to try to deal with it.

Laury was feeling pretty discouraged when we went over to the infusion center to get another blood draw and get her Hiccman Line dressing changed. She came back out after receiving the new dressing and was feeling much better. Once again, a nurse was Laury's angel. The nurse told Laury how good she looked and how well she was doing. Laury said, "Right", and the nurse said, "No, I see a lot of patients who have gone through a bone marrow transplant and you are doing really good." It is amazing how these angels get placed in our path just when we need them.

All our Love.

Tuesday, 7/8/2014 – Yet again

"And I got out of there without punching anyone, kicking anyone, or breaking down in tears. Some days the small victories are all you achieve." - Molly Ringle, Relatively Honest

Today was another long, frustrating day. We had hoped to be able to go the clinic in Naperville to have Laury's transfusion. The clinic informed us that Laury would have to be typed and cross matched today and the transfusion would be tomorrow. We called Dr. Odenike's nurse and she sent us back to U of C. Laury and I left at eleven and got home around seven. Lisa, our nurse, was able to get us into the infusion center to get typed and cross matched. The clinic has to do this every week, so even though the information was in the computer the last type and cross match was over a week old. This meant Laury and I had to wait while the typing was completed before receiving the blood.

While we were sitting waiting for the results, Paula, our transplant nurse, came to see us. She informed us that Dr. Odenike wanted to admit Laury to the hospital to receive her blood because the infusion center would not be able to give her both units of blood before it closed. I asked Paula if Dr. Odenike would be OK if Laury received one unit today and the other one on Thursday when we come back to clinic. Paula said that the doctor would probably not approve of that but she would check.

After Paula left I went to Sonya, the woman who pretty much runs the infusion center. I asked her if Laury's type and cross match had come back. Sonya said it had but that they were going to admit Laury to the hospital. I said that Laury didn't want to go to the hospital and that we had just gotten out a week ago, and that if we could get at least one unit of blood into Laury she could go home tonight. Sonya said, "I will get you back here in just a few minutes." and she did. Laury received one unit of blood and with the agreement to come back tomorrow morning at 8:00am, we were able to leave. Paula knows they messed up; they should have read Laury's numbers as soon as they came back on Monday and we were there in plenty of time to get two units of blood. Paula asked us to come even earlier on Thursday to make sure it wouldn't happen again. I asked her who was going to make sure that we didn't have the same thing happen and wind up sitting and waiting even longer on Thursday. Paula assured us that she would check the numbers as soon as they were available.

So we head back to U of C early tomorrow morning. I can see now why they say the hardest part of the recovery is when you go home. It is not because Laury is so tired and weak. It is because we spend so much time waiting and going back to clinic. It has been a very frustrating couple of days.

All our Love.

Wednesday, 7/9/2014 – Package deal

"I knew I was going to take the wrong train, so I left early." - Yogi Berra

Today Laury and I left the house at six fifteen in the morning to make an eight o'clock appointment at the infusion center. We arrived a little after eight but Sonya had us back in a room before eight thirty. She said to Laury, "I want to get you in, out and home." We echoed those feelings and thanked Sonya again for her help yesterday.

Laury was hooked up to the first bag of blood and the nurse asked if we wanted her to page Dr. Odenike to see if it would be OK to speed up the drip to complete the transfusion in an hour and a half instead of two hours. Laury said yes, and the nurse paged Dr. Odenike who responded with a yes. This was good news because we also found out Laury was to get two units of blood instead of one. This meant one less hour of sitting in the clinic today.

While the second bag of blood was going into Laury, Jean, our nurse practitioner, stopped by. We had an appointment with Jean for tomorrow at four thirty and she said that when she heard we were back today, she came to see us so we wouldn't have to make the trip tomorrow. Jean also told Laury that she managed to squeeze her in to do Laury's bone marrow aspiration on Friday. This, too, was good news, Laury really wanted Jean to do the procedure, but Jean originally did not have any open slots on Friday.

Jean also talked to us about the transition from hospital to home. She said that many times it can be difficult and sometimes the clinic doesn't make it easier by what happened on Monday. Jean said we will have good days and bad days; some as a result of health issues others because of office issues. She said they are all part of the package. Somehow, the way Jean put it made sense and we both felt much better.

Today restored our confidence in the clinic and the people who work there. They really are looking out for us and were not happy about what happened over the last two days. I guess we always knew this to be true, but as Laury said, "We are just a little full right now."

Thanks for all your encouragement and support again.

All our Love.

Thursday, 7/10/2014 – Rest stop

"Growth is a spiral process, doubling back on itself, reassessing and regrouping." - Julie Margaret Cameron

Regrouping is a good way of describing what Laury and I are going through today. Laury is trying to find herself, and the inner strength and calm she had and still has, and as for me, I am trying to get back into working full time and being a full time caregiver. To say that we have not gotten off to a smooth start is a bit of an understatement. But we are getting there.

Laury had a good session today with her therapist, Pat, and her energy healer, Nancy. Both of these healers helped Laury understand what is going on within her, spiritually and emotionally, and how to get back on track. Laury felt much better after these sessions. She had to be reminded that we are still early in the journey, and that it is OK to feel the way she feels sometimes. Laury used to say, before we went into the hospital, that she was on a healing sabbatical. Pat reminded Laury that she is still on that sabbatical. Just because we are home from the hospital doesn't mean Laury should stop taking naps when she feels the need, doing meditation, and restorative yoga. Laury has to continue to give herself permission to be sick. Laury can be her own worst critic sometimes and get frustrated with herself.

So today was a rest stop on the journey. No trips down to clinic, but a time to take out the refreshments, check the maps, read the travel brochures, and enjoy the sunshine. The trip continues tomorrow, hopefully with renewed energy and focus, and a better feeling of where we are and where we are going.

All our Love.

Friday, 7/11/2014 – Fluidity

"Small change, small wonders - these are the currency of my endurance and ultimately of my life." - Barbara Kingsolver

Bone marrow is an amazing thing. When it works correctly, it is moist, sticky and full of blood. Laury's bone marrow before the transplant was very dry, so dry in fact that the last time she had a bone marrow aspiration, they were not able to get any fluids. Laury had a bone marrow aspiration today, at the thirty day mark, and they were able to get fluid. This means that there has been significant change in her bone marrow - for the better. We will have the full results of the test on Monday, but the fact the technician was able to get what they did is very good news.

We spent the afternoon at the clinic today. Laury had blood drawn, and her numbers were good. No need for a transfusion. This, too, was good news. Laury admitted that now she has some anxiety when we go to clinic over whether she will need blood and they will want to admit her to the hospital again. Laury cried at the good news today.

Every visit we have to manage something new: changes to medication levels, new medications, stopping medications, program changes. Everything starts new each time we go. Laury and I are beginning to understand this and are getting better at asking what we need to do differently this time.

I asked Laury what she wanted to do this weekend, and she replied, "Find my routine". The routine includes handling change, feeling good about it, keeping our eyes on the landing spot, and remembering to have fun.

All our Love.

Saturday, 7/12/2014 – Stormy day

"The heart of man is very much like the sea, it has its storms, it has its tides and in its depths it has its pearls too" - Vincent van Gogh

Yesterday was an emotional and tiring end to a long week. We ended on a good note with the news of Laury's bone marrow. Today, however, Laury is tired, both physically and emotionally. Her hip is really sore from where they did the bone marrow aspiration. She is also still feeling the effects of having to take so much Benadryl to control the itching.

Yesterday was hard, emotionally for Laury. We went back to the 10th floor of the hospital to visit a friend that Laury had corresponded with. The journey was tiring for Laury. It is a long walk from the clinic to the hospital and from the elevators to the room. The journey was also emotionally tiring for Laury. I asked Laury how she felt going back to the 10th floor so soon after leaving. She was quiet, and said she was not sure how she felt, but she wanted to be there for her friend.

So today Laury has spent most of the day on the couch, reading and napping. She is worn out. But I know that even if she knew that she would feel this way afterwards, Laury still would have gone back to visit her friend. It is so easy to be self-centered on this journey we are on. Laury reminded me yesterday why so many people care about her, because she cares about them. No matter what.

All our Love.

Sunday, 7/13/2014 – Integration

"The deepest of level of communication is not communication, but communion. It is wordless ... beyond speech ... beyond concept." - Thomas Merton

The view from our room in the hospital was amazing; we could see the city, sun rise and sun set. It lifted our spirit at times watching the clouds, sailboats, and storms. We could see for miles. Coming home Laury and I have a different view: trees, garden, small animals and neighbors. Just like our change of view we have also experienced a change of perspective.

When Jesus healed the man with Leprosy he told him to go see the priest to be declared clean and re-integrated into the community. In the hospital we were part of a community, one that is focused on healing and sending people back to their community. Now that Laury and I are home we are beginning to be more integrated back into our community.

Jesus knew that to be completely healed you need to again be part of your community.

This weekend Laury and I spent some time re-integrating. Last night our friend, Joan, who is going through cancer treatment, stopped by to drop off some hats her daughter had made. Joan, like Laury, has lost her hair to chemo and wanted to share a couple of hats with Laury. They met at the back door, through the glass of the storm door. When Joan removed her hat to reveal her bald head, Laury gave her the "thumbs up" sign and Joan returned it to Laury. I wish I had taken a picture; there they stood talking, from my point of view looking like a bald-headed baby looking at themselves in a full length mirror.

Today we went over to Kelly's to look at where she needs a sprinkler system installed. Kelly then came back to our house and Laury and she sat outside and talked. Right after she left, John and Becky stopped by with some delicious pie. We sat around the living room and got caught up on their lives and happenings.

Laury was feeling better today and being able to meet with people and re-integrate is healing for her, and me. Laury welcomes visitors, and we will be honest if it is too much. You all are our community.

All our Love.

Tuesday, 7/15/2014 – Monday, Monday

"Gratitude doesn't change the scenery. It merely washes clean the glass you look through so you can clearly see the colors." - Richelle E. Goodrich

Yesterday had many things to make Laury and I tired and angry. We drove down to clinic in crazy-heavy rain, we waited for four hours for Laury to receive blood, and we got home after eight. Our plan of arriving early and having the nurse watch for Laury's results and determining if she needed blood failed again. This time it was due to the lab taking two hours to get the results back. Again we had to beg to get at least one unit of blood in Laury before we could go home. Laury and I were in the infusion center waiting room from one thirty to four thirty before they got us in.

As we sat there, Laury got more and more anxious about not being able to get the blood in time. It was very easy to get mad and upset. However, a few things happened to turn things around. First, we ran into our friend, Erin, the young woman with breast cancer that we used to see every Monday. Erin was there to start another round of chemo. She was supposed to have surgery this month but her doctor wanted another round to shrink her tumor more. Erin's surgery is now scheduled for a week after her son's second birthday. She certainly had more reason than we did to be upset, yet Erin was happy and glad to see us. She sat next to us and we talked about treatments, two-year-olds, and good places to eat around the hospital. She made the waiting worth it.

Our nurse and Dr. Odenike both came over to the infusion center to see us and to try to get us in earlier. They were concerned about Laury and knew that this was stressful for her. It was good to see that Dr. Odenike and her nurse were trying their best to make it better. Once we got back into the chair, Victoria our nurse was great. She treated Laury with such kindness and agreed to stay late to make sure Laury got her blood. Victoria called Laury "baby" with a true sense of love. Later Dr. Odenike came to see us again. Laury has some more changes to medications, and we are waiting to hear if we have to go back today or tomorrow to get Laury more blood.

After Laury and I were done in the infusion center we headed up to see Robin in the hospital. I asked Laury if she wanted me to push her in a wheel chair and she said yes. The chair made the long walk easier and faster. Robin greeted us with a smile, and we could see she was doing much better. After a short visit we headed home.

A long day, but instead of leaving with anger and frustration we left with gratitude. Grateful for friends, doctors, nurses, wheel chairs, light traffic coming home, and just being together on this journey.

All our Love.

Wednesday, 7/16/2014 – Patience

"Try looking at your mind as a wayward puppy that you are trying to paper train. You don't drop-kick a puppy into the neighbor's yard every time it piddles on the floor. You just keep bringing it back to the newspaper." - Anne Lamott

Today was a good day. Laury woke up with more energy, no itching, and feeling better about life. Laury and I are finding it is easy to lose sight of the fact that just because Laury is home from the hospital that we are far from over. This is not a sprint, but a marathon, or maybe a triathlon. We have finished the first leg of the race, and it may prove to have been the hardest, but we won't know that until we finish the other two legs. Everything we read told us that coming home and healing is the hardest part of this journey. Laury and I need to be reminded of that.

Laury still has a lot of healing to do. She is getting better, but it is not a straight line to the finish. We will have ups and downs, times when it will be easy to lose site of the ultimate goal: Laury's good health and long life. Going to the clinic is stressful and it is trying our patience. But it is only one day, and each day we complete a visit Laury is closer to the finish line. Laury and I are going to work on getting back to living day-by-day, with an eye on the finish line but not so focused that we forget to get through today with joy and happiness, regardless of what happens. We know the good days will outweigh the bad, and that as long as we are together and have your support we will get there.

All our Love.

Wednesday, 7/16/2014 – Walking

"The sum of the whole is this: walk and be happy; walk and be healthy. The best way to lengthen out our days is to walk steadily and with a purpose. " - Charles Dickens

We went for a walk today. Laury and I try to get out for a walk every day we don't have clinic. Some days Laury is not up for it and others the weather does not cooperate. Today we walked slowly, Laury's red blood numbers are still pretty low, but we made it around the block. Our walk has a purpose but not always a goal. We have a large hill near our house. Laury's goal is to be able to make it up that hill. We haven't set a time table for the hill it will happen when it is time.

Laury and I used to walk hand-in-hand; right now Laury needs both her hands free for her balance. One of my goals is to walk holding hands again. Simple goals, but we need them to help stay focused and help gauge our progress. Tomorrow we head back to clinic. Laury is scheduled for two more units of blood. This time Laury has a chair reserved and we are expected. Another goal for us is for Laury to no longer need blood. We know it will happen, but just like the hill, we do not have a time table, but it will happen when it is time.

All our Love.

Friday, 7/18/2014 – Today's angel

"Sophie: "Right. So no plans at all, then?"

Jenna: "Other than rocking in the fetal position for a while?" - Rachel Hawkins, Spell Bound

I wish I could say that our trip to the clinic yesterday went as planned: arriving on time, getting the blood results, chair waiting, Laury receiving two units of blood, seeing Robin and home by six. I wish I could say that but I can't. Laury and I did arrive a little before one, and Laury had her blood draw and we were waiting in the infusion center by 1:10. Little did we know that the plan had already come off its wheels. The technician that drew Laury's blood took her old blood band (a red band that shows Laury's blood type). The technician said that the bands are only good for 72 hours and Laury would need a new one. This meant that Laury would have to wait while the lab typed and cross matched her - a process that takes at least ninety minutes.

Paula, our nurse, came by to see us after we had been sitting in the infusion center waiting area for about an hour. Paula wanted to know why we were not back getting Laury's blood. We told her that Laury needed to be typed and cross matched again. Paula said that Laury's blood band was good for today and that she didn't need a new type and cross match, so she went back to talk to the infusion center. Paula came back out after a few minutes and asked Laury if she still had her old blood band. Laury said the technician had taken it. So Paula, Laury and I walked back to the lab to see if we could retrieve her old blood band. When we got there the technician said she had thrown it away. Paula asked her to check the trash can for the band and we all offered to go back and help her look for it. The technician unhappily said she would go look. She came back after a few minutes and said she couldn't find it. Paula, said in her heavy Spanish accent, "I am trying to make this all run smoothly for you, and I am failing!" We all laughed and said it wasn't her fault. We walked back to the infusion center and began waiting again for the typing results.

After about another hour, Helena from the infusion center came out and said that the lab hadn't even started on Laury's blood typing yet and it looked like Laury would not be getting blood today. Laury replied to Helena, "Oh shit, Helena!" Helena said, "I know, I was afraid to come out and tell you." Helena said she would call Jean our nurse practitioner who we were to see at four thirty, to see what Jean wanted to do. After about ten minutes we saw Jean walking toward us and she stopped at the front desk and gave Helena Laury's old blood band. Jean said that she had gone over to the lab and had gone through the trash until she found it.

Helena got us back into the infusion center but said she wasn't sure we had enough time to get two units of blood. Heidi, our infusion nurse, said she would make sure we got both units, and quickly ordered the blood to be delivered and we were off and running. Heidi left after one unit was in Laury and Victoria, who had stayed late Monday night for us, again stayed late to make sure Laury got her second unit.

While the second unit was going, Jean stopped by again to talk with Laury and to see how she was doing. She also gave us the results of the bone marrow aspiration. The bone marrow shows signs of making blood. This is really good news Jean said that the DNA test to see if the bone marrow is the new marrow won't be back for another two weeks, but she is confident that it is the new marrow. Jean also reassured Laury that she is right where she needs to be on her healing path. Laury was grateful for the news, and she said it felt good to be validated.

We left the infusion center and went to see Robin. We left the hospital at around seven thirty, and because of traffic we arrived home a little before nine o'clock. All things considered it was a good day.

All our Love.

Friday, 7/18/2014 – My turn

"The cave you fear to enter holds the treasure you seek." - Joseph Campbell

According to the web site Literary Devices, foreshadowing is a literary device in which a writer gives an advance hint of what is to come later in the story, so here goes. On Thursday while Laury and I were waiting in the infusion center, an older man sitting across from us, took out a blood glucose meter and checked his blood sugar. He then took out a needle and gave himself an injection in the back of his arm. Laury said quietly to me, "I really wish I hadn't seen that, it kind of made my stomach tingle." I said me, too, and you all know how I hate needles.

Yesterday, our nurse, Paula called and said that Laury would need to be given a Neupogen shot every day to help promote her white blood cell growth. Laury was on the Neupogen while in the hospital but now they wanted to start it up again. And you guessed it. I am going to have to give Laury that shot.

Paula contacted our local Oncologist, Dr. Ferris, to arrange to have the shot given out here and to teach me how to give it in the future. Laury and I went to the local infusion center and met with the nurse. Jessica, our nurse, brought us back to the room and took Laury's vitals. Laury's blood pressure was normal and her pulse was 58. I told the nurse that if she took my BP and pulse right now it wouldn't be too good. I was very nervous. The Jessica showed me how to draw the liquid into the syringe and make sure there are no air bubbles and how to push the shot into Laury's arm. It wasn't as bad as I thought it would be, but today I get to do it myself.

Laury promised to tell me if I hurt her or if I do a bad job - I will need this feedback to make sure I get better. I have seen Laury face so many fears during this journey, I can face this one for her.

All our Love.

Sunday, 7/20/2014 – Clean toilets

"When you work on the little things big things happen" - Rodger Halston

Today Laury was tired and a little down. Laury did not sleep well last night and she really felt it all day. I did manage to get her shot in without a problem. I can't say that I enjoyed it but it wasn't as bad as I thought it would be and Laury said it didn't hurt.

Tomorrow Laury and I head back down to clinic at U of C. We are trying something different, Laury is going to get typed and cross matched out here at the infusion center and then we are heading downtown. If they determine Laury needs blood, then we have the option of having the transfusion out here or downtown depending on how backed up things are at U of C. We will see how this works this week. We are still hoping that Laury's spleen will quit taking up all the new blood and that the transfusions will last longer. Ultimately, we want Laury's new marrow to start producing enough red blood cells that she doesn't need the transfusions.

Lyndsay came over for dinner and sat outside with us and talked and laughed. It picked Laury up and she felt the best she has felt all day. After dinner, Lyndsay cleaned the kitchen and cleaned the toilets while I finished cleaning the cat boxes. Small things, but it was really nice to see Lyndsay and to have her help. I feel like I sometimes need another day in the weekend to get everything done.

All our Love.

Tuesday, 7/22/2014 – If first you don't succeed

"Never confuse a single defeat with a final defeat." - F. Scott Fitzgerald

Plan B went down in flames yesterday, leaving Laury in tears and me with a skull-crushing headache. Laury and I went to the clinic here in Naperville yesterday morning and they took blood to cross and type match. The plan was that if U of C didn't have time to get Laury her blood they could send the order to Naperville and we would have the transfusion sent here the next morning. Laury and I also tried arriving earlier at U of C. We got there at eleven thirty, and Laury had her blood drawn by noon and we were sitting in the infusion center waiting room. Once again, this is where the plan came off its rails. We waited until four, to be taken back, which of course meant that they would not be able to get both units of blood into Laury. I paged Paula, our nurse, to see if we could get the order signed to have the transfusion done in Naperville. Paula showed up around five and said it was now too late to send the order. The infusion center ran one unit of red blood and one unit of Platelets into Laury and we left the clinic around seven thirty.

The day was not a total loss however. We saw our friend, Erin, and as usual she brightened our waiting. Also, Dr. Odenike stopped by with some good news. While the process is taking longer than any of us would like, Laury's bone marrow is engrafting. Dr. Odenike said the DNA test on the bone marrow shows that it is from the donor. Dr. Odenike also said that the white counts have come back up since giving Laury the Neupogen shots, proving the marrow can respond to stimulation. I asked Dr. Odenike where all the red blood was going that we are giving Laury and why it isn't lasting very long. She explained that Laury has two blood types going on in her system right now. Laury has some antibodies from her and some from the donor. Both of these groups of antibodies can attack the transfused blood and break it down. Dr. Odenike said until the new bone marrow produces enough blood and antibodies to remove the last of Laury's antibodies, this battle will go on. There is no good way of telling how long this will last. This is one downside of the blood type mismatch between Laury and the donor. Ultimately, things are progressing but slowly.

The other good news was that Dr. Odenike agreed that from now on we will get a CBC here in Naperville before we go down to clinic. The results of the CBC will be faxed to U of C and if they determine Laury needs blood they will fax the order back to Naperville and we will have the transfusion the next day in Naperville. No more coming to clinic five hours ahead of schedule. Dr. Odenike agreed that what we were trying to do didn't work, and it was too much on Laury and me.

Today we hope to recover from yesterday and get back at it. Laury asked me what she should image her body doing to help her healing. I said to me it sounded like a relay race. Her old antibodies need to hand off the baton to her new antibodies. Right now her old antibodies are still trying to run the race and her new ones are not up to speed. Thursday we try plan C. Wish us luck.

All our Love.

Tuesday, 7/22/2014 – Too tired

"Sometimes the most important thing in a whole day is the rest we take between two deep breaths." -Etty Hillesum

Today was for taking deep breaths. Laury was worn out from yesterday. She slept in late and spent most of the day on the couch. Laury and I have an appointment tomorrow at the infusion center in Naperville for another unit of blood. This will be our first test of the new plan. We both hope the experience will be more restful and run smoothly.

It is hard to see Laury have days that take the wind out of her sails. It is even harder when I feel I don't have any extra energy to give her. Today we both needed rest, time to regroup, rebuild and gain back some of the strength we expended yesterday.

I can't image how tired Laury must feel when I feel this tired. The weight is heavy today, but I know it will get lighter tomorrow.

All our Love.

Wednesday, 7/23/2014 - Mom

"God could not be everywhere, and therefore he made mothers." - David C. Gross

My mother died suddenly yesterday. My sister called to tell me. I have been feeling "off" the last few days, and the best way to describe it is "overwhelmed". I was sitting at the computer yesterday and I remembered something my mom said to me recently, "Sometimes you just need a good cry." I then got the call from my sister, and I had my opportunity for that cry.

You were right Mom, it helped. Thank you. I love you.

All our Love.

Thursday, 7/24/2014 – Decision

"Crying is all right in its way while it lasts. But you have to stop sooner or later, and then you still have to decide what to do." - C. S. Lewis, The Silver Chair

The last couple of days have been for crying and remembering. Laury and I also had our first experience with the infusion center here in Naperville. We had an appointment yesterday at ten thirty, and arrived at ten twenty-five. Laury and I were taken back right at ten thirty and the blood was started and we were home by one thirty. The center is quiet, the chairs are comfortable, and the nurses are nice. It was a very good experience. Today we went back to have Laury's blood checked before we go down to clinic this afternoon. Laury's numbers are good, so she does not need any blood. She feels better and has a little bit of an appetite back.

My mother's funeral is on Saturday in Michigan. I have decided not to go. It was a tough decision, one that I arrived at with some loss of sleep. But as I told my brother and sisters, Mom was grateful for the care I am giving Laury and would want me to take care of Laury first. Mom was a woman of very strong faith. She had no doubts that her parents, brothers and son would be waiting for her in heaven with open arms. When I tried to argue with my mom the last few nights, about being there for her funeral she would say to me, "I am fine, and happy, you need to stay with Laury." I almost never win arguments with my mom.

I thank all of you for your kind thoughts and prayers. We are spent emotionally, yet full of your love.

All our Love.

Friday, 7/25/2014 – Waiting

"So much of control is not authoritative action but mindful waiting."-
Cameron Conaway, Caged: Memoirs of a Cage-Fighting Poet

So much of what Laury and I are going through involves waiting. Many of you have asked, "How do you stand waiting so long, it would drive me crazy", or "I get tired just hearing about all your waiting." We discovered on Thursday that there are different types of waiting. Laury and I do not enjoy the long waits but they never seemed to bother us until they involved whether or not we would have time to get Laury blood. Many times we spent the better part of a day at clinic and would come home tired but never with the defeated spirit of waiting for blood left us with.

Yesterday, Laury and I went to clinic in the afternoon. We already knew Laury did not need blood and we just needed to be there a few hours early for our labs. The waiting was not bad, the anxiety over would we have time to get the blood, would we have to come back, why was it taking so long to get the type and cross match, all were not there. Laury and I could sit and enjoy our time together and wait.

Today we visited Laury's parents to see the progress Laury's Mom and her new gardener made. Laury's Dad said, "I am so glad you stopped by. Mo couldn't wait for you to see her gardens!" Laury's Mom had made a spice cake and gave us a big piece to take home. I couldn't wait to get home and eat some. Waiting can be a good thing. Next week Laury and I have a long day on Monday back at clinic, but we will be together and we will wait together.

All our Love.

Saturday, 7/26/2014 – In the Garden

"I come to the garden alone

While the dew is still on the roses" - Charles Austin Miles

My Mom was a gardener. She loved gardens and everything about them. In the spring Mom planted, in the summer she weeded, in the fall she harvested, and in the winter she planned for spring. Today was my Mom's funeral. Laury and I wanted to do something to let my mom know we were thinking of her and missing her. A few months back in the post, *Lightheaded,* I talked about a space that we made in our garden after a couple of box woods died. Laury and I had talked about what to plant there since we have been home from the hospital. Last weekend we were driving somewhere and I saw this beautiful garden of Astilbe and I said to Laury, "How about putting some Astilbe in that space?" Laury replied, "That would be beautiful and they would love it because it is so wet there." So last Sunday I planted, with Laury's direction, three new beautiful Astilbe plants.

Today we were looking at the new Astilbe garden and talking about what we could do to remember my mom. I said that Astilbe was one of her favorite plants. We decided to plant six more different types of Astilbe in the garden and rename the space, Mom's Garden. It felt good to weed, dig and plant today. I am not a gardener like Laury or my Mom. But working in the garden today made sense- it connected me with Mom. I know Mom would love this new garden and we will think of her every time we sit on the patio and see all the beautiful Astilbe.

Rest well my Mom, we will keep the garden weeded for you.

All our Love.

Tuesday, 7/29/2014 – F-bombs

"Under certain circumstances, profanity provides a relief denied even to prayer." - Mark Twain

Laury had a day yesterday where it seemed that every other word she said was F**K. Laury is not one to hold back her feelings and yesterday she let them fly. She was frustrated that her blood numbers were down again and that she needed two units of blood and platelets. There is not a lot I can do when Laury gets like this but to sit with her and let her ride it out. At one point after another string of profanity-riddled venting, I texted Laury, "I love you". She heard her phone and read my text. She said, "I think you sent this to me by mistake." I said it was no mistake that I just wanted her to not lose sight of the fact. Laury replied, "Just because I am saying F**K every other word doesn't mean I don't love you." We both chuckled.

Truth is that we are both frustrated that this is taking so long. Dr. Odenike again assured us that she is not concerned. Yes she too would like it to move quicker, but Dr. Odenike says with this process it just takes time. She reminded us that the DNA test shows that the engraftment has taken place and things are moving, however, just slowly.

Yesterday was a long day, it included Laury getting a unit of platelets, and a respiratory treatment, a dressing change, and meeting with Dr. Odenike. Today we have to go to the hospital out here to get Laury a unit of blood, and tomorrow to the local infusion center to get another unit. The hospital and infusion center are too busy to give Laury two units at one time.

Laury needs yoga, she needs a way to release the frustration and find her center. Rattling off a string of F-bombs may feel good for a short while, and I will never deny Laury that opportunity, but it doesn't last. I am sure today will be better and no one is better at finding her center than Laury-but yesterday was F**Ked up.

All our Love.

Tuesday, 7/29/2014 – Leaving

"As happens sometimes, a moment settled and hovered and remained for much more than a moment. And sound stopped and movement stopped for much, much more than a moment." - John Steinbeck, Of Mice and Men

Laury was very tired today; she felt the need for blood. We had an appointment for one unit today at the local hospital and one unit tomorrow at the local infusion center. I decided to go early to the appointment today in hopes that they could get us in with enough time to get both units of blood. The plan worked with the help of Karen, our nurse. Once again someone took it upon themselves to go out of their way and help us. When we told Karen our story she said she would call over to the infusion center and see if she could get the order changed to two units. Karen came back a few minutes later and said we were good to go.

With Karen's help Laury received two units of blood and now she has tomorrow off to just rest. Laury and I were once again the last people to leave the clinic and watched the cleaning crew start their shift. Laury and I have become used to coming into these situations with noise and movement, but leaving in silence. Almost every time we go to the clinic at U of C lately we are leaving after everyone else. We say hi to the cleaning crew and are amazed at how empty the parking lot is.

Today was no different; Laury and I arrived in the middle of the day and left after six to an empty clinic and quiet music playing. In some ways it is nice to be able to leave in quiet, being the only ones left, and going home after a successful visit. We are also thankful that someone was willing to leave even later than us. I hope they enjoy the silence as they leave, too.

All our Love.

Thursday, 7/31/2014 – Thinking about it

"Learn to be quiet enough to hear the genuine within yourself so that you can hear it in others." - Marian Wright Edelman

Yesterday was a quiet day, one that both Laury and I needed. Laury felt much better and was in a better mood. I needed the time to focus on work and to do yoga. Today Laury and I head to clinic at U of C. We hope that goes smoothly.

I am not a saint. I appreciate the sentiment and the complement, but I am just doing something for someone I love. I love Laury with all my heart. I have since the day we met. I would do anything for her. But I am also selfish. I want Laury back. As she says, "I miss my buddy". I was talking with my sister, Kim, and I told her I admire that she can give herself a shot every day, and Kim told me, "It is easy when your life depends on it". My life depends on Laury.

Laury admitted that some of her bad mood and frustration over the last few days was because she felt she kept me from being at my mom's funeral. My mom was happy for the love that Laury and I share; she understood it probably better than we gave her credit for.

I have thought about working in the shop, going on vacation, working a normal day, and other things that I "miss". But nothing compares to the time I have been able to spend with Laury. There is nothing I would rather be doing than sitting at her side. I don't think that makes me a saint - just someone in love.

All our Love.

CHAPTER SEVEN

August

Friday, 8/1/2014 – Smooth

"May you have warm words on a cold evening, a full moon on a dark night and a smooth road all the way to your door" - Irish Blessing

Smooth is the best way to describe yesterday. Laury and I went to the infusion center here in Naperville to get her blood draw and type and cross match. We waited for the results and found out that Laury needed blood and platelets. The nurse had already called our nurse, Paula, at U of C and placed the order, and we already had a chair for the next morning in Naperville to receive the transfusions. The entire process ran like it was supposed to.

Laury and I left for our U of C clinic appointment at three and arrived around four. Our appointment was for four thirty, so we checked in and went over to the infusion center for another blood draw. Usually, the technicians draw the blood from a vein even though Laury has a Hickman line. The reason for this is that the doctors are checking the level of Prograf in Laury's blood. For some reason when you receive Prograf through the Hickman line it hangs around the line for a long time and throws off the reading. Last Monday I asked Dr. Odenike if we could now begin using the Hickman line for the blood draw since it had been a month since Laury had received Prograf through her line. Dr. Odenike agreed, and said they would know if there was still Prograf hanging around if the numbers looked weird because the numbers have been very stable. One more small victory - no more sticks with the needle to get a blood draw.

At the infusion center Laury was called back after a very short wait. The technician drew her blood and we went back to the doctor's waiting area. After a short wait we were taken back to our room. Laury put her meditation tape on and asked me if I was going to play solitaire. I said that I was not going to play because Jean was going to be coming real soon. After about five minutes Jean, our nurse practitioner, came into the room.

We had a good visit. Jean again assured Laury that she is early in the process and things are moving in the right direction and that it was OK to get frustrated but to not stay there.

We left the clinic around four forty-five and were home around six thirty. About as smooth a running day as we can expect, we will take it.

All our Love.

Friday, 8/1/2014 – Giving

"We never think lightly of those who walk with us on our uphill days." - Richelle E. Goodrich

Today Laury and I went to the infusion center here in Naperville and Laury received a unit of platelets and a unit of blood. The room was private, quiet, new, comfortable, all of the things you wish for when you have to sit in a room for four hours. Our nurse Keely was kind, talkative, and caring- all of the things you want in a nurse.

Later in the early afternoon, Marinda came over to work with Laury on yoga. This is a true gift.

Laury and I are constantly amazed and humbled by the gifts people have given us over the last several months. You all have given your time, kind words, support and love.

Sometimes it is hard to feel good about what we are going through, and I will admit that I am tired today. But every time we feel overwhelmed there is someone there to help. This journey we are on is amazing and wonderful.

Thank you all again for being with us and giving such wonderful gifts.

All our Love.

Sunday, 8/3/2014 – Hungry?

"For is there any practice less selfish, any labor less alienated, any time less wasted, than preparing something delicious and nourishing for people you love?" - Michael Pollan, Cooked: A Natural History Of Transformation

It was a good, yet busy weekend. Laury was looking and feeling good. Saturday morning we went down into the city to get my hair cut. Laury and I stopped at the little bakery/restaurant across the street from the salon to order our usual cookie, and Laury ordered an iced Latte. The woman behind the counter remembered me but didn't recognize Laury in her hat and mask.

We came home and I began my chores for the weekend: grocery shopping, laundry, cleaning the cat boxes, etc. The weekends are busy for me. Grocery shopping has become a little more difficult lately. Laury still doesn't have much of an appetite and when she does eat it is in very small portions. I am used to planning meals and cooking most of them on Sunday so we have food already cooked when we get home from the clinic - I started this practice when Laury and I were doing yoga several nights a week. Now however, I am not sure what to make. I make stuff that I will eat during the week but I also have to make things that Laury can and will eat.

I have begun to make things Laury can pick at rather than sit down and eat all at once. For example, instead of making a bunch of chicken breasts on the grill, I roast a chicken then shred it up so Laury can take small pieces anytime she feels like it. I have been the main cook our entire marriage. I love to cook for Laury and for others. When the girls were at home we would have family dinner each night. It is hard when I ask Laury what she is in the mood to eat, I usually get, "I don't know, I probably will just pick at something." Most of our dinners now are me sitting down to something different than what Laury is eating. I still love it when Laury eats something that I have made and enjoys it. Friday night she was in the mood for a grilled cheese and managed to eat the entire thing. I was in heaven.

All our Love.

Monday, 8/4/2014 – Energy

"She was full of some strange energy that morning. Her every movement had purpose and life and she seemed to find satisfaction in every little thing." - Anna Godbersen, Envy

Today was a very good day. Laury had lots of energy. She woke up early and felt great. We went to the clinic here in Naperville this morning and got Laury's CBC and type and cross match. Her numbers were pretty good, much more stable than last Monday. Laury still will receive two units of blood tomorrow but we hope that this will get Laury up to a point where she can continue to feel well - not just maintaining.

Laury went for a walk to downtown Naperville with her friends Vicky and Kelly. They ran into Lyndsay while they were down there and Laury came home happy and energized. Laury said it felt like she was on vacation and that she had done well. It was good to see her out and walking and smiling and having fun.

Our trip down to the clinic at U of C was quiet. The waiting room at the infusion center was empty, and at one point Laury and I were the only people sitting and waiting. Laury got her blood draw and a dressing change. We then met with Jean, our nurse practitioner. Laury's spleen continues to shrink and everything still points in the direction of Laury's recovery. We hope that the blood numbers will begin to stabilize and Laury won't need the transfusions, but now that we are going to the infusion center in Naperville it is not so bad.

It is amazing to see Laury feel good. It sometimes is hard to imagine what it will be like when this is all behind us. I got a taste of it today, Laury smiling, talking, looking great and feeling great. It is what we are working for.

All our Love.

Tuesday, 8/5/2104 – Time

"The butterfly counts not months but moments, and has time enough"-
Rabindranath Tagore

Today we went to the infusion center here in Naperville for Laury to receive two units of blood. Laury and I arrived at nine thirty and left at two thirty. We didn't have the same private room we had last week but it was still nice. Laury and I found out today that if you are going to be there over lunch, the clinic brings around a menu and you can order lunch from a small selection provided by Corner Bakery. The lunch is brought in around twelve thirty and for Laury it is free.

While sitting there today, I wondered how time for us has become measured in things other than minutes and hours. Today the day was measured in two units of blood, yesterday in a clinic visit. I have noticed that many of the waiting areas and infusion areas have no clocks. I think it is because time isn't experienced in the same way in these spaces. "Does it really matter what time it is?" asked the song from Chicago. I can't think of another place where this is truer than the infusion center. Once you are there, the only thing that matters is getting what you need - no matter how long it takes.

Maybe this why Laury and I can sit for hours. It is not really minutes ticking away but life-giving blood going in.

All our Love.

Wednesday, 8/6/2104 – Cooperation

"Competition has been shown to be useful up to a certain point and no further, but cooperation, which is the thing we must strive for today, begins where competition leaves off." - Franklin D. Roosevelt

Laury had another good day today. She looked good, felt good and had enough energy to walk with Kelly again. Laury and I go to clinic tomorrow and we hope we will see Laury's numbers holding or improving.

Yesterday Laury and I visited with Pat, Laury's therapist. Laury can be very competitive - with herself. She sets up objectives and tries to meet and improve on them. This is one of the things that make Laury such a good teacher. Pat suggested to Laury and me that right now, where we are in this journey, it is not always good to set objectives. The doctors haven't talked about specific objectives, like when her red blood numbers should start showing up, when Laury will no longer need transfusions, etc. They know that each person and situation is different. All the doctors are looking for right now is continued positive movement.

Laury and I admitted that we want objectives sometimes, but for now we have to be comforted that the doctors are saying Laury is still improving. Today, when Laury was getting ready to go for her walk, she asked me if we still had our Pedometer so she could keep track of how far she walked and to try to do a little more next time. Laury then quickly changed her mind and said, "No I just need to go and do the best I can today." There is no guarantee that next time Laury will be able to go further, and what will be important is that she keeps going. Pat reminded Laury and me that it is better right now to cooperate with this journey and its ups and downs, instead of trying to compete with it.

All our Love.

Thursday, 8/7/2014 – Nineteen

"It is good news, worthy of all acceptation; and yet not too good to be true." - Matthew Henry

Laury and I went to the infusion center here in Naperville this morning to get Laury's blood checked. The results showed that Laury's numbers were stable and that she probably wouldn't need a transfusion tomorrow. We took this as good news and came home to get ready to go down to U of C.

We arrived at U of C, checked in and went to the infusion center to have another blood draw. Before they took Laury's blood Laury and I stopped in to see Robin, who was also in the infusion center receiving chemo therapy. We talked for a little bit then they took Laury in for her blood draw. After taking her blood, Laury and I went over to the waiting area to wait for our appointment with Dr. Odenike. After waiting for about forty-five minutes, Paula our nurse came in and asked us, "Did you get platelets today?" I said we had not, and just then Dr. Odenike came in, and she asked us the same question. Paula said to Dr. Odenike that we had not received platelets.

Dr. Odenike got very excited and said, "Your platelets were 13 from the blood test in Naperville, and here they were 19. I called the lab and they said they are going to do a manual count and probably revise the number higher." What this means is that Laury has produced platelets this week! This is a very positive sign, one we have been waiting for. Dr. Odenike said that we can't bank on this being steady progress, but she said, "For today we will take 19!" Laury and I were excited that we had good news and progress. Paula and Dr. Odenike were just as, if not more, excited than we were. Laury jumped up and hugged Dr. Odenike. Dr. Odenike said, "It has been a rough day, and this absolutely makes my day."

Laury and I drove home with smiles on our faces and excitement in our hearts.

All our Love.

Friday, 8/8/2014 – Why

"You are forgiven for your happiness and your successes only if you generously consent to share them." - Albert Camus

Today was nice. No infusion centers to go to, no appointments. Laury was able to take in the day. I didn't even need to hook Laury up to the IV pump because Dr. Odenike decided yesterday to go to every other day on the fluids. Laury was free to do yoga, have a Reiki session, and talk to friends.

It was nice to be able to share some good news. Yesterday, while Laury and I were at the infusion center in Chicago, I watched one of the nurses bring out an older man in a wheel chair. He was rather abrupt with the nurse telling her where he wanted to sit and that he wanted to be called back soon and to make sure they all knew where he was, etc. The nurse was very nice to the man despite his rudeness. I heard the nurse ask him, "Do you have anyone with you today?" The man answered no and she replied, "Why?" He asked her, "Why what:", and the nurse said, "Why don't you have anyone?" I did not hear his answer.

I know I have talked about how going through this by yourself would be overwhelming. But after yesterday I also realized that you need people to share the good news with, too. I couldn't wait to get home yesterday and post. I knew you all would want to hear it. I was not disappointed. Your comments have kept the good news alive today.

Thank you all again for being with us on this journey.

All our Love.

Sunday, 8/10/2014 – A short vacation

"Each person deserves a day away in which no problems are confronted, no solutions searched for. Each of us needs to withdraw from the cares which will not withdraw from us." - Maya Angelou

Yesterday, like most Saturdays this summer, I worked in the garden. I was removing spent flowers from the Hastas and doing some general weeding. I noticed that Laury did not come out to sit and watch me and give directions like she usually does. I found her sitting on the patio looking "forlorn" - she said she was bored.

I took a break for lunch and asked Laury if she wanted to go to Wagner Farms with me to get some fresh vegetables. Laury perked up and said, "Yes, that would be great!" We hopped in the car and took the short drive to the farm. There Laury talked with the owner and looked like she was having fun. When we got back home I asked Laury what she wanted to do now. Laury said that it felt good to go somewhere with the windows down and not be cold. Laury mentioned that we had talked about going to a small town near us called Geneva and to see our friends Candice and Gary and to walk around the town. Laury and I hopped back in the Mini and drove to Geneva. We stopped at our friends and saw their new front gardens and talked for a little bit. Laury and I then drove to down town, parked and walked to an ice cream shop. We sat outside off by ourselves and then walked a few blocks up one side of the street and down the other. Laury said she felt like we were on vacation. I agreed.

Later, our friends Joan, and Clyde, stopped by. Joan has been going through chemo and as she put it, "It was good to sit and compare notes." Joan is having surgery on Wednesday this week, she and Clyde will be in our prayers.

My Saturdays have been so busy this summer since we got home from the hospital that taking even a half of a day to just relax has been out of the question. But Laury and I both needed yesterday. A time to walk hand-in-hand and not think about all the stuff we have we have been through, or the things we have to do when we get home. It was nice to be together, on vacation, even just for a few hours.

All our Love.

Monday, 8/11/2014 – Romance

"The best love is the kind that awakens the soul and makes us reach for more, that plants a fire in our hearts and brings peace to our minds. And that's what you've given me. That's what I'd hoped to give you forever" - Nicholas Sparks

Yesterday was a beautiful day. I woke early before Laury and made cinnamon French toast for us. She woke to classical music playing and we sat at the bistro table and smiled at each other and remembered Laury and I are still in love.

Our friend, Kelly, was competing in a triathlon in Naperville so we walked down to the race area to show our support. By the time Laury and I got there the race was over, but we were with her in spirit. The walk took us along the river and we stopped several times to sit. Laury still gets tired and the walk was long. But neither one of us minded the short stops to listen to the water and see the light reflected off the leaves.

Yesterday reminded Laury and I that even though we still love each other, we are also in love with each other. We still need time to be together and show our love. It is hard to find romance right now, but sitting on the bench by the river and eating our French toast together it was there, and it felt good.

All our Love.

Tuesday, 8/12/2014 – Reminder

"No one is useless in this world who lightens the burdens of another." - Charles Dickens

All evidence points to Laury's marrow producing platelets. We had Laury's blood check yesterday morning in Naperville and again at the clinic at U of C and both places had Laury's platelets at 22. This is an increase from last week, so she is not just holding on to the platelets she was given, but actually producing them. Laury asked Dr. Odenike if we can say that these platelets are coming from her and Dr. Odenike said yes, and she is optimistic. Dr. Odenike laughed and said she went a little overboard last Thursday with the news, but she feels she is on this journey with us and she was excited by the progress.

While Laury and I were at the clinic at U of C yesterday, we stopped in the infusion center to get Laury's blood draw and dressing change. We also went to see Robin who was at the center to receive her chemo treatment. Laury stayed with Robin while she had her treatment and waited until Robin's daughters came back from getting something to eat. I was a little annoyed to be left by myself in the waiting area, but realized later that this is what Laury has to do. There is no way she was going to leave Robin alone and she was right to have stayed. I felt bad for getting angry. I, of all people, should know the importance of supporting each other. Thank you for the reminder, Laury.

All our Love.

Tuesday, 8/12/2014 – Hydration

"Water is the driving force in nature." - Leonardo da Vinci

Laury has been on hydration since we got home from the hospital. First we were giving Laury a full liter of fluid with Potassium and Magnesium every day. I would hook her up to a bag of fluids and a battery powered pump. The fluid line is connected to one of the lines of Laury's Hiccman catheter. We then went to a half liter every day for a couple of weeks and then to a half liter every other day. The reason the doctors want to keep the fluids in Laury is to make sure her kidneys stay flushed. Many of the medications Laury is on are not good for her kidneys, so they want to make sure they stay clear. Laury's kidney numbers have become stable and Laury has been able to again drink enough fluids on her own that the doctor decided today to take Laury off the extra fluids.

This is nice for Laury. The extra fluids, while good for her, made her get up several times at night to go to the bathroom. We are hoping that without the extra fluids Laury won't have to get up as often and will get a better night's sleep. It is amazing to watch the little things come into alignment. Laury's blood numbers being up means she feels better, feeling better means she eats and drinks more, eating and drinking more means she doesn't need the extra fluids, not needing the extra fluids means she will get a better night's sleep, which will make Laury feel better and keeps the process going. You begin to understand why this is such a balancing act, everything affects something else.

All our Love.

Wednesday, 8/13/2014 – Just Tired

"I must be overtired', Buttercup managed. 'The excitement and all.'

'Rest then', her mother cautioned. 'Terrible things can happen when you're overtired. I was overtired the night your father proposed." - William Goldman, The Princess Bride

Laury was tired today. She is not sure if it is "my red blood counts are low" tired, or something else. We will have Laury's blood checked tomorrow so we will know if it is the red counts. I don't think Laury really needs a reason to be tired right now. I think just "to be" takes a lot of her energy. It is hard not to over analyze how Laury is feeling we are always looking for something significant. "It could be this, it could be that, should we be concerned?" we can't help thinking.

I know I get tired just having to think about all the things that could be making Laury tired. So sometimes I think it is OK for Laury to just be tired, nothing more or nothing less. Laury and I just need to sit and catch our breath sometimes. It was good that we didn't have any place we had to be today. Laury could rest, regain her strength and be ready for another full day tomorrow.

We honor Laury's tiredness by letting it happen today, no worries, just tired.

All our Love.

Thursday, 8/14/2014 – Sip and eat

"When eating an elephant take one bite at a time." - Creighton Abrams

Laury and I went to the infusion center in Naperville at lunch time today to get Laury's CBC and type and cross match. Laury's Platelets are up over Monday and her white counts are only down a little. We had expected the white numbers to drop a little because we went from giving Laury a Neupogen shot every night to every other night. Laury's red blood counts were down and tomorrow she will receive two units of blood. This was also good news, because Laury was able to go the entire week without a transfusion. We hope this signals the beginning of the red blood cells coming from her new marrow.

This afternoon Laury and I went to clinic at U of C. We met with Paula, our nurse, and Jean, our nurse practitioner. Paula asked Laury how much she has been drinking. Laury was not sure but Paula said that she wanted to make sure Laury was getting at least two liters of fluids a day. Paula said Laury did not have to drink it all at once but she should sip fluids all day. Paula also asked about Laury's eating. Laury said that when her red blood numbers are up she can eat more. Paula then said, "OK, so now you need to sip and eat," in her heavy Spanish accent. Laury said, "If that is my prescription, then I will follow it. Sip and Eat!"

So starting tomorrow Laury is going to measure out two liters of water and make sure she drinks it all during the day. After her transfusion tomorrow Laury will probably feel more like eating, as well. Our new mantra for keeping Laury moving forward is: "Sip and Eat".

All our Love.

Friday, 8/15/2014 – Nap time

"No day is so bad it can't be fixed with a nap." - Carrie Snow

I got Laury up early this morning. We had an 8:30am appointment at the infusion center in Naperville for Laury to get two units of blood. I woke Laury at seven, as she had asked, and made sure she was awake. I asked Laury if I needed to come back and check on her in a few minutes to make sure she was awake and Laury said no. Laury promptly fell back to sleep. She did manage to get up in time to get ready, and off we went.

By nine Laury was hooked up to her first unit of blood and by one we were on our way home. We ordered a lunch for Laury while at the infusion center but it never showed up. The nurse said the lunches were running late, so I said someone could eat Laury's meal. As we walked out of the infusion center Laury was a little wobbly, so we walked slowly and carefully back to the car.

I suggested a Kreger's brat for lunch and Laury said that it sounded good. We stopped, and Laury got a brat and I ordered the pulled pork sandwich. We came home and ate our lunch on the patio. Laury ate her entire brat, something I have not seen her do for so long that I can't remember her ever eating an entire brat. After lunch Laury said she was ready for a nap. She went to the couch on the patio and I went back upstairs to work. I came down around four, calling it a day and Laury was still on the couch. Laury said she had been able to nap and that she must have needed it. I would have loved to have been able to join Laury. Today was a perfect day to nap outside, and I was glad she was able to take advantage of it.

All our Love.

Saturday, 8/16/2014 – Connecting us

"We cannot live only for ourselves. A thousand fibers connect us with our fellow men; and among those fibers, as sympathetic threads, our actions run as causes, and they come back to us as effects." - Herman Melville

Today I got up early to run the Mini over to the dealership for some work. I brought home a brand new Mini loaner and Laury and I decided to take it for a drive. We drove about an hour and half to the small town of Woodstock. (The movie Groundhog Day was filmed there.) There was a farmers' market going on in the town square and we stopped at an outdoor bistro and had lunch. After lunch Laury and I walked around the market and bought a way too big bag of caramel corn - the lady assured us that you can freeze it. We then stopped at an ice cream shop for a cone. Laury ate most of her lunch and cone.

Laury also bought a felt hat made by an old woman at the market. It fits Laury perfectly and will be nice and warm. Our drive home was nice and we stopped a couple of times for Laury to use the restroom. I realized as I watched Laury walk into the McDonald's to use the rest room how fragile she still is. Laury has made a ton of progress, but watching her walk and seeing her from a distance- it is still not her, not completely. Laury is feeling much better, but by the time we got home she was exhausted. We both took a nap and then sat out on the patio.

I spoke with my sister, Jann, and she brought me up to speed on the progress of dealing with my mom's estate. It was nice to hear about some of the people who came to my mom's funeral looking for me.

Jann also told me how much everyone up in Michigan enjoys and looks forward to reading my posts. This really makes Laury and I feel good. Your comments and hearts mean so much, and help us maintain a connection through all of this. Laury and I look forward to the day when we can go and visit and renew the connections in person.

All our Love.

Monday, 8/18/2014 – Dan and Laury

"That's the worst way to miss somebody. When they're right beside you and you miss them anyway." - Pittacus Lore, I Am Number Four

Sunday was a nice day. I did the rest of my chores in the morning and then Laury's parents brought us lunch. We sat outside on the patio and ate and talked. It was nice to have the break and enjoy the good food. After Laury's parents left Laury and I took a nap. Laury has been able to sleep during her naps, something she wasn't able to do before.

The rest of the day was quiet, sitting together outside and talking and enjoying the breeze.

I admitted to Laury that I miss her. I miss her energy, her strength- not that she is not here, but she is not who she used to be. Laury said she misses her too. We both know Laury is still there and will come back, most likely even better, but there are still times when we miss her. I think part of what we have been doing on the weekends lately is to reconnect as a couple, as Dan and Laury, not patient and caregiver. We miss that.

All our Love.

Tuesday, 8/19/2014 — Amazing

"Wonder is the beginning of wisdom." - Socrates

One of the young nurses we had at the hospital told us that the scariest part of the job is that many of the patients know more about their disease then she does. I am sure this is true. You can't live with a disease, have it impact your life, and not learn more about what it is and how it works. Laury and I have always asked questions about her disease and the bone marrow transplant process. Laury and I know by now that even though there is a tremendous amount of science that goes into all of this, there is still space for unknowns and amazement.

Laury's hair has begun to grow back at the same time her eye lashes have begun to fall out. We know that the chemo kills fast growing cells like hair, but why does it do it at different rates, and how is the eye lash different from the hair on her head?

I have been wondering where the B positive blood type is coming from now that Laury's old bone marrow is gone. How is it that every time we have Laury's blood checked it is still B positive? I did some research and I know the blood type is determined by the presence or absence of the A and B antigens. These antigens are produced by the bone marrow and the lymph nodes. I asked Dr. Odenike yesterday, "If Laury's bone marrow is now producing A positive antigens, why is her blood type still B positive?" Dr. Odenike replied, "We are not sure exactly how that works." She said at some point, the new A antigens will overpower the B antigens and Laury's blood type will change. Dr. Odenike finds the entire process amazing, and so do we. Laury's progress is slow but still moving in the right direction.

It is important every once in a while to just wonder at the amazing process that is going one inside her.

All our Love.

Wednesday, 8/20/2014 – Yum

"All you need is love. But a little chocolate now and then doesn't hurt." - Charles M. Schulz

Laury told Pat at our session yesterday, "It was a really good day today." Mandy from school stopped by and Marinda gave Laury another Reiki treatment. Laury said her energy was good and most importantly, emotionally she felt up. Laury has been feeling a little flat lately and it was good to hear she felt better today.

There are still some side effects from the chemo that are bothering Laury so it easy to understand her frustration. Laury's eyesight is not good right now. Her distance vision is actually better than it was before the chemo but up close she can't see much. The lack of up-close vision makes it hard to read or do beading. The doctor says that Laury should start seeing some improvement in her vision in about a month.

Another side effect of the chemo is that Laury lost her tastes, nothing tastes the same or it doesn't have any taste at all. Laury says that tastes are starting to come back. Last night Laury said she could taste the butter on the potatoes and the chicken had good flavor. Getting her taste back is critical to helping Laury eat more and gain back the weight she has lost.

Laury says it is hard to eat when things don't taste the way they should. Last night after dinner Laury had a brownie with ice cream, and she said she could really taste the chocolate. I think if she can now taste the chocolate, we are in good shape. I will just cover everything with chocolate - isn't that what we all really want to do anyway?

All our Love.

Thursday, 8/21/2014 – The past

"I can only note that the past is beautiful because one never realises an emotion at the time. It expands later, and thus we don't have complete emotions about the present, only about the past." - Virginia Woolf

Yesterday was another really good day for Laury. She woke feeling good emotionally and physically. Laury and Kelly went for a walk and I think she came back with more energy than she left with. Laury told me she ran into one of her students while on their walk downtown. The student happened to be the one who made one of the blankets given to Laury by her class. Laury said they couldn't hug but they both stood close to each other and cried. Laury said, "What a gift, seeing her, of all my students."

In the early afternoon Laury and I went to an appointment with Dr. Ferris here in Naperville. Dr. Ferris is Laury's oncologist who has been working with U of C to order the blood transfusions here in Naperville. Dr. Ferris had not seen Laury since February, so Laury felt that we should meet with her, if for no other reason than to thank Dr. Ferris for all her help. Dr. Ferris was very glad to see Laury and kept telling her how good she looked. We kept thanking Dr. Ferris for going out of her way to help and for making the transfusions work here in Naperville. Dr. Ferris said she was glad to help and would continue to help any way she could. Dr. Ferris asked Laury and me how long we have been together and we said thirty-two years, and she replied, "You two are a remarkable couple". That made us feel good.

Before Dr. Ferris came in, her nurse took Laury's vitals and updated her medical history. The nurse asked Laury, "Any changes in your history since we saw you last?" Laury replied, "Just a bone marrow transplant." Then the nurse and Laury both said together, "That is enough!" I said to Laury, "Think about it, you now have ET, Myelofibrosis, and a bone marrow transplant - in your past!" Laury quietly said, "That is remarkable, isn't it?"

Laury and I left the visit with a little more energy in our steps.

All our Love.

Thursday, 8/21/2014 – Rain

"Last night

the rain

spoke to me

slowly, saying,

what joy

to come falling

out of the brisk cloud,

to be happy again

in a new way

on the earth! - Mary Oliver

Laury and I woke to the sound of rain this morning, something we haven't heard for a while and we welcomed it. Rain is a gardener's best friend. Our gardens needed the "natural" rain - more so than the water from the sprinkler. Today Laury and I didn't follow the usual plan of going to the infusion center in Naperville to get Laury's blood work done before we headed to U of C. The appointment at U of C had been moved up to twelve twenty so we figured that there was no reason to get Laury's blood checked because we would get it done at U of C, and if she needed blood it could still be ordered in time for tomorrow. Laury's white and platelet numbers are still holding steady, but she will need a red blood cell transfusion tomorrow. This is when I discovered the flaw in today's plan. The type and cross match of blood is only good for seventy two hours. This means that the blood typing Laury had done in Naperville on Monday is not good for a transfusion on Friday. Also, Naperville can't use the type and cross match from U of C, after leaving U of C Laury and I had to go to the infusion center in Naperville to get Laury typed and cross matched.

Laury and I left the house at ten for the U of C appointment, earlier than normal because of the rain this morning, and after stopping at the Naperville infusion center we got home around four. We did stop at Kreger's and got a couple of pulled pork sandwiches for a late lunch / early dinner. After eating our sandwiches Laury and I both decided it was not too late for a nap and we crawled into bed. I opened the window a little so we could hear the rain. I did not sleep but it was nice to just lie there and listen to the rain and relax.

The rain slowed down our commute to the city and back, but it paid us back in a nice afternoon nap.

All our Love.

Friday, 8/22/2014 – Strength

"Some people believe holding on and hanging in there are signs of great strength. However, there are times when it takes much more strength to know when to let go and then do it." - **Ann Landers**

Laury and I went to the infusion center this morning here in Naperville. Laury needed to get a transfusion of red blood cells. We were told yesterday that Laury would receive two units. Laury did not think she needed two units and asked our nurse Jessica to call Paula at U of C and see why they felt she needed two units. When Laury and I arrived at the center this morning, Jessica told us that after talking with Paula, they decided that Laury would only get one unit.

I wanted Laury to get two units, to get and keep her strength up over the weekend. Laury just felt she got too much blood last week and she didn't need that much this week. I love seeing Laury advocate for herself; she knows her body really well. I trust that if Laury feels she doesn't need the blood then she probably doesn't.

School started this week, and I expected Laury to be a little down about not being able to go back. I know Laury misses her friends and working with John. But when I asked her how she was feeling about school starting Laury said, "I am not ready. I know I can't go back yet, and I couldn't do it right now." The doctors would like Laury to take the entire school year off, but Dr. Odenike agreed to reassess Laury in December to see if she might be ready to go back. Laury is not setting December as a goal to go back. I think Laury just wanted to hear that there is a small possibility that the door hasn't been slammed shut.

While we were in the room today waiting for the transfusion to complete, Laury asked me, "Why do people think I am brave and strong? I am just taking this one day at a time and dealing with whatever comes up." That is Laury's strength, taking one day at a time. It's a strength Laury has shared with me and I am forever grateful.

All our Love.

Sunday, 8/24/2014 – Friends

"Why did you do all this for me?' he asked 'I don't deserve it. I've never done anything for you.' 'You have been my friend,' replied Charlotte. 'That in itself is a tremendous thing." **E. B. White, Charlotte's Web**

One of the most amazing things that has come out of this journey is the reconnection Laury has had with her friends. Some she hadn't seen or spoke to in years, others Laury sees often but has reconnected at a new and different level. Yesterday, Mardy and Brian, friends of Laury's from college, came down from Port Washington to visit. We haven't seen them in years, but as with all good friends, as soon as Mardy and Brian walked in the door it was like we had just seen them the day before. Laury had so much energy yesterday, and the visit made her feel so good. We went to lunch and sat outside and talked and got caught up on our lives. We managed to finish lunch right before a large storm hit, which was good because we were sitting outside, since Laury still can't be in crowded places.

After lunch we came back to our house and talked and watched the storm. It was a short visit since all of us did not want Laury to expend too much energy. After Mardy and Brian left, I thought Laury would be ready for a nap instead, she asked me if I wanted to go look at gas logs for our fireplace. I said, "Maybe next weekend, the store is closing in less than an hour. But if you really want to go we can." Laury said she really wanted to go and so we did. We came back home and Laury still had more energy than I have seen her with in a long time.

Laury has always been an extrovert, and it is good to see visits from good friends energizing her again. Thanks again, Mardy and Brian, for coming to visit. It was a great day.

All our Love.

Monday, 8/25/2014 – Hot and cold

"Laughter is wine for the soul - laughter soft, or loud and deep, tinged through with seriousness - the hilarious declaration made by man that life is worth living." - Sean O'Casey

Laury has been cold ever since her chemo treatments. Laury and I sit together in our bedroom watching TV, me in shorts and a T-shirt and Laury with a hat and sweater on wrapped in a blanket. We keep a quilt in the car for our trips to U of C. When it is hot and I have the air conditioner on, Laury uses the blanket to stay warm. Laury hasn't been able to do her yoga at home because she says it is too hard to relax when she is so cold.

Yesterday we ran some errands and Laury asked if it was too hot to open the windows and sun roof in the car. I said it was, but we opened them anyway. We went for one place to another, me sweating and Laury enjoying the warmth. Our last stop was Target, where we got a couple of things and as Laury and I were walking out of the store, we looked at each other and laughed. I was carrying a fan for me and Laury was carrying a space heater for her. We chuckled and I said, "Well that pretty well sums us up, doesn't it?"

All our Love.

Tuesday, 8/26/2014 – Time off

"Time is too slow for those who wait, too swift for those who fear, too long for those who grieve, too short for those who rejoice, but for those who love, time is eternity." - Henry van Dyke

Yesterday Laury and I once again found ourselves sitting and waiting in the infusion center at U of C. We were there to get Laury's blood taken and her line dressing changed. As usual, the center was over booked and there were a lot of people waiting. We already had Laury's CBC results from Naperville earlier in the morning. The only question we had was whether or not Jean, our nurse practitioner, would recommend Laury get a red blood transfusion.

After an hour of sitting and waiting Laury saw, our beautiful smiling friend, Erin, come out of the infusion center. We hadn't seen Erin in a few weeks and it was good to see her. As soon as Erin saw Laury she said, "I knew there was a reason for the chemo taking so long today!" Several weeks ago I noticed the water jar that Erin carried. It was made up of a Mason jar with straw in the top. Laury has had several of these types of cups, but made of plastic, and they always get ruined in the dishwasher. When I saw the jar Erin had I asked her where she got it. Erin told me that her friend makes them, and I asked her if she would have her friend make one for Laury. Erin had been carrying Laury's jar with her for the last several weeks hoping to see us. After giving Laury her new water jar, Erin sat with Laury and talked. Once again she helped the time go by in the waiting room.

Laury was finally taken back for her blood draw after an hour and half wait. We then went over to see Jean. The visit with Jean was short. Jean decided that Laury needed two units of blood today - hopefully enough to get her through the weekend, and that we didn't need to come back to U of C until a week from Thursday. Laury and I go to the infusion center here in Naperville this morning for the blood. We will still get Laury's blood checked here in Naperville on Thursday and Tuesday of next week but we don't have to travel down to U of C. This was great news, to have a few days off and not have to go to Chicago, but Laury and I are also a little nervous. We wish we could go on a vacation somewhere, but the doctors don't want Laury too far away in case something happens. We are going to enjoy the next week off. Maybe I will have time to clean the garage!

All our Love.

Wednesday, 8/27/2014 — Eggs

"It may be hard for an egg to turn into a bird; it would be a jolly sight harder for it to learn to fly while remaining an egg." - C. S. Lewis

Yesterday Laury and I spent from nine thirty to two thirty at the infusion center here in Naperville. Laury received two units of blood, enough we hope to get her through the weekend. I spent two and a half hours of our time there on a conference call. I had to have my phone on mute because the room Laury and I were in didn't have a door and we were right across from the bathrooms. I logged into the call, and just as I was stating my name to let everyone know I was on the call, someone flushed the toilet. Fortunately, there were enough people on the call that nobody could tell where the sound came from. Laury's chair today was heated, so she didn't need a blanket to stay warm. Laury told the nurse that this was her new favorite room. She really liked the chair and she could see the gardens. I still would prefer a room with a door.

The nurse told us that earlier in the year there had been a group of small ducks running around the garden. Everyone was concerned because the garden is on the second story and they wondered how these little ducks were going to get back down. The nurse said they decided to go out and gather the ducks in a box and take them to a wildlife center. The nurse said, "They were so small, we wondered how they even got up there in the first place." I replied, "Eggs." The nurse looked at me confused and said, "Eggs, I don't understand?" I said that the mother probably had a nest in the garden. The nurse replied, "Oh God, we never thought of that!"

All our Love.

Friday, 8/22/2014 – Future

"That's how you know you love someone, I guess, when you can't experience anything without wishing the other person were there to see it, too." - Kaui Hart Hemmings, The Descendants

Yesterday was another good day for Laury. She continues to feel good and I believe her strength is increasing. Laury talked about learning to do things to keep her busy and occupied now that she is feeling better. Laury's days are not the same. While she still has a long way to go, she is feeling like she can do more. Laury did yoga in the morning using her new space heater to keep her warm. She said the heater worked great and the yoga felt good.

Laury says she has lost a lot of strength and flexibility, but I am sure it will come back. Laury spent the afternoon with Kelly getting gelato and enjoying the weather.

I spent most of the day on and off conference calls, really unaware of what Laury was doing. The day was a glimpse of what our future looks like. I going off to work again, involved in new projects, and Laury at home working on things that make her feel good and get her strength back. I will miss spending so much time with Laury; she brightens my days.

All our Love.

Friday, 8/29/2014 – What day is it?

"The advantage of a bad memory is that one enjoys several times the same good things for the first time." - Friedrich Nietzsche

"I keep thinking today is Friday", Laury said to me more than once yesterday. We both have been messing our days up this week. Laury and I have become so dependent on the calendar to tell us where and when to be somewhere, we easily get confused when the routine changes. Yesterday Laury and I went to the infusion center in Naperville to get Laury's blood checked like we always do on Thursday mornings. Her blood numbers are holding steady, so Laury doesn't need a transfusion today. What threw us off was that Laury and I didn't go to U of C yesterday and Laury had her transfusion on Tuesday. Next week is even more confusing. We have Laury's blood checked on Tuesday and if she needs blood we are scheduled for a chair on Wednesday.

Jessica, our nurse yesterday, said, "Oh Labor Day, I am not sure you are worth it." She said that it is not really like a day off because on Tuesday they will be scrambling to find space for the sixty patients that they would have had on Monday.

Laury has been keeping our calendar on-line, but even that doesn't help sometimes when we forget what day it is.

As Laury and I finished dinner last night I said, "Crap, I forgot to submit my time sheet and it is the end of the month and they have to be posted by 5:00pm on Friday." Laury said, "I will finish cleaning up and you go do your time sheet." I ran upstairs and filed my time sheet. It wasn't until we went to bed that I remembered yesterday was Thursday. I laughed and

Laury said, "What is so funny?" I said, "Today is Thursday. My time sheet is not due until tomorrow."

I guess we may have gotten a little too good at this "One day at a time" thing.

All our Love.

Saturday, 8/30/2014 – Head to toes

"You cannot hide in a hat; you will be noticed, especially by men. To men, you become a lady when you don a hat--one who they rush to open doors for. To women, you become an inspiration, reminding them that they have a closet full of hats they have not had the courage to wear." - Unknown

Laury's hair has started to come back in. It is very fine, and as Laury says, "It hasn't yet reached the Yoda stage." Laury has been wearing a hat ever since her hair fell out. Laury almost never wore a hat before and with the help of her mother's extensive hat collection, she managed to find a hat that she feels good in. Lately Laury has been getting compliments from men on her hat. Women have always told Laury they liked her hat, or that she looked good, etc. But now men have been stopping and telling Laury they like her hat. On Tuesday when Laury and I were leaving the infusion center an older man said to Laury from across the room, "I like your hat. It looks like you are ready for a round of golf." Last week when we were in the fireplace store, one of the employees came by and said, "I love your hat and outfit." Our friend, Bob as we were leaving their house after dinner said, "I like that hat." I know it makes Laury feel good that women think her hat looks good, but when men say it, it makes Laury feel even better.

Yesterday Laury and Kelly went for a pedicure. Laury still has to be careful with germs and bleeding, so pedicures have been off limits. However, Czar, the local salon, has private rooms and Laury was able to bring her own polish, and the woman was very careful. Laury came home with a new coat of polish and feeling like a million bucks. Later Laury called me into the bathroom to show me her last eyelash, still hanging on for dear life.

The hat and toes are small things, but they make Laury feel better. It is hard to see what this process has done to Laury's body and skin, so the fact that she gets complemented on her hat or her toes means a lot. It makes going through this a little easier.

Thank you all for your complements and encouragement.

All our Love.

Sunday, 8/31/2014 – Cleaning

"True life is lived when tiny changes occur." - Leo Tolstoy

Yesterday I cleaned the garage. The garage is also my shop. My shop is something that I had put aside when we started this journey in February. Every day I pulled the car into the garage this spring and summer I would say to myself, "I need to clean my shop." The weekends have been full of cleaning and chores but I never seemed to be able to get to the garage.

Once I started cleaning it was like a time capsule. There were items I had left on the work bench from Christmas, tools left out from various small jobs around the house. The space is my most personal area in our home. It felt good to get it cleaned out. But it felt more than good, I felt that I was regaining part of my life; part that had been put aside to become Laury's caregiver. Laury sat in the driveway and read while I worked in the shop.

Most summers, Laury is in the garden while I am in shop, Laury in her most personal space and me in mine. Since February, both of these places have been lost to us.

Cleaning the shop was a milestone. I can now start thinking about designing and building things again. This is another step toward a time when our life won't revolve around Laury's health. We are getting there, slowly but surely.

All our Love.

CHAPTER EIGHT

September

Monday, 9/1/2014 – A Bargain

"The best things in life are beyond money; their price is agony and sweat and devotion ... and the price demanded for the most precious of all things in life is life itself - ultimate cost for perfect value." - Robert A. Heinlein, Starship Troopers

Laury and I spent most of the day at home today. In the afternoon we went to see Lyndsay's new apartment. It was good to see how Lyndsay has already made it into a home. It was a short drive and we drove with the air conditioner on and Laury's window open - a good compromise of hot and cold. Most of the day I spent going over and entering medical bills and receipts. It had been a while since I put all of the medical statements from our insurance company in the spreadsheet to see what has been paid.

I keep a total of what has been billed, not what the insurance company paid and not what we owe. Most of the statements say we owe nothing and we would like to keep it at that. However, Laury and I are not sure what, if any, additional bills from U of C we will get after insurance is done paying.

The spread sheet currently has over six hundred and fifty entries and the items I added today brought the total amount billed to the insurance company to over one million dollars. This total doesn't include any bills from the month of August, so we expect the number to keep going up. I noticed something strange with the numbers and I mentioned it to Laury. If you look at all of the expenses, the cheapest thing on the list was the doctor bills. The tests, drugs, and hospital room are all incredibly large numbers. The only numbers that look reasonable are the doctor bills. Almost two-thirds of the expenses on the statements are for drugs. This is amazing, and the drug numbers don't include all of the drugs that have been purchased at our local pharmacy.

I am not holding my breath or losing any sleep over the final bills. They will be what they are, and Laury is still a bargain.

All our Love.

Tuesday, 9/2/2014 – Dad

"I believe that what we become depends on what our fathers teach us at odd moments, when they aren't trying to teach us. We are formed by little scraps of wisdom." - Umberto Eco

My father passed away last night. His passing wasn't a big surprise; he had been "fading" in a nursing home for the last several years. When my sister called with the news of my mother's death, even she said that she thought it would be my dad, and not my mom who died first.

My brother and sisters all believe that Dad stayed around so long after his stroke because he couldn't leave Mom. Even though we weren't sure he understood that mom had passed, he must have at a very deep level.

My dad and I didn't always get along- no surprise for a father and a son.

We had a major falling out several years ago and we really didn't speak to each other for quite a while. My dad and I came to terms with each other a few years ago after he had his stroke.

I owe a lot of who I am to my dad. He taught me how to treat women, to open doors for them, to respect, care for and love them. He also showed me that it is OK to show your emotions. My dad would cry at birthdays, Christmas and while talking about his grandchildren. My dad was also an artist. His drawings, paintings, and carvings are all over our house, and he was always proud of the art that all of us created.

Most importantly, I never doubted he loved me. Even when he was angry with me and we weren't speaking, he loved me.

All our Love.

Thursday, 9/4/2014 – Grumpy

"...being in a bad mood with your friends beats being in a bad mood without them." - John Green, Let It Snow

Yesterday, Laury was feeling better and in a grumpy mood. She didn't want to have to go get a unit of blood and, told our nurse, Jessica on Tuesday that she would be fine without it. Dr. Odenike disagreed and we went to hospital to get the blood. Laury and I had to go to the hospital because the infusion center was full, playing catch-up from the holiday. We arrived on time and Laury immediately told the nurse that they should run her blood in an hour and a half, not the two hours they normally do. Laury told the nurse she could check her prescription if she didn't believe her. Laury wasn't rude, but she was not happy to be there. After waiting a while, Laury said, "We have been here forty-five minutes and I haven't even gotten my blood yet. This is taking too long!" I took a deep breath and said nothing.

Laury is feeling better, and she has more energy and she is getting bored and frustrated by all of the limitations that are still placed on her. So in some ways it is good that Laury was grumpy. It shows that she is ready to move on. When I was leaving for yoga last night I asked Laury if she was going to be OK while I was gone. She replied, "No, damn it, I want to go with you! I am going to talk to Dr. Odenike. She has got to lift some of these restrictions!" I gave her a kiss and was glad to be going alone.

Today Laury is in a better mood. We head down to the U of C this afternoon. I am sure Laury will ask about what she can and can't do, but most importantly she will follow what the doctor tells her. It doesn't mean, however, that Laury will always like it, but that is OK - it just means she is getting better.

All our Love.

Friday, 9/5/2014 – Control

"To be in hell is to drift; to be in heaven is to steer." - George Bernard Shaw

Laury was in a better mood yesterday. She had an energy healing treatment, which Laury says always helps her feel better. We went to the U of C yesterday afternoon. On our way, Laury said she was going to have her blood draw done from her arm. She said she was tired of waiting in the infusion center to have it done from her Hiccman line. This decision turned out to be a good one. When Laury checked in, the receptionist said there was a two hour wait in the infusion center to draw blood. After getting back to the doctor's waiting area, Laury went into one of the rooms to have another blood draw, this time from her Hiccman. Laury has been part of a study that the hospital is doing on preventing infections. Laury was given a drug (or placebo) as part of the test while in the hospital and they have been checking Laury's blood periodically since she has been out. Yesterday was the end of Laury's participation in the trial.

Once Laury and I were taken back to our room, Paula stopped by. She told us that she had not received any results from Laury's blood work in Naperville this morning. We told her it was because we had canceled the appointment since we didn't need to have Laury's blood typed and cross matched again this week. Paula said, "Oh, great. They are usually so good, I was wondering what happened."

Laury's blood numbers are good. Her white counts were down a little but her platelets were up to almost 30 and her hemoglobin was at 8.3. This means that Laury will not need a transfusion. It also means that she went an entire week only getting one unit of blood. Laury and I are hopeful this is the start of the red cells coming in but we can't be sure yet.

Laury asked Jean if she could cut back on going down to U of C to once a week. We would still have Laury's blood checked here in Naperville on Tuesdays but we would only go to clinic on Thursdays. Jean said it sounded OK to her but she would talk to Dr. Odenike and Laury could talk with Dr. Odenike on Monday when we see her next. Laury also mentioned and showed Jean her stomach and back. Her skin is very dark, almost black in some places. Jean called this, "Chemo bronze". Basically, it is the dead skin cells from the chemo. Laury said she has never been so tanned.

As we were leaving, Laury said she felt better because she felt heard. Laury says that so much of this journey is out of her control. Laury said she has watched her body change, her life change and just wanted some control back. I understand those feelings. I think sometimes we just need to shout at the universe, in hopes of being heard.

All our Love.

Saturday, 9/6/2014 – Normal days

"Don't cry because it's over, smile because it happened." - Dr. Seuss

The last couple of days have been spent in quiet and remembrance. Laury did not require a blood transfusion on Friday so we were free to make the day our own. I had taken a couple of days off work because of my father's death. Friday, Laury and I went shopping for a piece of furniture for the sun room to keep her beading supplies together. Laury and I went to several thrift stores and the outlet stores to try to find the "perfect something". Laury is walking faster now, but when we got into the stores she slowed way down. Laury said the combination of not being out for so long and not being able to see well made her want to just slow down and take everything in.

We found a little metal multi-shelved unit that worked great, and Laury spent most of last evening decorating it. Laury loves to decorate. In the summer it is with flowers, and the rest of the year it is with things in the house. It is not unusual for me to come home and have a room rearranged, or things moved from one room to another. Having a new piece in the sun room to decorate gave Laury a much needed something to do.

On Friday Laury and I also went to my favorite tool store to look at the new table saw I am going to buy. I have wanted a new saw for a while and I received enough money from my Mom's life insurance to buy the one I wanted. I thought about what to buy with the money and I wanted to get something that I would have forever. With my Dad passing, getting the table saw made a lot of sense. I think Mom would approve.

Today Laury and I went to the city to get my hair cut. It was good to see and laugh with Magen. When we got home I saw our neighbor Doug out cleaning his boat. I went over and talked with him for about an hour. It was good to see Doug and catch up. It seems like the entire summer has gone by without talking.

It is nice to have some days that don't revolve around getting Laury to an appointment. The last couple of days have been nice, but they also have been filled with memories of my parents. Thank you again for all your loving and kind thoughts. Together we move forward.

All our Love.

Sunday, 9/7/2014 – A good hiccup

"Though I lack the art to decipher it,

no doubt the next chapter in my book of transformations is already written.

I am not done with my changes." - Stanley Kunitz, The Collected Poems

Laury has always gotten the hiccups easily. There were times when Laury said she had them three or four times in one day. Having the hiccups is not new to Laury, however, since she had the bad throat pain, she hiccups in her sleep. Laury will be sleeping and begin hiccupping, and the really funny part is that she has six hiccups at a time. I have gotten to the point when Laury starts hiccupping that I count them, each time it is six hiccups and then she goes back to sleep. I mentioned the strange, exact number of hiccups to the doctor and she just laughed. Go figure. I guess it is something that will work itself out over time, like so much of these side effects.

Laury's taste and sense of smell are improving. Today when I brought in some chicken off the grill Laury said, "Those smell great!" Laury also can now taste sharp cheddar cheese again - one of her favorite types of cheese. It is encouraging to see these little things reappear, and it also makes planning meals a little easier now that Laury can taste more things.

Today Laury and I took a long walk. We went into town and Laury got a Starbucks and we walked along the river. Laury didn't need to stop as often as we did last time. Laury's legs are getting stronger and we are hoping that her red blood counts are staying up. Laury and I go to the U of C tomorrow afternoon. We are hoping that Laury's numbers will have improved and the red will finally have begun to come in- something we have hoped for for the last couple months. Laury and I tell each other that this time will be the time. We have to be right sometime.

All our Love.

Monday, 9/8/2014 – Reality check

"Reality is one of the possibilities I cannot afford to ignore" - Leonard Cohen, Beautiful Losers

"Our visits with Dr. Odenike are always a reality check. I don't always like what she has to tell us, but I know she is there with us", Laury said to me yesterday. We had just left the U of C and our visit with Dr. Odenike. Laury and I hoped to be able to change our schedule to once a week at the clinic and for Laury to be able to go to yoga and to bring the cats down from upstairs. All of these were vetoed by Dr. Odenike. Laury is making progress but we are still not far enough along to drop some of the precautions against infection and diseases.

We asked Dr. Odenike what the significance is of the 100 day mark. She said that most significant complications of a bone marrow transplant show up in the first 100 days. Once Laury is beyond that mark the risks begin to drop. Given Laury will reach her 100 days this month, Dr. Odenike agreed that after that point we can start going to the clinic once a week. The cats and yoga studio will have to wait until December.

Laury's white counts are well within the normal range and her platelets continue to rise. Laury's red blood still has yet to make a significant appearance. Laury will get a unit of blood today. Laury continues to feel better, even though she has had some episodes of nausea lately. The nausea is most likely caused by all the medications she is taking. The reality is that we are not out of the woods yet. Laury told Dr. Odenike that the yoga studio is her community and she misses it. Dr. Odenike said the community is important to Laury's healing, but for now it will have to come to her.

Laury is still on the right path, and as Dr. Odenike said yesterday, "You have done and continue to do all the right things. We don't want to do anything to ruin that." It is our reality. We don't always like all the restrictions, but they have gotten Laury this far and we are not going to let anything stop us from continuing.

All our Love.

Wednesday, 9/10/2014 — Smile

"I wondered if my smile was as big as hers. Maybe as big. But not as beautiful." - Benjamin Alire Saenz, Aristotle And Dante Discover The Secrets Of The Universe

Yesterday Laury was feeling the effects of her low hemoglobin. She was glad we were getting blood. Laury can get nauseous and shaky when her numbers get too low. Laury and I went to the infusion center here in Naperville and Laury received a unit of blood. Laury was not in a hurry today or impatient. She quietly sat while the blood flowed in. After getting the blood we returned home and I went back upstairs to work. Laury said she tried to take a nap but couldn't sleep, so she sat outside for a while.

Laury has had some tears lately when she talks about how things are going. Laury said she is having trouble with receiving again. She feels that she should be giving more and she can't. Laury can't help feeling she is letting some people down, like her students and her co-teacher John. Laury knows she is not really letting anyone down, but I think when she is not feeling strong it catches up with her.

Last week when Laury and I went to the infusion center at CDH the nurse who helped us asked Laury a lot of questions about her transplant. The nurse told Laury the reason she was asking all the questions was because her thirty year old son was going to need a bone marrow transplant. The one piece of advice that Laury gave her was for her son to start preparing as soon as possible. Mental and emotional preparation is as important if not more important than being physically prepared. As Laury said to the nurse, "He will have to learn to receive."

There is a school picture of Laury from her first teaching job, that I come across occasionally. I have always loved the picture; Laury always looks at it and comments on her big hair, her weight, etc. Yesterday, after dinner, I went outside to put the cars in the garage and put the cushions away ahead of the storm. Laury was standing at the sink in the kitchen and I could see her. I watched her for a while and I then stepped up on the small deck so she could see me. Laury looked at me and smiled. The same smile in the picture I love. I knew she was feeling better, stronger.

Thank you for all of your words of encouragement and love. There are still days when this journey is a little too much, the reality too real. It was good to see the smile. It showed me that Laury is still there, and I am still in love with the same woman in that picture.

All our Love.

Thursday, 9/11/2014 – Forgetting

"If you wish to forget anything on the spot, make a note that this thing is to be remembered." - Edgar Allan Poe

Chemo-brain is something we have heard about and have talked about ever since Laury started chemotherapy treatments back in February. Laury and I both will joke when one of us says something silly or forgetful: "Oh must be chemo brain." It is funny at times, but other times not so much. Laury was telling me about a conversation she had with a friend who is going through chemo and Laury said to me, "We were talking about chemo brain and then we forgot what we were talking about."

Laury and I agree that sometimes it is the chemo therapy that has affected her short term memory and as she says, her executive functioning. I also think that Laury and I have so much on our minds and in our schedule that is only natural to forget things- like what day it is.

Yesterday Laury was frustrated because she forgot that Kelly was off work on Wednesday and she could have done something with her instead of sitting home. Laury was bored yesterday and it would have been good for her to get out and do something. Laury was pretty hard on herself for forgetting, but I am not sure that I knew what day it was yesterday. I have noticed that I can easily forget things these days. Last weekend I went to ACE to pick up some things for the house. I made a list to make sure I wouldn't forget anything - then I forgot to take the list with me.

So if Laury or I don't return a call, or reply to a text or email, please be patient. We probably just forgot. But we will never forget all of the love you have all shown us.

All our Love.

Friday, 9/12/2014 – Confusion

"God turns you from one feeling to another and teaches by means of opposites so that you will have two wings to fly, not one" - Rumi, The Essential Rumi

Yesterday, like the last several Thursdays, Laury and I went to the infusion center in Naperville to have Laury's blood checked then down to the U of C. Laury's platelets continue to rise and her white counts were down, but this was not unexpected because we switched to only giving Laury the Neupogen shots on Sunday and Thursday nights. Laury's hemoglobin was 7.2, so we left Naperville expecting that Laury would be getting a transfusion today.

We traveled down to U of C and Laury had her blood taken again. Laury has been having her blood drawn from her arm rather than her Hiccman line to avoid the long waits at the infusion center. Laury and I met Paula after Laury's blood was taken again, and Paula said Laury's hemoglobin at U of C was 7.8, so Dr. Odenike decided not to give Laury blood. We were surprised and concerned, but also happy that we didn't have to spend several hours in the infusion center, and Laury would have the day off. I was concerned that Laury's hemoglobin might get too low by Monday the next time we have it checked. Paula and Jean felt that this is unlikely to happen.

We met with Jean and discussed Laury's progress. Jean says that even though the red blood still has not shown up, everything is still progressing. I asked Jean if there was something like the Neupogen (which stimulates the white cells growth) that could be given to Laury to stimulate her red blood growth. Jean said there is, and it is called Epogen. I asked Jean why we were not giving it to Laury. Jean replied, "Because Laury's Epogen levels are normal. It would be like pouring water into a full glass." I said, "So the body produces this hormone naturally, and giving Laury more would mean that the body would just rid itself of the unneeded extra." Jean said, "Exactly."

Jean again told us that the spleen is still probably taking up some of the red blood cells. Even though the spleen has gotten smaller, its job is to filter the blood of foreign matter and the transfused blood can be viewed by the spleen a threat. Everything is acting the way it is supposed to, but right now that means things are confusing. The spleen is not sure what is good blood and what is bad, and the antibodies are not sure was is good and what is bad. Jean assured us that all the signs say this confusion is being figured out internally and eventually the red will show up and reach normal levels.

The body is an amazing thing, always trying to bring itself into balance. Sometimes we just have to relax and let it figure it out on its own.

All our Love.

Saturday, 9/13/2014 -Normal couple of days

"What may look normal to a spider , will look like a chaos to a mosquito." - Reddioui Islam

Yesterday was a quiet day. Laury spent most of the day on the computer or watching TV. Her eyes were bugging her, making reading and beading out of the question. I was working, so we couldn't go anywhere to entertain Laury. Now that Laury is feeling better, she is in need of things to do that don't require good eyesight or being around groups of people. Laury and I will take movie and TV show suggestions. We have a Roku and Amazon Prime, Laury has access to tons of movies and shows, but it is hard for her to go through all of the lists and pick something out.

Today, Laury and our daughter, Lyndsay, went to the bead store. Laury was excited to get out of the house, but was also excited to have Lyndsay help her pick out beads. I stayed at home and did some tree trimming. I am trying to keep the raccoons off the roof, so I trimmed a few trees that I thought they have been using to get up there. I worked in my shop for a while and Laury sat in the driveway and watched me. It was a little strange to have her there just watching. She is usually off doing her own thing when I am running the power tools. Laury said it felt good to see me working in my shop.

Later in the afternoon, our friends, Candice and Gary, stopped by. It was good to see them and talk and catch up. They both commented on how good Laury looks and sounds compared to when they last saw her. It was good to get an opinion from someone who hasn't seen Laury in a while. Candice said that Laury sounded more like herself. I guess that is something I had noticed and but it hadn't registered. Laury speaks with much more energy and force now, more like her old self- another sign of her getting better.

Not a lot happened that last two days. It was kind of nice.

All our Love.

Sunday, 9/14/2014 – Full day

"I arise full of eagerness and energy, knowing well what achievement lies ahead of me." - Zane Grey

Yesterday was an energetic day. Laury and I started the morning with a two hour walk downtown. We walked to Starbucks and I went in to get Laury's coffee while Laury took a call from her friend, Michelle. We then walked to the River Walk and on the way ran into our friends, Bill and Diane. It was good to see them and hear about their summer which included their son's wedding. We then sat in the sun and Laury finished her coffee.

Laury and I then walked to the Apple store to pick up some software I ordered online that morning. Laury waited outside and watched the people and dogs walk by. We then walked home and Laury Skyped Keri. After eating some lunch, Laury and I went to Wagner Farms to pick up our tomatoes that we are going to can this week. We then went to Glen Ellyn to see Laury's parents. Laury and I walked her mom's gardens and saw all the work and new plants that Laury's mom and her gardener had put in. The gardens look beautiful. There is something to this gardening thing- Laury keeps saying her Mom looks ten years younger since she has been able to get in her gardens again. Laury tried on some of her Mom's cold weather hats. Some of which gave us a good laugh. It is funny how some hats look great on one person and completely silly on someone else.

After leaving Laury's parents we went to Batavia to see Lyndsay. I gave her a hanger I built for a macramé shelf that Lyndsay wanted to hang in her new living room. We didn't stay long and headed back home in time for dinner.

It was a long day with lots of running around. Laury's energy was good through it all. I think I was ready for bed before Laury was. I think this is what I have to look forward to when she completely regains her strength. I won't be able to keep up with her.

All our Love.

Tuesday, 9/16/2014 – Waiting

"Being with you and not being with you is the only way I have to measure time." - Jorge Luis Borges

Laury asked Dr. Odenike yesterday during our visit, "What do I need to do? What does my body need right now?" Dr. Odenike replied, "Time." Laury and I were disappointed yesterday to learn that Laury's hemoglobin was 6.2 and she will be getting two units of blood today. Every time we have Laury's blood checked Laury and I hope that this will be the time when the red blood numbers will show an increase. It wasn't yesterday. We tell ourselves not to go into these tests with expectations, but it is hard at this point not to.

I again asked Dr. Odenike if everything is OK and if we should be concerned. Dr. Odenike says that things are just progressing slowly and she knows it is frustrating. Dr. Odenike explained that what most likely is happening is that Laury's antibodies are still attacking the new stem cells before they have a chance to grow into red blood cells. Dr. Odenike ordered a special blood test for our visit on Thursday to see if this is happening. I asked her if there something we can do if this is going on. Dr. Odenike said there are things that can be done, but right now it is too early and the treatments to suppress these antibodies would leave Laury very vulnerable to infection. Dr. Odenike thinks we just need to give the process more time.

As we were driving home, Laury asked me if I was tired of waiting for her to get better. I said, "I have my entire life to wait for you." Laury and I will have to be patient and give this more time, but at least we know things are still going in the right direction.

All our Love.

Wednesday, 9/17/2014 – Listen

"To walk quietly until the miracle in everything speaks is poetry, whether we write it down or not." - Mark Nepo

Yesterday we spent several hours at the infusion center here in Naperville while Laury received two units of blood. Much of our time there was spent in silence; me working and Laury reading. The nutritionist stopped by to talk with Laury about how she was eating and about how to get more protein into Laury's diet. I sat and listened to Laury describe her difficulties with taste and still not having much of an appetite.

Now that Laury is feeling stronger I find that when we are with the doctors and nurses, I am doing more listening than talking. I used to be the one to answer the questions on how Laury was feeling, or what was going well and what wasn't. It is hard not to correct Laury when I think she is mistaken or confused on something the doctor has asked her. I am finding that once again my job as the caregiver involves being a good listener.

Sometimes I need to listen to be able to remember the instructions the doctor has given Laury. Other times Laury just wants to vent and needs someone to listen to her. A lot of the time I need to listen to what is not being said. Laury tells me much of how she is doing by how she acts and what she does, not by what she says. I have had to learn to read these signs and know when to ask Laury questions and when to stay quiet and just listen. Many times Laury's actions are much more enlightening than her words.

The other night I woke up in a mild panic. I wasn't sure Laury was in the bed next to me. I reached out carefully, not wanting to wake her if she was there, just to make sure. She was there, very quiet, too quiet. I then became concerned that Laury wasn't breathing. I again reached out to see if I could feel her breath. I couldn't. I laid there sure Laury was OK but not absolutely sure. I pushed my toes on to her toes, she didn't move. I then said to Laury very quietly, "Please give me some sign you are alive and well." Laury began to snore. It was all I needed to hear. I went back to sleep happy.

All our Love.

Thursday, 9/18/2014 – Brother Andrew

"You do not need to know precisely what is happening, or exactly where it is all going. What you need is to recognize the possibilities and challenges offered by the present moment, and to embrace them with courage, faith and hope." - Thomas Merton

We had the carpet in the family room and the furniture in the living room cleaned yesterday. This is not usually something that is very interesting or causes me to run to the computer to tell you all about it. However, this simple event, like so many on this journey, proved to have a life of its own. One of the young men who came to clean heard Laury telling the crew chief her story. The young man introduced himself to Laury as Brother Andrew. He is a monk who studied at the Thomas Merton Center. Thomas Merton is one of Laury's favorite authors and he has taught Laury much about contemplative prayer.

Brother Andrew asked Laury if it was OK with her that he carry her story back to his abbot and add her to their prayer circle. Of course Laury said yes and was honored by the gesture. Laury was standing at the refrigerator looking for something to eat when she said to Brother Andrew, "One of the most difficult parts of this healing is that I am an extrovert and I am having to live this introverted life right now." Brother Andrew relied, "You can live your extroverted life by examining your introverted moments and taking them into your being at a deep level."

Laury told me all of this after the crew left and said to me, "I can't get out to meet these people, so now they are being sent to me."

All our Love.

Friday, 9/19/2014 – Freedom

"Nothing is more difficult, and therefore more precious, than to be able to decide." - Napoleon

Like every Thursday for that last three months, Laury and I had Laury's blood checked in Naperville in the morning and went to the U of C in the afternoon. Laury's white blood counts were stable and her platelets were up to over forty thousand. Laury's hemoglobin was 9.2 which is great, reflecting the transfusion she had on Tuesday.

Laury felt strong yesterday. Laury is trying to find ways to get some freedom back into her life. So much of her daily routine is dictated by others right now. As we were getting off the elevator at U of C yesterday, I asked Laury if she was going to get her blood drawn from her arm or her Hiccman line. Laury said, "I hate having the blood draw from my arm, but I won't sit and wait in the infusion center." I said that I didn't mind waiting at the infusion center for them to draw it from her line. Laury replied, "I have to have some freedoms, and I choose not to wait. If I don't have some control over this process then I will go insane." I understand Laury's frustration. This journey has been about letting go and receiving, but at some point you want some of your life back. Laury recently received an invitation to the annual survivor's banquet at U of C. Laury is excited to go and in particular wants to hear the discussion on life after transplant. I think now that Laury is beginning to feel stronger, she is ready to move on. I know we are not out of the woods yet, but we can begin to think about a life after transplant and what that looks like.

I have not regretted the freedom we have given up on this journey. Laury and I have both gained other freedoms that were worth the trade.

All our Love.

Sunday, 9/21/2014 – A year

"Hope

Smiles from the threshold of the year to come,

Whispering 'it will be happier'..." - Alfred Tennyson

Yesterday Laury and I canned tomatoes. This is something we have done together for the last several years. It is an all-day affair, and this year I made a batch of my Mom's celery sauce. Our son-in-law, James, had asked me to make a batch, since he ran out of the jar I sent him and Keri home with last year.

Laury and I didn't can tomatoes last year because we were so busy with Keri's wedding. We usually put up twenty five to thirty quarts of tomatoes. Laury and I get two boxes of tomatoes from Wagner Farms and spend an entire day peeling and stuffing the tomatoes into jars. We give some of the tomatoes away to friends and family, and most Laury and I keep and use in dishes throughout the winter. The tomatoes really taste good in January and February.

It was good to be able to can this year. Laury stood next to me at the sink like years before and we talked and made a mess. It was also a little sad, because I remember canning with my Mom, making her celery sauce brought back these memories. Laury and I were watching TV and I heard the ping of the jar signaling the last jar had sealed. I said to Laury, "There goes the last jar. We are done canning. What a difference from a year ago." Laury said, "Yes, this time last year I knew things were changing with my health." I said, "I knew before this time." and Laury asked, "Why didn't you say something?" I replied, "I knew you were focused on Keri's wedding, and I also knew you had to arrive at that conclusion in your own time." Laury said, "Thank you for that."

It has been a long, happy and sad year. Today marks Laury's one hundredth day after transplant. Laury and I are not sure where we thought we would be today. I thought that today would be a logical place to conclude the posts, but I think we have a little farther to go together, so I will continue. I think we are going to celebrate by going for a walk and buying Laury a purse she saw at one of the stores downtown. Maybe we will go get a Bundt cake. Whatever Laury and I do to celebrate, we will think of all of you who have helped so much and carried us through this last year.

We thank you all again for your love and support.

All our Love.

Monday, 9/22/2014 – Refreshed

"May you be forever blessed for that moment of bliss and happiness which you gave to another lonely and grateful heart. Isn't such a moment sufficient for the whole of one's life?" - Fyodor Dostoyevsky, White Nights and Other Stories

Yesterday was a beautiful day. Laury and I went for a long walk into town and walked through the Fine Arts Fair that was going on. Laury ran into a few people she knew and was able to bring them up to date on her progress. The people we met all said that seeing Laury had made their day. Later in the day Laury's friend from Germany, Kathy, stopped by for a short visit. It was good to hear Kathy and Laury catching up and laughing about things they did many years ago. Laury also spent time on the phone with her sister and her friend, Mardy. Afterwards Laury said to me, "That is amazing! I spoke to all three of my bridesmaids today!"

Later in the afternoon, Laury and I went to the Library to pick a TV series that Laury wants to watch, and to pick up her new purse- Laury's 100 days purse. We had a nice dinner of roast chicken and sweet potatoes. Laury said she could taste everything! It was a nice day, perfect for connecting and celebrating our friends, connections and Laury's continued progress.

Thank you all for the well wishes. We head down to the U of C this afternoon. Laury is getting another bone marrow aspiration. This can be a painful procedure as they take some bone marrow by going through the hip bone. We are back at it today, but the weekend refreshed and renewed us for the week ahead. Thanks.

All our Love.

Tuesday, 9/23/2014 – Hats

"We just know inside that we're queens. And these are the crowns we wear." - Felecia McMillan

Yesterday Laury and I went to the infusion center here in Naperville to have Laury's blood checked. Her numbers are still good and her hemoglobin was 8, so no transfusion today. Laury and I headed down to the U of C earlier than normal because Laury had a bone marrow aspiration at two. We arrived around one, and after waiting a little while in the lab for Laury to get her blood checked again, they were ready for her procedure.

While we were at the lab waiting, there weren't two seats together, so Laury sat next to an older gentleman and I sat across from her. After sitting there for just a minute the man turned to Laury and said, "I like your hat. It is really sharp." Laury told the man that the hat belongs to her Mom, and she likes it too. The man told Laury that he bought a bowler hat when he was in England. He says he does not wear it often but he thinks it is special like Laury's. Laury said she wears the hat to keep her head warm, and the man replied tapping his bald head, "Me too!" They both laughed.

Laury's procedure went well. She was pretty sore afterwards and walking a little slow. Laury walked to the bench by the elevators and I went to the receptionist area to work out our schedule for next week. We are now only going to have to go to clinic once a week. While I was standing there I saw AJ, one of the receptionists, and I complemented her on her new hair style. She thanked me and said, "I didn't recognize Laury without her mask on." Funny how for AJ, people with masks are the norm.

When I caught up to Laury she told me that a woman had stopped and told her she liked her hat. The lady said to Laury, "I saw you walk in a while ago and I thought to myself, that it's a really sharp hat and she looks great in it". Laury told her she liked the woman's hat too, and she liked her bald head. The woman said that she liked her bald head, too. Laury then said to her, "Here's to bald heads and healing!" The woman replied, "The healing is already there." Laury said, "Amen" and the woman walked away. But right before she turned the corner she stopped and looked back at Laury and said, "It is already there."

Amen to that - the healing is already there.

All our Love.

Wednesday, 9/24/2014 – Healing day

"We hunger for quiet times; we find in them a womb to renew our strength." - Virginia Ann Froehle

Feeling the effects of the bone marrow aspiration, Laury was tired and sore yesterday. She decided to "go with it" and let herself be quiet and heal. When I asked Laury at the end of my work day what she had done all day, she replied, "Healed." It was good to see Laury recognize that she needed the time and the quiet to allow her body to recover. Laury has had the procedure before and even gone to work the next day, but her body has been through a lot and it needs a little more help now to rebound.

After I finished working yesterday I went up to Trader Joe's to get a bottle of wine. Laury and I sat out on the patio and Laury enjoyed a small glass of wine and the beautiful weather. We talked a little but mostly watched the chipmunks running around the patio and the large hawk that came to the top of the maple tree. We had nowhere we had to be. It was a good day for Laury's healing.

All our Love.

Thursday, 9/25/2014 – Surrender

"Pray, and let God worry." - Martin Luther

Laury spent another day yesterday taking it easy and letting herself heal. She spent most of the day reading and listening to a book on tape. I could see Laury felt better and was comfortable with being quiet and listening to what her body needed.

I went to yoga last night. It was a restorative class, just what I needed. Linda, our instructor, said to us after we had gotten into a difficult and sometimes painful pose for me, "I want you to think of the word, surrender. Surrender to the things you can't control and trust you will be supported." Listening to her I was able to relax and get into the pose. So many times on this journey Laury has been asked to surrender and trust that she will be supported. And she has been, we have been, by all of you. Thanks for reminding me of that Linda. Great practice.

All our Love.

Friday, 9/26/2014 — Knowing

*"Our first experience of life is primarily felt in the *body.* ... We know ourselves in the security of those who hold us and gaze upon us. It's not heard or seen or though it's felt. That's the original knowing."* - Richard Rohr, Everything Belongs: The Gift of Contemplative Prayer

Yesterday Laury and I went to clinic at the U of C. Laury's hemoglobin is low so she has to get a unit of blood today. The visit with Jean, our nurse practitioner, went well. All the signs are still good and the fact that even though Laury needs blood today, it has been ten days since her last transfusion. The results of the two additional blood tests were back. Laury's Epogen level is high, signaling that her body knows it needs red blood cells and it is producing the hormone to tell the marrow to make more. This is good news. It means that this part of the internal process is working just fine. The second test was to see if Laury has an antibody that is attacking the new red cells. The results were back from the lab, but

Jean said she would have to talk to Dr. Odenike to understand what the results mean. We will see Dr. Odenike next Friday and will find out more then.

It would appear that Laury's body knows what to do and is doing it. Her body knows it needs red blood and is using all of the facilities it has to produce them. Unfortunately, right now Laury's body also thinks that this new blood is foreign and is trying to destroy it to protect her. Right now I think Dr. Odenike wants Laury's body to figure it out on its own rather than to take action to suppress the antibodies. Dr. Odenike is confident in Laury's body's ability to figure it out and reach a normal state. It just needs time. It is all a miracle to me.

All our Love.

Sunday, 9/28/2014 – Friend fixes

"The glory of friendship is not the outstretched hand, not the kindly smile, nor the joy of companionship; it is the spiritual inspiration that comes to one when you discover that someone else believes in you and is willing to trust you with a friendship."
- Ralph Waldo Emerson

Friday Laury received a unit of blood at the infusion center in Naperville. We arrived at eight thirty and were home by eleven thirty. I was not feeling one hundred percent and had some work I had to get done by the end of the day. Laury and Kelly took off on a walk downtown. I didn't see Laury again until after six. She and Kelly walked to several stores and had a coffee and a coffee gelato. Laury was looking for a top to wear under her shift dress to the Celebration of Life party we are going to next weekend at the U of C. Laury is very excited to go to the event and has been planning her outfit for weeks.

While Kelly and Laury were walking around downtown Naperville, they ran into an old friend, Nikki. Nikki was not aware of the journey Laury has been on and after Laury told her, Nikki said, "When you showed me your bald head I just thought you were still the rebel and had shaved your head." They all laughed. Kelly and Laury also ran into Bob and Vicky, and Bob's brother who is in town visiting.

Yesterday I painted the front window frames in preparation for getting new replacement windows. Laury sat near me soaking her toes and keeping me company. Yesterday there was also a nice Guestbook entry from Laury's friend Ed. Ed was part of the group that Laury went to Africa with. He, too, was unaware of Laury's current journey. Laury was touched to hear from him. Later last night our friends, Joan and Clyde, stopped by. Joan is starting another round of chemo and is still recovering from her cancer surgery. Laury and I were tired when they arrived and we weren't sure we were up for their visit. But as we all sat and talked about our experiences and what was to come we gained strength. As they were leaving Clyde said to me, "I need these fixes."

The last two days have been full of "friend fixes". Each one has added something to our life and our journey. Each one of our interactions with friends is special and keeps us going.

Thank you all for being our friends.

All our Love.

Monday, 9/29/2014 – Our future

"I was doing something I'd never done before. And what will I be able to do tomorrow that I cannot yet do today?" - Elizabeth Gilbert, Eat, Pray, Love

Yesterday morning Laury and I took our long Sunday morning walk. We stopped at Starbucks and I went in to order Laury's, 'tall single shot pumpkin spice latte, two espresso shots, one regular, one decafe, no whipped cream", hoping I could get it straight. I did pretty well, but they somehow gave us a Grande instead of a tall I really have no idea why they are not called small, medium or large. We walked along the river walk to our favorite talking spot. The spot is near a small waterfall under one of the covered bridges.

Laury wanted to talk about our future. She has been thinking about what she wants to do when she is healthy enough to work.

Laury and I haven't talked about our future much lately. We have been focused on living day by day. It was good to talk about what our possibilities are and what we want out of the rest of our lives together. We can never be sure what the future holds for us. We do know that we have a future now and it is exciting to talk about it.

All our Love.

Tuesday, 9/30/2014 – Content

"Sometimes we go along, thinking

"Ah, this is it - this is what true peace feels like..."

Then, in a moment of grace, something shifts in our hearts,

and in awestruck wonder, we whisper,

"oh my, I just didn't know there could more..."

— Kate Mullan Robertson

The last two days can best be described as content. Laury has been content to quietly go about her day and let her body get what it needs. On Monday Laury was feeling tired. She said she played too hard over the weekend. Laury watched TV, beaded and listened to her book on tape. Laury also took a long nap- so long that I came down twice from my office to make sure she was OK. I see a difference in Laury's tiredness. It is not the overwhelming exhaustion of the early days when she was first home. The tiredness now looks more like Laury has done a lot and she needs a rest. After the rest she is restored.

Today we had Laury's blood checked. Her numbers were stable and her hemoglobin was 7.5 so she and the doctor agreed to wait until Thursday to see if she needed blood. Laury came home and then went out with her friend Vicky to run some errands. I came down later in the afternoon and she was resting in the chair in the sun room watching a movie on the Kindle. Laury seems more at ease, better managing her ups and downs of energy. It appears to me that there has been shift in how she manages her days and how she feels. Laury still needs to see people, to talk and spend time with friends, but she seems more content to have these quiet days. It makes me feel good to see Laury happy in this situation and not frustrated with what she can't do, but enjoying what she can.

All our Love.

CHAPTER NINE

October

Thursday, 10/2/2014 – Ice Cream

"Without ice cream, there would be darkness and chaos." - Don Kardong

Laury had a very good day yesterday. The morning was quiet and in the afternoon she had a good visit with her friends Marinda and Karen. Later in the afternoon Kelly stopped by. It was the type of day that energizes Laury without taking too much physical energy. Last week, while Laury was receiving blood at the infusion center here in Naperville, the Nutritionist stopped by to talk with Laury about her diet. The Nutritionist and Laury talked about how to get enough protein and calories during this time of healing. Laury has taken care to eat right for the last several years. Her eating habits have focused on maintaining a healthy weight with the right balance of foods.

Now, however, since she is feeling better and more active, she actually needs to eat to put weight back on. She has lost several pounds and since she didn't have a lot of fat to begin with, she lost mostly muscle. The nutritionist told Laury that she needs a minimum of sixty grams of protein per day, but she also needed more calories than just protein. Laury and I were talking about this last night while eating dinner. I said to Laury that it is almost like she is pregnant. She needs to be eating for two right now, her muscles and her new bone marrow. Laury liked that analogy and said she could get behind that view. Laury said to me, "I have been craving mint chocolate chip ice cream."

This morning while getting her blood checked, Laury mentioned this conversation to Jessica our nurse and Jessica said, "Eat all the ice cream you want right now. I wish someone would tell me that."

I am going to go to the store to get some mint chocolate chip ice cream. There have to be some benefits of going through this.

All our Love.

Friday, 10/3/2014 – Survivor

"Some part of me can't wait to see what life's going to come up with next! Anticipation without the usual anxiety. And underneath it all is the feeling that we both belong here, just as we are, right now." - Alexander Shulgin

Yesterday Laury's sister and mom came over to help Laury finish her outfit for the Celebration of Life banquet on Saturday. Laury has been excited about attending this event since we received the invitation a month ago. She has been cleared by Dr. Odenike to attend and Laury is looking forward to talking with other people who have been through a transplant like she has. Planning her outfit has taken up many hours of Laury's time over the last couple of weeks. It is good to see her so into this, a chance to dress up and socialize.

Today Laury and I have a long day. Laury is receiving two units of blood this morning and then we will drive down to the U of C to meet with Dr. Odenike. Tomorrow, I get my hair cut in the city in the morning and then we drive back home and get ready and drive back to the U of C for the banquet.

When Laury asked Paula and Dr. Odenike if she could attend, she asked them, "Am I considered a survivor? It is so soon after my transplant." Both Paula and Dr. Odenike said that yes Laury is considered a survivor. I guess we never really thought of "surviving" the transplant. It was something Laury was going to get through and come out even healthier than when she went in. Laury and I are happy to be attending the banquet with others who have gone through this and are alive and happy. Tomorrow will be a big day and a big deal for Laury; a day to celebrate her and her new life.

All our Love.

Saturday, 10/4/2014 – Islands in the sea

"We are like islands in the sea, separate on the surface but connected in the deep." - William James

Today was a great day. Laury stayed home to get ready for the celebration while I went into Chicago to get my hair cut. Laury had decided that getting back at ten thirty would not give her enough time to get ready by eleven, when we wanted to leave. I raced off to the city and Laury took her time getting herself together. When I got home I jumped into the shower while Laury was finishing her makeup and putting on her outfit. Laury looked fabulous. It's the first time I have seen her in makeup since the transplant- not that she needs makeup to look fabulous- but I could tell it made Laury feel special. The outfit was great and yes I took some pictures, although all they show is my inability to take a good picture, not how great Laury looked.

We arrived in the cold rain a little early and got lucky with a parking spot right across the street from the International House where the banquet was happening. Laury and I met Paula in the large hall and also one of the nurse practitioners who had worked with us during the transplant. The food was mostly little sandwiches and fruit and vegetables. It was the best food we have ever had at U of C. Laury and I sat with a couple from Indiana. He had been out of transplant for six years and he kept telling Laury how good she looked and couldn't believe she was only 114 days out. Rich and Carol from the Growing Place showed up a little later and sat with us, as well. Rich went through a bone marrow transplant last year.

Most of the speakers told us things we already knew, but it was good to hear again. Dr. Odenike talked a little, but was cut short when the keynote speaker showed up. Near the end of banquet they had an open mike session where people got up and told their story. Laury talked briefly through tears about how thankful she was for everyone at U of C and what a beautiful place the hospital was to heal.

It was good to hear these stories, many of which sounded more difficult than what Laury went through. There were two other people who spoke that had Myelofibrosis. One was a woman named Lori and the other was a man named Steve. Laury wanted to meet Lori so we hung around after to track Lori down and talk. It was amazing to see all of these survivors and caregivers. It is not something that I could have appreciated a year ago. I think for Laury it was uplifting to see and hear she is not alone and there is another side to this journey, and we are well on the way to getting there.

All our Love.

Sunday, 10/5/2014 – Heroes

"I am of certain convinced that the greatest heroes are those who do their duty in the daily grind of domestic affairs whilst the world whirls as a maddening dreidel." - Florence Nightingale

The last two days have been full, long and fun. Friday started at eight o'clock with Laury receiving two units of blood at the infusion center. We left the center at one and came home to eat lunch before heading down to the U of C at two. Laury and I left the University of Chicago at six and were home by seven thirty.

Friday's visit with Dr. Odenike was good, informative, uplifting and sad.

Dr. Odenike reviewed the special blood test that Laury had two weeks ago. It shows that Laury is making antibodies that are killing the A positive blood cells. Dr. Odenike said that she would consult with her colleagues about possible actions, but she felt that the best thing to do is wait. Laury said, "I feel strong, I feel good." and Dr. Odenike replied, "You cannot underestimate the importance of that to healing. I have some patients whose blood numbers are perfect and I am watching them waste away. I tell them that the transplant was a success but they say they don't feel good and are not happy and they are failing." Dr. Odenike said that the reason for waiting is that she is convinced that Laury's body will figure out what to do and make the correction on its own and that the other courses of action are too risky.

Dr. Odenike also told us that the latest bone marrow aspiration showed that 100% of the DNA in Laury's marrow is from her donor. Laury's bone marrow and blood now has the Y-chromosome. This is good news. It means the marrow is working and will eventually overcome the remaining antibodies to allow Laury's red blood numbers to rise.

A month ago there was a story in the paper about a man who had been taken off a plane in Nigeria because he was sick and a local doctor on a hunch tested him and found he had the Ebola virus. The entire hospital was placed in quarantine. I asked Dr. Odenike, who is from Nigeria, if she knew anything about the incident. She told us that the doctor, whose name is Adadevoh, was the daughter of one of her medical school professors and her parents live in the town where the hospital is. Laury asked Dr. Odenike to write down the doctor's name so she could pray for her. On Friday Laury remembered to ask Dr. Odenike how Adadevoh was doing. Dr. Odenike replied, "She is in heaven." Laury began to cry and said, "I have been praying for her every day." Dr. Odenike said back to Laury, "Don't cry, you have been praying for her soul. I can't believe you were so concerned about her with all that you are going through." Dr. Odenike went on to tell us that Adadevoh, in doing her job as a doctor, saved hundreds of people from the Ebola virus and prevented it from taking hold in Nigeria. She is considered a hero. Dr. Odenike said to Laury, "I try to tell my son that none of us are guaranteed any time on this earth. But, if we have touched one life and made a positive impact on that life, then our existence has had meaning."

In the last two days Laury and I have met many heroes: doctors, nurses, and other patients. But since February, you all have been our heroes. You have touched our lives and have made a positive impact on us during this journey. I thank you all again.

All our Love.

Tuesday, 10/7/2014 – Eyes

"The eye through which I see God is the same eye through which God sees me; my eye and God's eye are one eye, one seeing, one knowing, one love." - Meister Eckhart, Sermons of Meister Eckhart

One of the lasting side effects of Laury's chemo treatments is her eyesight. Laury has been unable to see close up even with her glasses on. The doctors say it will come back and not to buy new glasses right now because Laury most likely won't need the same prescription when the side effects are gone. I mentioned, as others have, about getting a cheap pair of reading glasses. I showed Laury some at Walgreens when we were there a few weeks ago. Yesterday, Laury and Kelly went for a walk downtown and they looked at cheap reading glasses. Laury said she found a pair, but they were too expensive, so they went back to Walgreens.

Kelly described the task of picking out the glasses to me like this: "Laury picked up a pair of 1.0 and said "Wow!" and then she tried the 1.25 and said, "Oh Wow!" and finally Laury tried the 1.5 and said, "Holy shit I can see!" They came home with the 1.5s.

This morning Laury and I went to get Laury's blood checked at the infusion center. Laury's numbers are good and she doesn't need a transfusion tomorrow. We will have the blood checked again on Thursday when Laury and I go to the U of C. After we got home, I went upstairs to my home office to work. I came down a little later to get a glass of water and Laury was sitting at the computer. She was sitting so far from the screen that she had to lean way in to reach the mouse. I asked her why she wasn't wearing her new glasses. Laury replied, "They don't work on the computer." I was confused by this and Laury said, "I checked and the glasses only work for my nails and reading a book."

I believe her but it still doesn't make sense to me. At least Laury's nails will look good.

All our Love.

Thursday, 10/9/2014 – Caregiver

"only someone who is ready for everything, who doesn't exclude any experience, even the most incomprehensible, will live the relationship with another person as something alive and will himself sound the depths of his own being." - Rainer Maria Rilke, Letters To a Young Poet

The last few days have been pretty simple. Laury is feeling good, and strong. I work upstairs all day and see her at breaks and lunch. Laury's sister is in town and she and Laury's mom have stopped by. I heard them laughing and enjoying their time together. Laury is content to read and has been using her new "Cheaters" to overcome the chemo eyesight.

Things are getting to feel more like normal. Our lives still are focused on Laury's health but it doesn't seem to have the intensity that it has for the last several months. Laury and I both knew and hoped it would get to this point, a life where every moment is not dictated by a medical schedule. It means my role as caregiver is changing. Laury is capable of doing so much more now and making her own decisions, that my roll has been greatly reduced. It feels a little strange. I know we still have a long way to go, but Laury has come so far and every day she gets more strength and independence.

I have read and heard stories of how to be a good caregiver. I have not heard anyone talk about what it is like to stop being a caregiver. I am not ready to stop yet, nor do I think Laury is ready, either, but I can see glimpses of what it might be like. It looks joyful, but a little sad. I love taking care of Laury.

All our Love.

Friday, 10/10/2014 – The hill

"It is easier to go down a hill than up, but the view is best from the top." - Arnold Bennett

Yesterday was a full day, like most of our Thursdays, of late. Laury and I went for a walk at lunch around our neighborhood. If you remember, back in a previous post I talked about the hill near our house and how Laury was not ready to take it on at that point. Yesterday we avoided the hill again until we were headed home and Laury and I were going to turn down the street to avoid the hill and Laury said, "I think I want to try the hill. I will just take it slow." So we did. Laury made it to the top and we continued on home. She said it felt good.

Laury and I also started our new once-a-week plan that meant we didn't have Laury's blood checked in Naperville in the morning. Instead, we wait until we have it checked at the U of C, and they call Naperville to order the blood, if necessary. This is the opposite of what we have been doing, so there was some concern that it might not work. We arrived at our usual time about an hour before our appointment and had Laury's blood checked. After about an hour of not hearing from Paula, I called her. I learned from her voice mail message that she was out of the office for a week. I began to wonder if she had left instructions for the person covering for her on what to do with Laury's results and who to call. I went to the reception desk and asked them who was covering for Paula, and they told me Linda was, and I asked them if they could page her for me.

After another fifteen minutes of not hearing anything we were taken back for our appointment with Dr. Odenike. It was now four forty-five and Jessica at Naperville had told us she needs to hear from the U of C before five to get the blood ordered. So this time I paged Linda to have her call me directly. After a few more minutes of not hearing from Linda, I called Naperville to try to talk to Jessica. I was told that Jessica had left for the day, and after trying to find another nurse for me to talk to, the receptionist came back on the phone and told me that she had found a note from Jessica to us if we called. Jessica called Paula when she didn't hear from her, and then hearing Paula's message Jessica called Linda and got Laury's blood results.

Once again Jessica went over and above to make sure everything went the way it was supposed to. The good news through all of this is that Laury didn't need blood. Laury has gone the whole week without needing blood. It is too early to say whether this means the red blood cells are coming in, but a week without a transfusion is good news, no matter what.

The hill and blood are more small steps on this journey. We celebrate them and hope and plan for more to come.

All our Love.

Sunday, 10/12/2014 – The patio

"I know this much: that there is objective time, but also subjective time, the kind you wear on the inside of your wrist, next to where the pulse lies. And this personal time, which is the true time, is measured in your relationship to memory." - Julian Barnes, The Sense Of An Ending

Yesterday I cleaned the patio and got it ready for winter. I put the table and chairs away in the playhouse and cleaned and winterized the fountains. At times while I was working I tried to remember doing this same job last year. I know it was later in the season last year because Laury wanted the patio to be set up for Keri's wedding. But, I really couldn't remember. What I did remember was the feeling I had this time last year that Laury's health was quickly deteriorating. I had seen some changes earlier in late summer, but as Keri's wedding approached, I began to notice them more. I also remember the feeling of fear that was always with me. I was never afraid of Laury not surviving a transplant. I was afraid that she would wait too long to agree to the transplant. This always present fear was something I couldn't share with Laury. I knew she had to arrive at the decision to do the transplant on her own. I do remember relief when Laury finally admitted to me that it might be time for a transplant and that she no longer feared it.

A lot has happened since I last put the patio furniture away for winter. The fear is gone, and every day I see Laury getting stronger and healthier. I think I will always remember these times. Fear is not soon forgotten, but I will have Laury by my side when the memories hit and I will have the knowledge that the fear was unfounded.

All our Love.

Monday, 10/13/2014 – Kind words

"A kind gesture can reach a wound that only compassion can heal." - Steve Maraboli, Life, The Truth, And Being Free

Laury and I have experienced so many acts of kindness toward us over the last several months it is hard to keep track. I have tried to point them out in my posts and to give thanks. All of these gestures small and large have made this journey so much easier.

Last week I had been feeling the need to go see my sisters and friends in Michigan. I also wanted to see my parent's house before it is sold. I guess I was grieving. I asked Laury if she thought she was up to making the drive and staying a day or two. Laury said that she thought she could make the drive and wanted to support me going. When we met with Dr. Odenike last Thursday I asked her if Laury could be cleared for this short trip. Dr. Odenike was very nervous about letting Laury go, but understood our need for connection and closure, so she reluctantly agreed.

On our way home, Laury and I talked about when we might go and how long we would stay. After much discussion, we agreed that right now is not a good time to go. Laury and I want to see everyone, both family and friends, and to try do that in small groups (Laury still can't be in groups of more than four at a time). This would take more time and strength than we both felt Laury has to give right now. It was a tough decision.

The next day my sister, Kim, called to tell me she was a grandmother again. We talked about the new baby and how things are going with the sale of Mom's house. I told Kim that we had been thinking of coming up but we weren't sure if it would work. Even before I told her that we had decided not to come, Kim said, "We would love to see you both, but I don't think it would be good for Laury to risk it. She has done so well, I would hate to have something happen. You will be able to get up here and see everyone soon enough." These simple words were so kind and loving. Laury said to me when I told her what Kim had said, "Kim gave me words. I have felt that I have been holding you back and have been feeling guilty and bad. Kim's words make it OK."

Thank you, Kim, for understanding and speaking those words of kindness.

All our Love.

Tuesday, 10/14/2014 – Step backward

"He was angry; not as the irritable, from chafing of a trifle; nor was his anger like the fool's, pumped from the wells of nothing, to be dissipated by a reproach or a curse; it was the wrath peculiar to ardent natures rudely awakened by the sudden annihilation of a hope --dream, if you will-- in which the choicest happinesses were thought to be certainly in reach. In such case nothing intermediate will carry off the passion --the quarrel is with Fate." - Lew Wallace, Ben-Hur

Laury had her blood checked today. Her hemoglobin is down to 6.3 so Laury will need a transfusion tomorrow. Laury is angry and frustrated with this; she had plans for tomorrow that she does not want to break. It is hard not to be disappointed when we build our hopes up that maybe this time the red numbers will be up. As Laury pointed out to me, the things she planned to do tomorrow are just as important to her and to her healing as getting blood. Dr. Odenike might not agree, and we most certainly can't wait until Friday for the transfusion.

I think it is hard for Laury when she feels so good to have these blood results. Her first reaction was that the numbers were wrong. Laury said she feels too good for the numbers to be true. This is what makes this part of the journey so frustrating. You feel you are making progress and there are measures of that progress and sometimes they don't agree. It makes it hard to know what to do, or in my case what to say. I know this is a small setback when compared to other things that could have happened. I also know that Laury's plans for tomorrow can be rescheduled, but it doesn't help the frustration and the disappointment. This is not and never has been a straight step by step always moving forward journey. Today was a step backward day. Tomorrow we will move forward again.

All our Love.

Thursday, 10/16/2014 – The "hole"

"Sometimes I wish I could walk around with a HANDLE WITH CARE sign stuck to my forehead." - Elizabeth Wurtzel, Prozac Nation

Yesterday was a little better day. Laury received two units of blood. We arrived at the infusion center at eight thirty and were home by one. I spent most of the time there working and Laury read and listened to a book on tape. This was not the way Laury had wanted to spend the day, but she admitted in the morning she really felt the need for blood, so it was a good thing Laury was getting some.

On Tuesday, when I came downstairs after work, Laury apologized to me for getting so upset about having to get blood. Laury said she was disappointed and fell into the "hole" again on the news of her needing blood. Laury asked me, "I couldn't believe I fell into the hole again so quickly. Do you think I am still really weak?" I said that falling into the hole is not a sign of weakness. She has been through a lot and to be disappointed was natural. I went on to say, "Falling into the hole is OK, staying there is not. You didn't stay there very long this time. I think this shows you are stronger than you give yourself credit for."

I think Laury is incredibly strong and has been doing an amazing job getting better. It is understandable to get down sometimes. I know I do, too. The waiting for the red blood cells is proving to be harder than either of us thought.

All our Love.

Friday, 10/17/2014 — Two steps forward

"Go back?" he thought. "No good at all! Go sideways? Impossible! Go forward? Only thing to do! On we go!" So up he got, and trotted along with his little sword held in front of him and one hand feeling the wall, and his heart all of a patter and a pitter." - J.R.R. Tolkien, The Hobbit

Yesterday Laury and I went to clinic at the U of C and met with Dr. Odenike. Ever since Laury received her stem cell transplant she has been taking the anti-rejection medicine, Cellcept. Laury has been taking nine Cellcept pills a day and I just refilled the prescription for another thirty days. So of course, yesterday Dr. Odenike told us Laury can stop taking Cellcept. This is good news because it means that the doctors feel the transplant has engrafted enough that there is no chance of rejection. It is also good news because the Cellcept capsules are big and taking nine a day was a pain for Laury. It is just too bad we now have almost 270 of them that will go to waste. Dr. Odenike also mentioned that Cellcept sometimes can suppress the blood counts, so we are hoping that being off of it will raise Laury's red counts.

As a result of the transplant Laury no longer has any of the antibodies for common diseases. As a result, over the next two years Laury will have to go through the same set of vaccinations as most children. We received another piece of good news yesterday. Laury was far enough along to receive her first inoculation. So yesterday Laury received a shot, against pneumonia. She wasn't crazy about getting a shot but it did mark another positive milestone on this journey.

Compared to earlier in the week yesterday was a "two steps forward" day.

All our Love.

Sunday, 10/19/2014 – Hair, nails and table saw

"Where there is love there is life." - Mahatma Gandhi

This weekend was full. Yesterday Laury and I went to the city to get my hair cut. We usually go every three weeks, but because Magen is busy next weekend we went a week earlier.

Laury asked Magen to look at her hair and Magen cut it with scissors! Laury's first haircut since June not done by my razor. After we left the city and came back to Naperville Laury and I stopped at Whole Foods to look for something to strengthen Laury's nails. Laury's nails have been splitting where the new growth is coming in. It is like looking at the rings on a tree - you can see in her nails when she received her chemo. This line is now growing out and where the new meets the old nail they can split. Laury found a product that is made just for this problem and she says it looks like it is working. Laury also bought some makeup at Whole Foods, tinted moisturizer and blush. Laury wants to start fresh with her makeup and wants to make sure the stuff she puts on her face is good and healthy. It is funny Magen and Heather, the woman at Whole Foods, both said that Laury didn't need any makeup. Since they both sell makeup it must be true!

Later on Saturday, Laury and I went to Berland's House of Tools and I bought my new table saw. It was hard for me to pull the trigger on this sale. The saw is very expensive and I just kept thinking I should use Mom's money for something else. But, on Saturday I heard my mom say, "Just buy the damn saw, I want you to have it." I think it is a fitting way to use the money from her life insurance - a tool my Dad would have appreciated, too, and Mom would be happy knowing that this saw is very safe. I pick the saw up on Tuesday. I am not sure how I am going to get the boxes out of Doug's truck when I get home - the saw weighs 600lbs.

Today, John, Laury's co-teacher, stopped by to pick my old saw. It was great to give the saw to John whom I know will use it and enjoy it and his kids will also reap the benefits. Today is also Laury's Dad's birthday. He turns 88. Laury just kept saying, "88 wow." It was nice to go over to their house and sing happy birthday. Laury and I both have a new appreciation for birthdays. May he have many more.

All our Love.

Tuesday, 10/21/2014 – Adjustments

"I have often wondered whether especially those days when we are forced to remain idle are not precisely the days spent in the most profound activity. Whether our actions themselves, even if they do not take place until later, are nothing more than the last

reverberations of a vast movement that occurs within us during idle days." - Rainer Maria Rilke, Letters On Life: New Prose Translations

The last couple of days Laury felt tired. She has had some nausea since Saturday. We both thought Laury probably overdid it over the weekend and needs blood. We had her blood checked this morning and her hemoglobin is 8.0 so it is not her blood. But, her blood pressure was 90/60 which would explain the feeling of being tired. Laury asked Jessica, our nurse, this morning to check with Paula at U of C to see if maybe we need to reduce Laury's blood pressure medicine. Laury started taking blood pressure medicine a few years ago. Laury's doctor thought that the high blood pressure was more situational with all that she was going through. While in the hospital, the doctors upped Laury's current blood pressure medication and put her on another one. Before she left the hospital they took Laury off the second medication. We now are thinking that perhaps Laury needs the remaining medicine reduced back to its pre-transplant level.

We should find out more today. Laury also has been itching since she was in the hospital. The itching has been up and down but it never went completely away. However, Laury told me yesterday that the itching is gone. Laury and I were pretty sure the Cellcept had been causing the itching but, now that she if off it we are sure. This is great to not have Laury itching, especially at night. I recently told a friend that with Laury constantly itching it was like sleeping with a chipmunk - she was always moving around.

We keep moving forward, making small adjustments as we go.

All our Love.

Wednesday, 10/22/2014 – Friends

"One's life has value so long as one attributes value to the life of others, by means of love, friendship, and compassion" - Simone de Beauvoir

Yesterday Laury was feeling better. She still feels a little light headed at times but she has her energy back. Paula, our nurse, has Laury taking about half the blood pressure medicine she was taking. We will have to wait and see if this helps. Laury and her friends, Robin and Vicky, went to the Morton Arboretum yesterday to walk around and to just be together outside. They brought a wheelchair for Robin but she walked quite a bit on her own. Laury said the colors were beautiful and it was just good to be with her friends and enjoy their connections.

Laury related a story to me this morning. She and Vicky and Robin were sitting on a bench near the main building of the arboretum talking. A friend of Laury's came walking by and Laury called to her. She stopped and talked with Laury for a few minutes. Laury was relating Robin's story to this friend, how Robin was going through much of the same things that Laury had just gone through. The friend after hearing the story said to Laury, "What a gift to have you there for Robin." Laury turned to Robin and Robin said, "I have always looked at it that way." Laury said she cried, "I have never looked at it that way," she said to me.

Later when Laury got home, she and I went to pick up my new table saw. My neighbor, Doug, graciously loaned me his truck to bring the saw home. The guy at the tool store used a fork lift to get the biggest box into the truck. There were about ten boxes all together and the big one weighs about four hundred pounds. We got home and I started unloading all the boxes and dragged the big box to the back of the truck. I was not sure how I was going to get it out of the truck and on to the ground. Laury said to me, "Doug will probably have it all figured out by time he gets home." Doug is an engineer and the type of friend who comes over to help me unload the truck even before he changes his clothes. Doug and I found in Doug's garage a couple of 2X4's screwed together that were perfect for ramps. After some heaving and lifting we safely got the box on the floor of the garage. My weekend project is to assemble the saw and make a first cut.

Friends are gifts. Whether we are to others, like Laury for Robin, or like Doug for me, we can't live without our friends. All of you.

All our Love.

Friday, 10/24/2014 – Community

"The truth is a community is as big or as small as your heart lets it be." - Genevieve Dewey, The Good Life

Yesterday was a clinic day. Laury and I left the house around two, as usual, and got home a little after seven. Laury received another breathing treatment to prevent respiratory tract infections. We also had Laury's blood checked and her hemoglobin was down a little from Tuesday to 7.4, but not low enough for her to need a transfusion today. Laury's white counts continue to increase and her platelets were above fifty thousand. Having platelets above fifty thousand means Laury is out of the danger range for bleeding. Laury can now begin to do inversions in yoga, like downward facing dog, without worrying about having her ears, eyes or nose bleeding. This is good news, especially for her caregiver, since I would have had to clean up the blood.

Yesterday, before we left for clinic, Susan, our friend from yoga stopped by. Laury was excited to see her. Even though it was a short visit Laury said it was special and it made her feel good. Laury misses everyone at our yoga community. On Sunday Laury and I were at Eddie Bauer exchanging a coat and we ran into Mary, another friend from yoga. Laury started to cry when she saw her. Laury told me afterward that her reaction surprised Mary. Laury hadn't realized how much seeing her friends means to her.

Yesterday, while walking through the infusion center at U of C to see Robin, I saw and said hi to many nurses and receptionists. It was good to see them. They are part of our community too.

Laury continues to slowly improve every day. She feels good and is happy to be giving back to the community again.

All our Love.

Sunday, 10/26/2014 – Inspector Lewis

"And the moral of the story is that you don't remember what happened. What you remember becomes what happened." - John Green

In 1996, while doing a major addition to our house, we experienced the Great Flood. After twenty three inches of rain in twenty four hours the floor drains in our basement spewed raw sewage and flooded the entire space with a foot of the smelly and disgusting stuff. For years after, every time it rained hard I would smell sewer and go check the basement to make sure everything was OK. It took me a long time to love thunderstorms again and to be able to sleep through them.

After Laury received her new stem cells in the hospital she had trouble sleeping. At night (more like early evening) she would take several sleep aids to fall asleep. After Laury fell asleep, I would retire to my couch/bed and watch something on the Kindle. I discovered a PBS Mystery series call Inspector Lewis. Since there were several seasons available, I watched a new episode every night. It was good for my brain to have something to focus on instead of the events of the day. I would try to figure out who the murderer was and I would enjoy the scenery (The show is set in Oxford shire).

When we got home there was one episode of the series I had not seen. I wanted to watch the show but it felt weird to be watching at home. I finally decided to watch the show one night after Laury went to bed. I sat in the chair with headphones on and instead of the Kindle, I watched on the big screen TV. Since then, the new season has come out and Laury and I have watched two new episodes. We watched one last night. After the show I admitted to Laury that it still feels weird to watch the show. Laury asked me, "Good weird or strange weird?" I said, "Strange weird." The show took me away in the hospital but now it takes me back. The memories are not necessarily bad but they are not all good either. I will admit that watching the show last night did not feel as weird as the previous two times did.

Yesterday at lunch in a small cafe in Geneva, Laury told me that at one point last week she thought to herself, "I think I feel better now than I did this time last year." Laury's greatest fear of the transplant was that it would leave her in a weaken state, something less than she was before.

We both are healing. The experience of the transplant will not soon leave us but we progress and create new experiences. I can't wait for the next episode of Inspector Lewis.

All our Love.

Wednesday, 10/29/2014 - Kindness of strangers

"We feel the love of strangers every day in the things they do that affect us without our knowledge." - Cassia Leo, Bring Me Home

When we had Laury's blood checked on Monday, her hemoglobin was down to 6.3. So yesterday Laury and I spent the afternoon at the infusion center where Laury received two units of blood. Our nurse, Barb, joked when seeing us that we should have chairs with our names on them, we are there so often. Being at the infusion center again and Barb's comment got Laury and me thinking about how much we depend on the kindness of strangers for Laury's healing. We have gotten to know the doctors, nurses, technicians, and even receptionists, so Laury and I don't really consider them strangers anymore. But, there are many other people whom we come in contact with that make this journey easier, who we really have no idea who they are.

I did a rough calculation, and Laury has received over 40 units of blood since her transplant. Each one of these units was donated by a stranger- someone we will never meet. If it hadn't been for this stranger's generosity, Laury wouldn't be here. For years, our friend Joan has organized blood drives at our church. We sometimes would tease Joan and say she was more interested in our blood then us. But now I understand the importance of what Joan and others like her are doing.

So Laury and I want to put out a long overdue heart felt thank you to Joan, and others like Joan, who organize blood drives. We also want to especially thank those who have given blood. Forty of you have saved Laury's life. Thank you and bless you all.

All our Love.

Thursday, 10/30/2014 – Socially full

"Time doesn't take away from friendship, nor does separation."
- Tennessee Williams, Memoirs

I have written before that one of the best things that has come out of this journey is Laury's reconnection with her friends. Yesterday, Michelle, a friend of Laury's from Junior High back in Ohio, came to visit. Michelle was in Chicago for a short visit and took time to come out to Naperville to see Laury. The last time the two had seen each other was about twenty five years ago. Laury said, as with other re-connections, "We picked up like we had never been apart." Michelle stayed for a few hours and met Lyndsay, who was fifteen months old last time they met. Later after I had left for yoga, Michelle left and Kelly came over. Laury, Lyndsay and Kelly rearranged the living room furniture, another sign Laury is feeling better. After Kelly and Lyndsay left, Laury called our friend Joan back. Joan had called to invite Laury to a Taize service at our church. Laury and Joan talked for several minutes and caught up on each other's progress.

Laury came up to me in the newly-rearranged living room after she was off her call and said, "It was a great day. I felt good. I am full of blood and socially full."

All our Love.

Friday, 10/31/2014 – Imagination

"your brain is wider than the sky" - Emily Dickinson

Yesterday Laury and I went to the clinic at the U of C. These visits with Dr. Odenike have become a little routine, checking medications, blood levels, etc. However, we always learn something. As Laury often says, "Dr. Odenike gives us words to what is happening." Yesterday was no different. We are still waiting for Laury's new red blood cells to arrive. Dr. Odenike described to us a possible treatment to suppress the old antibodies that are attacking the new red blood cells. Dr. Odenike said she was not ready to have Laury go through the treatment; there are still too many risks. The treatment would further reduce Laury's ability to fight infections and might also harm the new bone marrow graft. Dr. Odenike believes that patience is still the right course of action.

Pat, Laury's therapist, has helped Laury visualize what is going on in her body to help focus Laury's healing energies. Laury always asks the doctors what she should visualize her body doing to heal. Yesterday, while talking with Dr. Odenike about this battle going on inside Laury between her old antibodies and her new blood, I said to Dr. Odenike, "It seems like there are two armies fighting. The old antibodies have a bigger army right now but they do not have any replacements. The new antibodies are outnumbered right now but they are building reinforcements every day. Sooner or later, the new will win." Dr. Odenike said that this was a very good visualization. I asked Dr. Odenike if we will know the new has won when Laury's blood type changes, and Dr. Odenike replied, "Yes, you can't be both B positive and A positive at the same time." While driving home Laury and I were talking and I said, "I can see how this is going to happen. We will be sitting in the infusion center and the nurse will be reading the information off the bag of blood as they always do, and she will say, "Patient is A positive, and the donor blood is O." At that point Laury and I will both go, "Wait, did you say Laury was A positive?" and when the nurse confirms this we will yell and scream,

"They won!"

We need to keep that image in our heads moving forward - it will happen.

All our Love.

CHAPTER TEN

November

Saturday, 11/1/2014 – Happy Halloween

"Love is that condition in which the happiness of another person is essential to your own." - Robert A. Heinlein, Stranger In A Strange Land

Yesterday was a cold and snowy Halloween.

I had forgotten to get Halloween candy last weekend when I went grocery shopping. I was busy at work this week and somehow couldn't find the time to go get the candy, so yesterday afternoon, Laury and Kelly went to Oswald's to pick up Laury's prescriptions and get some candy. Since I am the one who usually buys the candy, I should have told Laury how much to buy. Laury came home with four bags of candy, which I knew was not going to be enough. While in the parking lot of Oswald's, Laury spotted Michael, one of our yoga instructors. Laury asked Kelly to stop the car and Laury yelled to Michael. Kelly said to me, "It was like a scene from a love story movie. There is Laury running across the parking lot to meet Michael and Michael running to meet Laury, and they end in a hug." Laury said it was great to see Michael and to hear him say how good she looked and to encourage her to continue her yoga.

Later, the kids started coming to the door around five. Most of kids at that hour were small and accompanied by their parents. Laury loves handing out the candy and seeing all of the costumes. This year she couldn't get that close to the kids so she stayed in the big picture window and I handed out the candy. I told Laury, "This is an introvert's worst nightmare, having all these strangers come to our front door." We laughed. One small group of boys came to the door while their parents waited in the driveway. As one of the boys ran back to his mom, he yelled, "He was kind of nice." I yelled back, "Hey, I am really nice!"

We ran out of candy about seven and had to turn all the lights off to keep the kids from coming to the front door. We both felt bad.

Laury and Vicky went over to Robin's yesterday morning to celebrate Robin's birthday (it is today). Robin has a cold so this meant that Laury could not get too close. The original plan was for Laury to stay outside while Vicky delivered the birthday presents. The cold weather made this plan impractical and so Robin came up with an alternative idea. Laury and Vicky sat in Vicky's car and Robin sat in hers in their driveway and they talked and shared across the open car windows. When Laury left our house she told me that they wouldn't be too long, so after two hours I texted Laury to make sure everything was OK. Laury said they couldn't believe they spent two hours in the driveway in running cars talking. They had a blast. Love will find a way.

When Laury got home from Robin's there was a package of fresh homemade pumpkin bread from our friend across the street, Mary Anne. All of these things made for a very happy Halloween.

All our Love.

Monday, 11/3/2014 – Wisdom and courage

"Without courage, wisdom bears no fruit." - Baltasar Gracian

I did not have to give Laury a Neupogen shot last night. Dr. Odenike decided on Thursday that Laury no longer needed the shot to stimulate her white blood cells. The hope is that without the Neupogen, Laury's body will produce more red blood cells. We talked with Dr. Odenike about stopping the shot two weeks ago but she was not ready to have Laury stop. Dr. Odenike said, "Give me another week. I am never really sure you don't need it until we stop the shot and find out for sure."

Laury and I have talked, and sometimes laughed about the courage associated with these shots: whether it took more courage for me to give Laury the shot than for Laury to let me give her the shot. One of the things we didn't talk about was the courage that Dr. Odenike and the other doctors have in treating Laury. Laury's disease, like many others that are treated at the U of C, is very rare. There are no set rules on how to treat the disease and how things will go. I think Dr. Odenike was being very honest when she said to us two weeks ago she was a little nervous and not ready to stop the shots. All of the wisdom and learning that exists at the U of C still doesn't mean the doctors are sure of what to do. Dr. Odenike frequently says to us, "I will consult with my colleagues on this." I would be concerned if she pretended to know all the answers. It takes courage to say to us, "I am not sure."

Dr. Odenike like many of you have commented on how much courage it takes to go through this journey. However, I am glad that Dr. Odenike and others like her have the wisdom and the courage to treat patients like Laury.

All our Love.

Tuesday, 11/4/2014 – Side by side

"My love for you spans over the lines of my past, present, and future. You are what I love remembering, what I love experiencing, and what I love looking forward to." - Steve Maraboli, Unapologetically You: Reflections on Life And The Human Experience

We had Laury's blood checked this morning. This is the first blood test without Laury taking the Neupogen shot. Laury's white blood counts were good and her Platelets increased to eighty thousand. Laury's hemoglobin dropped from 8.3 to 7.3 but it is not as big a drop as last week. Laury and I don't know if this means the red are beginning to come in or it is just the timing of the blood tests. We will have to wait for the blood test on Thursday to see if it is a trend.

I asked Jessica, our nurse, this morning if she ever checks Laury's blood type results when they come back. We get the CBC results within ten minutes, so we usually wait for them. The type and cross match take longer and Jessica says she usually checks those results later in the day. I asked her if she would call us if Laury's blood type changes from B+ to A+. Jessica said she would and she expects that there will be a big party when it happens. I don't know about the big party, but there will be celebration.

Laury was excited and pleased with her blood results today. When we got outside the cancer center she yelled, "Yes!" Laury said she feels good and she was positive that her numbers were good. I trust that Laury knows her body very well. Laury admitted to me that when I left for yoga last night she was really dizzy. Laury didn't want to tell me because she wanted me to go to yoga. Laury sat very still the entire time I was gone, and when I came home she said she got up to greet me and she was not dizzy. The dizziness is most likely caused by her blood pressure medicine. The doctors have cut it in half, but both Laury and I feel she no longer needs the medication.

Today at lunch time Laury and I went for a walk. The wind was cold and Laury's face and ears got cold, so we cut the walk short. Laury said while we were eating lunch that she could still feel the cold in her face. I said it was probably because her skin is so new, like a baby's. Laury looked at me kind of funny and said, "Oh yeah."

Every day we are still on this journey together. Laury and I are never sure what the day will bring: good blood numbers, red cheeks from the cold, time together to enjoy lunch. I do know that I love Laury and no matter where this journey takes us, I will be at her side.

All our Love.

Thursday, 11/6/2014 – Moments

"Love the moment for its simplicity, it may give or take nothing from you, but in the blinking of an eye it will have changed so many things forever." - Steven Redhead, The Solution

We head down to the U of C today for clinic. Watching Laury the past two days, I am pretty sure she is going to need blood. So is she.

Lately, Laury and I have reflected on the past year. It is hard not to, so much has happened. To say it was a big year is an understatement. Laury and I both know that we are not going to live in the past, and are happy for the future.

This morning Laury and I sat down with the calendar and tried to figure out when I can take some of my unused vacation days before the end of the year. We both chuckled that we have to plan around when Laury is likely to need blood. So the days will be used up one at a time, rather than in clumps. We can't plan on going anywhere for more than a few days at a time.

The dreaming Laury and I are able to do now is what we both want from our future. So much of our planning for the last several years has revolved around if and when Laury was going to need the transplant. Now that the transplant is behind us we are thinking about things like retirement and where we want to live. We still don't have any big plans, but it is fun to start thinking about it.

Each day Laury and I have moments that remind us that things are moving forward. Some days it feels like the day after Christmas; all of the big buildup and planning for the event. Now it is past, what to do? I think this hit Laury harder than me. She prepared so much for the transplant that when we got home I don't think Laury was quite sure what to do next. However, lately I have noticed Laury becoming more engaged in the future- thinking about it, talking about it, enjoying the thought of it.

As much as the future is exciting now, we are still living in the moment, day to day not wanting to miss a thing. The other day Laury called me down to see the group of doves on our outdoor chairs resting after each had taken a bath. They all seemed so content and happy. Laury said, "The only thing that would ruin this moment is if the hawk showed up." We laughed, and agreed that would pretty much wreck the moment.

We are still able to smile at simple things and notice the beauty of everything and everyone around us. Hopefully, that will never change.

All our Love.

Friday, 11/7/2014 — Another gift

"A wonderful gift may not be wrapped as you expect." - Jonathan Lockwood Huie

Today I am writing from the infusion center in Naperville. Laury is receiving two units of blood. Her hemoglobin dropped from 7.6 on Tuesday to 7.3 yesterday. This is a small drop and we could have waited until next week for blood. Laury decided to get blood today so she could feel good over the weekend.

Last week Dr. Odenike ordered the same antibody test she ordered last month to see if the old antibodies attacking the new blood were going away. Yesterday we got the results. The antibody numbers did not change. We hoped that they would show signs of going down. Dr. Odenike still feels the best thing to do is wait. The white counts are holding, even without the Neupogen, and the platelets continue to climb. I feel we are approaching the critical mass point where the new antibodies are going to take over.

Dr. Odenike agreed to take Laury off her blood pressure medication. This is a milestone for two reasons. One, Laury gets to stop another medication. Two, Laury started the medication when her blood pressure went up after her diagnosis. Laury's blood pressure used to get really high when we would go to the clinic. We called it "white coat syndrome". Laury would check her blood pressure at home and it would be normal, but as soon as her blood pressure was taken by a nurse or doctor it would be high. Laury went to our family doctor to talk about the possible course of action. Our family doctor felt the blood pressure was due to the anxiety and stress of the disease. He prescribed a beta-blocker that worked really well. When Laury went into the hospital for the transplant she needed to increase the medication and the doctors put her on another medication to counteract one of the other medications that raise blood pressure. Once the other medication was stopped, Laury was taken off the second blood pressure medication, but she has remained on the beta blocker.

Laury's blood pressure has been dropping over the last few weeks and she has had some dizziness when lying down. Laury and I both felt she no longer needed the medication, and yesterday Dr. Odenike agreed. The fact that Laury doesn't need the medication anymore means her stress and anxiety about the transplant are gone. A wonderful gift and another sign of progress.

All our Love.

Sunday, 11/9/2014 – Birthday celebration

"I love you without knowing how, or when, or from where. I love you simply, without problems or pride: I love you in this way because I do not know any other way of loving but this, in which there is no I or you, so intimate that your hand upon my chest is my hand, so intimate that when I fall asleep your eyes close." - Pablo Neruda, 100 Love Sonnets

Today is Laury's birthday. I am filled with love and gratitude that she is here with me this year. It is hard not to think back on Laury's last birthday. As Laury says, she was in denial that her body was changing. Laury and I saw doctor Dr. Baron the same week as her birthday last year and he confirmed that her spleen had started to grow. That visit was really the official beginning of our journey to transplant. Dr. Baron asked to see Laury after the holidays, but after a few weeks, Laury called him to move up the appointment because she wasn't feeling good, and we both felt we needed to see him sooner.

Laury had been working with her therapist, Pat, to wrap her head around the disease and to try to hold it off for as long as she could. By her birthday, there was no doubt that the disease was changing and moving fast.

Those worries are not here this year. Last night, Vicky and Bob asked us if we wanted to meet them for a drink at the Irish pub near our house. Initially Laury said no, thinking I would be tired and "in for the evening". But I wanted to go and celebrate Laury's birthday with our friends. We all realized that Laury couldn't go into the pub with all of the people, so we asked if we could sit outside. The server gladly brought us drinks and menus. We sat out in the forty degree night and drank and had our dinner. It wasn't our longest dinner together, but my beer sure stayed cold. Laury and I walked home happy that we had gone and grateful for friends willing to brave the cold for us.

Today Laury's parents came over to wish Laury well and drop off her gifts. We hadn't realized that the Naperville Marathon was going through our neighborhood this year. Laury's dad called to say our street was closed and to get directions on how to get here a different way. I walked up to the policeman at the corner to asked how to direct Laury's parents and the officer told me he was from Lisle and had no idea what streets were closed. Laury's parents finally were able to find their way here after about thirty minutes of driving around. They were going to get here no matter what. We were all glad they made it.

Keri and Lyndsay, our daughters, both are not feeling well, so Laury didn't Skype with Keri and Lyndsay didn't stop by. Laury was able to talk to them for a short while. It was sad for Laury not to be able to talk with them longer but she was grateful that they are taking care of themselves and hopefully will be feeling better soon.

Tonight I have planned a simple meal. Laury and I quietly celebrate her birthday and her new health and I will be celebrating her.

All our Love.

Monday, 11/10/2014 – Nature walk

"Those who contemplate the beauty of the earth find reserves of strength that will endure as long as life lasts. There is something infinitely healing in the repeated refrains of nature -- the assurance that dawn comes after night, and spring after winter." - Rachel Carson, Silent Spring

Yesterday I took the day off to relax and enjoy some time with Laury. We saw our friend Bill on Saturday and he told us about the nature trails he walks during the week. One trail, in particular, sounded fun. You can see where the Herons nest in the trees. Laury and I decided to go for a long walk to see the nests. It was a beautiful day here, about 55 degrees, but the wind was cool. Laury and I walked for about two hours; an hour and a half out and thirty minutes back. We went really slowly on the way out to take in everything and to be quiet in hopes of seeing some wildlife.

Laury and I couldn't find the "off" trail that takes you closer to the nests, but we could see them from a distance. The nests are huge and way up at the top of the tree. There are several nests together like a small village. We can't wait to see the nests when they are full of Herons.

Laury said that being out in nature felt so healing. She said she felt happy, and strong and loved my stories of being out in the woods when I was young. It was nice not to have anything else on the schedule for the day so we could take as long as we wanted. Lately, especially for me, there is always something to do next. It makes it hard to stay focused on what we are doing here and now. The walk yesterday was here and now time, one step after another, with nothing else to think about but the next turn.

Laury and I returned home after our walk and ate some lunch and took a nap. Later we did a little yard work. The day went by fast but each moment felt long enough.

All our Love.

Wednesday, 11/12/2014 – A mistake

"Yesterday, I got lost.

You did too.

So what?

People get lost all the time.

It's just a matter of finding yourself, and treasuring that." - Maddie Hample

We had Laury's blood checked yesterday morning. Laury's white blood counts were down a little and her platelets had dropped, as well. Laury's hemoglobin was good at 8.5. I was a little disappointed with the white and platelet numbers. I guess I let that disappointment show. Laury asked me as we were leaving the infusion center, "So what do you think of the numbers? What don't you like about them?" I wanted the numbers to keep increasing and for Laury's progress to be linear. The white and platelet numbers, even though they were down, are still within the same range as before. We forget that a blood test is just a snap shot. The difference between sixty thousand and eighty thousand platelets can be the difference between the morning and the afternoon and who is looking at the slide.

The most frustrating thing about Laury's healing is just when you think you have it figured out, it throws you a curve. What do these numbers mean? Probably nothing. We will have them checked again tomorrow and the numbers will most likely be back where they were before. Laury still feels great, looks great and I have no reason to believe that she isn't continuing to heal and making progress. So if anything, yesterday showed a lack in my progress. I am still expecting to understand fully what is going on and wanting things to go a certain way. I guess I forgot what a learning experience this journey has been and continues to be.

All our Love.

Friday, 11/14/2014 – Questions

"The job is to ask questions — it always was — and to ask them as inexorably as I can. And to face the absence of precise answers with a certain humility." - Arthur Miller

Yesterday we went to clinic at the U of C. Laury had her blood checked and her numbers were down a little more from Tuesday. I hoped that the numbers would be stable or have come back up. Laury's white numbers are down to the point where I had to give her a Neupogen shot last night to stimulate some more white cell growth. Laury's platelets after several weeks of increasing dropped. It is hard not to be discouraged by the blood numbers. Dr. Odenike said to us, "It can be so nerve wracking. You watch the numbers and keep hoping for improvement. This is only one blood test. Let's wait until next week to see what happens." Dr. Odenike pointed out that the trend is still upward and Laury still feels good and looks good.

I asked Dr. Odenike what could cause the numbers to drop. She replied that it could be many different things, such as, something Laury ate. Certain chemicals in foods can lower your blood counts. It could be a virus, or nothing. Dr. Odenike said that if a virus shows up in the blood work (she will have the results today) then they will start Laury on medication. Dr. Odenike said she would call us if anything shows up. She didn't think it was a virus because Laury is not showing any other signs of a virus like a fever or nausea. Laury is scheduled for another bone marrow aspiration in early December. If the numbers keep dropping Dr. Odenike said they will either pull the procedure up or do a blood test to try to see what is going on with the marrow.

I asked Dr. Odenike if it was possible that the graft was failing. I hated asking the question because I knew any discussion of this would scare Laury. Dr. Odenike said it is highly unlikely, as most graft failures happen within the first 100 days. Dr. Odenike doesn't think the graft is in danger and again told us we need to wait another week and not to get too concerned.

I have to be honest Laury and I are disappointed and a little concerned with the numbers. We both feel that the numbers will come back up and we are still on the right path. However, it is hard when it seems like all you can do is wait and see. Laury and I have always trusted the doctors and how Laury feels. We need to keep that trust moving forward this week.

All our Love.

Sunday, 11/16/2014 – Act of kindness

"Never underestimate the power of kindness. It is very contagious. A person whose heart is saddened by the troubles of this world, the loss of a friend or family member, a hard day's work, or the struggle of provision can experience joy through a simple act of kindness. - **Amaka Imani Nkosazana**

Laury has a small statue of a kneeling woman with her arms open sitting on a table that she can see while sitting at the computer. This statue was loaned to her by her therapist Pat and it is called "Adsume" and it represents being open to receiving. Laury says that she has had to learn to receive the gifts and love of others on this journey. I have had to learn to receive as well.

Yesterday Laury and I went to the city to get my hair cut. Magen was her usual funny, joyful self that always lifts our hearts with her kindness and caring. We stopped on our way home at Laury's parents to pick up some cookies that Laury's mom had baked. The visit was brief because I needed to get home to finally take care of the leaves in the back yard. We have a lot of trees in our back yard and every year it takes me almost an entire day to blow, rake, and gather all of the leaves so the city can pick them up. The forecast had been saying for days that we were going to get snow so I needed to get the leaves picked up yesterday.

When Laury and I arrived home, I noticed a big pile of leaves on our patio and I heard a leaf blower going in our back yard. I thought Laury had hired someone to come take care of the leaves to help me. When I walked into the back yard, I saw our neighbor Pete working away. He stopped his blower and we had an opportunity to talk. Pete said he noticed that I hadn't picked up the leaves and he thought that I must be busy with something else or I would have done it already. Pete said he was home alone with nothing to do so he thought he would help me out and take care of our leaves. Laury and I were speechless with gratitude. Pete asked if I minded if he continued to help me. I told him he did not have to continue but I was very grateful when he said he would.

The two of us working together cleaned up the front and back yard of leaves in less than two hours. Every time I saw Pete wheel a can of leaves to the front yard I thanked and blessed him. When we were done, I came in so amazed and energized by his act of kindness that I immediately started thinking of what I could do to repay him. Then I saw the statue and I was reminded that sometimes the best way to repay kindness is to just receive it with no strings attached and to say thank you.

So again, Pete, thank you - you have no idea how much your help meant to me yesterday. Bless you.

All our Love.

Monday, 11/17/2014 – Lilly and Autumn

"Until one has loved an animal, a part of one's soul remains unawakened." -Anatole France

Every morning since we returned home from the hospital, I have gone upstairs and have been greeted by Lilly, our cat, crying at the door. She was happy to see me and would always run to the food dishes. Maybe Lilly was happier to be fed. We have two cats, Lilly and Autumn. Lilly is the social one. If you have been to our house you have most likely met Lilly; she likes to meet everyone. Autumn is the older of the two and she is very shy.

One of the hardest things of this journey is keeping the cats upstairs away from Laury. The cats didn't understand why all of sudden there was a door placed between them and us and the rest of the house.

Lilly would sit with her nose against the glass and cry at anyone who would walk by the stairs. Every week when we saw Dr. Odenike we would ask her when we could let the cats out. Last Thursday Dr. Odenike finally agreed. Yesterday morning I went upstairs and opened the door and told Lilly and Autumn they were free. Lilly immediately ran downstairs and began checking out every room and crying as she went as if to say, "Hello dining room, I have missed you!" Autumn took her time, not sure what to make of her new found freedom, but eventually she too joined us.

Yesterday afternoon Laury and I sat by the fire place, with Lilly in her lap and Autumn in mine. Everything was right in the universe.

All our Love.

Tuesday, 11/18/2014 – Pauses

"A pause; it endured horribly." - F. Scott Fitzgerald, The Great Gatsby

The last few days have been filled with kindness, reunion, and waiting. Laury's blood numbers last week gave us pause. We both were concerned what the numbers would be when they were checked today. Laury and I felt off balance. I think we have become a little too sure of the progress, maybe taking it for granted. Laury and I knew, and now we know it again, we have to be able to deal with the unexpected on this journey. The journey didn't end last week, it just paused. It left us a bit stranded, not completely sure what to do. I guess there is no such thing as a "seasoned" traveler on this journey. Every day we start off anew.

Laury and I just got back from the infusion center and Laury's numbers are back up to where they were two weeks ago. Laury's white counts are above two and her platelets are at eighty thousand. Laury's hemoglobin is 6.3, so she will be getting two units of blood tomorrow. Laury cried when the nurse read us the results.

We both deep down had known that last week was a pause, a step backward, that would only last a short time. But it still was difficult and nerve wracking, not knowing for sure.

Maybe last week was to remind Laury and me that still so much of this journey is out of our control. We can't get to the point where we know what is going to happen. We can have a good idea of how things are going and the overall direction, but not completely. Healing is never a straight line. But, even in the pauses, there is healing.

Laury and I learned that we still can face these pauses together and with all of your help and support we move through them.

All our Love.

Thursday, 11/20/2014 – Same as before

"Accept the things to which fate binds you, and love the people with whom fate brings you together, but do so with all your heart." - Marcus Aurelius, Meditations

Several years ago, at Laury's grandfather's funeral, the minister told a story about when he visited Laury's grandfather in the hospital. The minister had come to visit after Laury's grandfather had cancer surgery. The minister said they talked about many things, and Laury's grandfather even walked him to his car when he left. The minister said it wasn't until he was driving away that he realized that he never had the chance to ask Laury's grandfather how he was doing. The talk had all been about how the minister was doing.

Yesterday we went to the infusion center here in Naperville. Laury received two units of blood. For us it was an ordinary day: get to the infusion center at eight and leave around one. I watched Laury interact with the nurses and technicians as they came into the room to check on her. We have been there so many times, we know everyone by name and Laury easily picks up where she left off in her talks. We hear about weddings, kids, family, vacations and holidays. I wonder if everyone that comes into these rooms hears these stories, or does Laury bring them out. I have been amazed at how Laury can make connections with anyone. It must have been like that with her grandfather in being truly concerned about others.

Laury has had a few moments over the last week were the sight of the Hiccman line, the blood tests, the sitting and waiting has been enough. She cries, "It has been so long, too long." But Laury doesn't stay there. She moves on and tries to makes it a good day not only for herself but for others around her, too. We have read that to getting through this journey means trying to make things as normal as possible, keeping your life as much like it was, as possible. Laury and I now know that this is not possible if you look at the things that you can no longer do. But, it is possible if you approach each day the same way you always have, with love and compassion.

All our Love.

Friday, 11/21/2014 – Spirit

"I admire some people for their brilliance and I respect others for their strength. But I am indebted to those who can rekindle my spirit." - Steve Goodier

Yesterday Laury and I went to clinic at the U of C. It turned into a very long visit, and we got home around eight. Laury felt strong all day and cleaned out her closet before we left. It is amazing to see Laury do so much and have so much energy even though her hemoglobin is 8.5. I shake my head at what she will be like when she reaches a normal hemoglobin level.

One of the reasons the visit yesterday went so long is that Laury needed a Pentamidine treatment. These treatments are given every four weeks to help prevent upper respiratory tract infections. Laury was due for her treatment yesterday, but Dr. Odenike had forgotten to order it ahead of our visit, so we had to wait for the respiratory therapist to come up after our visit with Dr. Odenike. The therapist was an older Indian woman and she recognized Laury. She was the same therapist Laury had two months ago. Laury and I smiled at remembering this woman had come into our room last time and asked me if Laury was my mother, and Laury hearing this said to her with a smile, "You're fired!"

I left the room and went to sit in the waiting area for Laury to complete her treatment. After about twenty minutes Laury came out with the therapist and said to me, "This is a beautiful woman". The therapist replied, "Look at that, a beautiful woman calling me a beautiful woman." Laury and the therapist exchanged hugs and well wishes and the therapist went to the elevators.

Laury began to tell me through tears about her interaction with the therapist after I left the room. Laury said the therapist had seen the order come down for her treatment and she recognized Laury's name and said, "I love her, I will stay late and do the treatment." Laury wasn't sure she had heard her correctly so after her treatment she asked the therapist, "Did you say you loved me?" The woman said, "Yes". She went on to say that the last time she had sensed Laury's spirit and compassion, but this time she said that it was there for everyone to see. The therapist went on to tell Laury about how she came to this country with her husband who is a professor at U of C. She said they arrived in the country with one suitcase, and have been grateful ever since. As Laury recounted the story to me she looked at me with tears in her eyes and said, "Do you believe this? I can't ask for these people to be placed in my life."

Laury and I then went to the hospital to visit Robin. Robin is on the 10th floor in the same ward Laury was in. We walked in and were greeted by Megan, who recognized Laury, and came running around the desk to give her a hug. We also visited with some of the other nurses who had worked with Laury. There were a lot of tears and laughter. The nurses were all glad to see Laury. We spent a few minutes with Robin. Laury gave her a fake plant to brighten her room and some bracelets she had made for her. We didn't stay long, as we were hungry and Robin was tired.

There have been many visits to the U of C that have been this long or longer. Most have taken so much energy that we could barely make it home. But, yesterday's visit gave us more energy than we came in with.

All our Love.

Sunday, 11/23/2014 – Tears

"Tears are the words that the heart could not express, silent truths the eyes do confess." - Aisha Mirza

Many of the medications that Laury takes have side effects. Most of these side effects have been minimal, and Laury has been able to deal with them. One side effect that has given Laury the most difficulty is she has not been able to cry. I should say she hasn't been able to cry like she used to, at joy and at pain. Lately this side effect seems to be going away. Laury has been shedding tears a lot lately - mostly tears of joy. Laury says it is good to feel the tears to be able to have them flow again, even if she is not always sure why they are there.

On Friday, Laury and Kelly went to Czar's to get a pedicure and manicure. Dr. Odenike approved Laury going as long as the technician was careful. Laury came home afterwards feeling so good. She said the people at Czar treated her so special that she wanted me to tell you all about it. Her nails are at the stage where they are thin and splitting because of the chemo, and as Laury says, they just don't look good. Her nails now look great.

While she was at Czar, Laury ran into Debbie, one of the owners. Laury said it was good to see her and they both cried and hugged. Laury asked me, "Why do people cry when they see me?" I said it was probably because they were so happy to see her.

I am not sure we ever really know why we cry sometimes. There have been times on this journey when it would have been great to cry, to get out the anger and frustration, or the happiness. But the tears didn't come. Other times Laury or I would find ourselves crying for no good reason. I don't usually like to see Laury cry, especially if it is because of something I did. But lately to see her tears has been uplifting. I know Laury is getting back to more of herself. Laury without tears is not a complete Laury.

All our Love.

Wednesday, 11/26/2014 – Thankful

"Happy, even in anguish, is he to whom God has given a soul worthy of love and grief! He who has not seen the things of this world, and the heart of men in this double light, has seen nothing, and knows nothing of the truth." - **Victor Hugo, Les Miserables**

Monday Laury and I went to the infusion center to have Laury's blood checked. Laury's white counts were way up and her platelets were holding steady. Laury's hemoglobin was down to 7.3 but not as big a drop as we had expected. Because of the holiday, if Laury didn't get a transfusion Tuesday or Wednesday the next time she could get one would be next Tuesday. We both felt that was too long to go so Laury received a unit of blood yesterday.

Yesterday we had a new nurse, Lauren. Laury and I met Lauren before but she has never been the nurse taking care of Laury. Lauren told us she was very excited to meet and take care of Laury. Lauren told us that she had worked six years at Northwestern Hospital in their transplant ward. She said whenever they get a patient at the infusion center that is a transplant patient, she wants to work with them. Lauren kept telling Laury how amazing she looked. She couldn't believe how good Laury looked and felt for having "just" gone through a transplant. It was nice to get another perspective on the timing of this journey- that six months is "just" in terms of a transplant. As we left the infusion center, we thanked Lauren for her good care and she thanked us for our time with her. I hope I never get used to having a caregiver thank us.

After the transfusion, we came home and changed into warmer clothes and walked downtown to meet Laury's brother, Bobby, his wife Jodi, and their daughter, Caitlyn who are in town for Thanksgiving. On our way to meet them, Laury and I tried to think of place we could eat. Laury still needs to avoid crowds and eating with a mask on is not possible. We noticed that the little Thai restaurant was not full, so we recommended it for lunch. Jodi had never eaten Thai food so she was game to try it. We sat around a table in a mostly empty restaurant and had a good lunch. After lunch, Bobby, Jodi and Caitlyn wanted to do some more shopping. Laury and I walked back home.

A little while later Bobby, Jodie and Caitlyn came over to our house to spend some more time with us. It was fun to sit and talk and laugh, and we probably kept them a little too long, since Laury's parents were waiting for them to come back for dinner.

The last few days have been filled with mixed emotions for Laury and me. We have so much to be thankful for this year. We would love to celebrate Thanksgiving with Laury's parents and her brother's family. We usually have Thanksgiving at our house and Laury and I both felt we were not up for hosting it this year. So we are staying home and having Lyndsay, Rich and Kelly for a bowl of my mothers' potato chowder. I can't help thinking about my sisters and their families in Michigan, celebrating this year without my Mom. I would love to be up there with them. I think about all of you and how much you have given Laury and me this year, and how thankful we are to all of you.

We are also thankful for all of the care we have received this year, given by such loving people- some of whom we have met and some we will never meet.

We truly wish all of you a happy Thanksgiving.

All our Love.

Friday, 11/28/2014 – A great Thanksgiving

"He mentioned a dear friend Morrie had, Maurie Stein, who had first sent Morrie's aphorisms to the Boston Globe. They had been together at Brandeis since the early sixties. Now Stein was going deaf. Koppel imagined the two men together one day, one unable to speak, the other unable to hear. What would that be like?

"We will hold hands," Morrie said. "And there'll be a lot of love passing between us. Ted, we've had thirty-five years of friendship. You don't need speech or hearing to feel that." - Mitch Albom, Tuesdays with Morrie

Yesterday was not a conventional Thanksgiving Day for Laury and me. Instead of the turkey and a large table full of people, we had Lyndsay and our friends Kelly and Rich. We served bowls of my mother's potato chowder and drank wine with Kelly's homemade Pecan pie and the French Silk pie Rich always brings.

Rich has been part of our Thanksgiving for over thirty years. Rich and I met while I was working at the local tennis club and finishing college and Laury and I were dating. When Laury and I were first married we tried to go to our families for the holidays. The first year we went to Laury's family for Thanksgiving and my family for Christmas. The next year Laury and I reversed it. The second year while at my parents' house I called Rich on Thanksgiving to see how he was doing. Rich's family is on the east coast in Boston and New York. Rich would go home for Christmas but was alone on Thanksgiving. After talking to Rich that year, and finding out he was alone, I said to him, "That will never happen again. Next year you are spending Thanksgiving with us." I told Laury about my conversation with Rich and she said, "He can't be alone. Next year he will spend it with us." I told her that I had already extended the invitation to Rich.

And so it began. Every year since then, with a few exceptions, Rich has been with us on Thanksgiving. It started with just the three of us and grew to four, then five, with the girls coming. Then as Laury's parents started joining us, it grew bigger, but Thanksgiving always starts with the call from Rich confirming he will be with us. On this year's call we told Rich that we wouldn't be having the big meal- just a small gathering with soup and he replied, "I don't care what you serve, I just want to spend the day with you guys."

The day started with me making some cinnamon French toast for Laury and me for breakfast. Kelly arrived around noon and she and Laury had a Mimosa - a tradition of Kelly's family at Thanksgiving. Lyndsay showed up next, and then later, Rich. Lyndsay had shrimp and mashed potatoes - she is a vegetarian, while the rest of us had the soup and homemade biscuits from Kelly's dad.

The meal was not the big event of the day. The time spent talking, remembering, laughing, and watching football made the day. It was a great Thanksgiving.

All our Love.

Sunday, 11/30/2014 – A gift from Mom

"That was the nature of presents. You kept them in the giver's stead. They were a small part of that person to keep." - Paul Magrs, Exchange

Friday morning Laury slept in until 11:15. If I needed any confirmation that having a quiet Thanksgiving was a good idea, it was that. Laury feels good but still doesn't have all of her energy back. Later on Friday we went over to Laury's parents to spend some more time with Laury's brother and his family before they went back to Dallas. When Laury and I got there, Laury's family were all eating lunch, and for a second we hoped they were having left overs and we could join them. Laury and I must admit that we missed the turkey leftovers most.

Yesterday, I worked in my shop finally completing the assembly of my new table saw. I had set a goal to complete the assembly this weekend. Most weekends I set very modest goals because I know that I never can get done everything that needs to get done.

The saw had been staring at me every time I opened the garage door. I think I had been avoiding finishing the job. I was talking with Linda, our yoga instructor, before my class on Wednesday and she asked me what I was doing to take care of myself. I said that I had been doing some more reading, yoga and projects, but I had not gotten into the shop. It was the first time I verbalized that I was having trouble working on the table saw. Linda said to me, "That makes sense. It is the finality of what it represents." I think I had been looking at the saw as representing Mom's death.

Yesterday, while I was waiting for the shop to heat up, I sat in the chair and stared at the table saw. I wanted to finish it but I had trouble starting. Once I began, it was hard work but it was also very freeing to finish. After about two hours, the saw was fully assembled. It was exciting to see it finally done. There are some final adjustments I need to make once I place the saw where I am going to use it, but I can use it now.

The saw no longer represents my Mom's death; it represents yet another gift she has given me. She has given me so many over my life that I am sure this will not be the last.

All our Love.

CHAPTER ELEVEN

December

Monday, 12/1/2014 – More progress

"Every now and then I sit and watch the sun rise to remind myself how it's done—peacefully, steadily, warmly, and in beautiful color." - Richelle E. Goodrich, Smile Anyway: Quotes, Verse, & Grumblings For Every Day Of The Year.

Sometimes Laury's progress is in something so small that I can overlook it. Yesterday, Laury asked me to help her get some Christmas decorations out of the closet under the stairs where she keeps all that stuff. We had talked about what we were going to do for Christmas decorations this year. Laury still can't have a real Christmas tree and any real greens in the house. Laury loves to decorate the house for Christmas. If you have ever been here for the holidays you will see the house is nothing short of a wonderland. Laury knew she was not going to do as much decorating this year as years past. Traditionally, Laury begins decorating on Thanksgiving this year it was the day after. Laury is trying to only use decorations that can be cleaned. This restriction left a problem of what to do with the banister. Every year it is covered with fake garland and lights. Yesterday Laury decided that she would take the fake garland out and wash it in the bathtub so she could do the banister. It was fun and reassuring to watch Laury get into "decorating" mode again. She gets lost in what she does and can spend hours quietly moving around and placing things several times until she gets them just right.

Today Laury and Kelly went to the Growing Place to get greens to decorate the planters outside. Vicky is going to do the work tomorrow because Laury still can't touch the live plants. Laury getting excited to decorate is progress; Laury decorating is real progress.

Today when I came down from working upstairs to make my lunch, Laury said to me, "I made a taco from the corn tortilla, cheese and the cold slaw you made yesterday. I could taste all the flavors! They said it would take six months before my tastes were finally back. They are back!" Another small sign of progress.

I am reminded that Laury's progress is measured sometimes in big things, but most of the time it is in the small things that give us the best indication of how things are going.

All our Love.

Wednesday, 12/3/2014 – Still waiting

"Wait, the most positive and infinite word ever made." - Sagar Gosavi

I am writing this post from the infusion center here in Naperville. Laury had her blood checked yesterday and everything was down again. Laury's white counts dropped and she is now neutropenic and we have to be more careful about infections. Her platelets were down a little and her hemoglobin was at 6.7. Laury is receiving two units of blood this morning.

Yesterday, after receiving the blood results, Laury and I left the infusion center feeling a little down again. We have seen these ups and downs, but each time we have Laury's blood checked we hope that this will be the one that signals the turning point. After we got home Allison came over to give Laury an Ayurvedic oil treatment. Laury said it was wonderful and very relaxing. In the afternoon, Vicky and Kelly came over to construct a Christmas arrangement in our outside container. Laury stayed inside while they worked. The arrangement is beautiful, and festive. Thank you Vicky and Kelly for bringing more holiday cheer to our home.

Laury continues to feel good. Yesterday we asked Jessica, our nurse, about the numbers going up and down. Laury asked her if she has ever seen this in other patients. Jessica replied that she has but, "You have a spirit about you that makes you feel good no matter what the numbers are." Jessica again reminded us on how well Laury is doing and that a lot of people (myself included) would not be happily walking around if our hemoglobin was at 6.7.

The waiting is tough. It has been a long time- almost six months since Laury received her stem cells- and yet, when we look back, it seems just like yesterday. There are things that we wouldn't have experienced if we hadn't been waiting.

All our Love.

Friday, 12/5/2014 – Pep talk

"My destination is no longer a place, rather a new way of seeing." - Marcel Proust

Laury and I went to clinic yesterday at the U of C. Our appointment was with Jean, our nurse practitioner, whom we haven't seen in a couple of months. While waiting for our appointment, Laury talked to me about her blood numbers. Laury said that she is tired of looking at the numbers; the excitement when they go up and the disappointment when they go down just add anxiety to her life right now. I said that Laury didn't need to look at the numbers. There are plenty of other people who are. But we both agreed that not looking doesn't solve the problem.

Seeing Jean proved to be just what Laury needed yesterday. Jean is always very positive, and yesterday even more so. She came into the room and immediately told Laury how good she looks. Jean asked Laury how things have been going and always counters anything negative with "Yes, but you are only six months out of a transplant." Laury has never been comforted by talks of how it could be worse. She is always about what she is feeling and experiencing. But sometimes I think we do need to be reminded of all the things that could have gone wrong and how really amazingly well Laury has done. Jean has a way of delivering this message that Laury can hear and take in. When we discussed that Laury's white counts were down a little more so I would have to give her a Neupogen shot, Jean added, "They will bounce right back up after the shot, they always have." When we asked Jean about how long this was taking, she said she just saw a patient whose red cells just came in last month after waiting a year. Laury asked Jean how he felt about it taking so long and Jean replied, "He is living his life. He is fine and happy."

While driving home, Laury admitted that she still can fixate on the negative aspects of this journey. She believes the reason for this fixation is a lingering fear of death. Laury asked me to point out to her when she is being too negative. I said I would try, but sometimes I fall into that trap, too. It is good to have someone like Jean look us in the eye and tell us how good things really are. Even a star patient like Laury needs a pep-talk once in a while.

All our Love.

Sunday, 12/7/2014 – Living

"Go forth into the busy world and love it. Interest yourself in its life, mingle kindly with its joys and sorrows." - Ralph Waldo Emerson

The last few days Laury and I have been busy. It is so easy to get caught up in blood numbers that we forget that we still have each other and we still have our life together. Friday, Linda came over to give Laury a yoga practice at home. It was something that Laury needed to help free up her sore shoulder. Thank you, Linda for your time and care. Later in the day, Laury and Kelly had Vicky over to our house to celebrate Vicky's birthday.

Yesterday Laury and I went into the city to get my hair cut. We stopped on the way home and picked up the grapevine Christmas balls from the Growing Place. Laury usually decorates the balls for her mom, but this year she still can't handle the live greens so we had them done. When we got home Laury asked me to move the cement deer from the patio to the benches next to the back door to become part of our Christmas decorations. I also put a spotlight on the container in the front yard. Later, over Skype, Laury taught our daughter Keri how to make a Christmas bow, Laury was thrilled to be asked and had fun teaching Keri. Last night Keri sent us pictures of her and James's apartment decorated for Christmas, including the bows she made.

Today I did a lot of cooking, including some of my Mom's beefy tomato soup for Laury's parents and Robin. Laury and I ran the soup and Christmas balls over to her parents and we stopped at Robin's on the way home to deliver her some soup and homemade biscuits, as well.

Sometimes when I sit down to write I try to think about what happened to us over the days that was significant, mindful, and worthwhile. So much of Laury's and my thoughts and actions seem to revolve around Laury's healing. It would be easy to be self-centered and measure every event in our life based on this benchmark of healing. But, I realized sitting down tonight that what we did over the last few days was to live; not focus on Laury's health but on each other and our friends. This is the way it is supposed to be.

All our Love.

Tuesday, 12/9/2014 – I am happy

All the same," said the Scarecrow, "I shall ask for brains instead of a heart; for a fool would not know what to do with a heart if he had one." "I shall take the heart," returned the Tin Woodman; "for brains do not make one happy, and happiness is the best thing in the world." - Frank L. Baum, The Wizard Of Oz

Today we had Laury's blood checked. Laury's white counts are back up and within a good range to fight infections. Laury's platelets rebounded, as well, and are above sixty thousand again. Laury's hemoglobin did not drop as much as it has in the past two weeks. The hemoglobin was down to 7.3, but we decided to wait until Thursday to see if she needs blood.

All in all, Laury and I felt pretty good about the numbers. We said to Jessica, our nurse, that we hope that one day soon she will call us to tell us that Laury's blood type has changed. Jessica said, "I check it every time you come in. I want to be the one to call you with the good news." Jessica is just as excited about our journey as we are.

This week will mark six months since Laury's transplant. Laury and I had hoped to have done some things, seen some changes, and accomplished some goals by now that we haven't. Not having accomplished these things has at times left us feeling defeated. But, the past few days I have been reminded of how happy we are just being together. I love watching Laury decorate the house for Christmas. Yesterday, Laury came up to my office to tell me she was leaving to do some shopping with Kelly. Laury told me how comfortable I looked and how good I looked to her. Her compliment gave me a familiar funny warm feeling in my stomach. I have heard Laury say several times throughout this journey, "I am happy." I guess it is my turn to say, "I am happy too."

All our Love.

Thursday, 12/11/2014 – Thank you, thank you

"Here are the two best prayers I know: 'Help me, help me, help me' and 'Thank you, thank you, thank you." - Anne Lamott

Laury and I just got back from our clinic visit with Dr. Odenike. Laury's numbers look great, her white counts are up, her platelets are above seventy thousand and her hemoglobin had only dropped from 7.3 on Tues to 7.2 today. We were all excited about these results. Paula, our nurse, came in to our room and exclaimed, "Have you seen your platelets!"

Tomorrow marks six months since Laury received her stem cells. As a result, Dr. Odenike is taking Laury off Prograf, her anti-rejection drug. This means that since Laury has shown no signs of Graft versus Host disease, Laury no longer needs to have her immune system suppressed. Once off the Prograf they will watch Laury closely for four to six weeks for any signs of graft versus host, but they are not expecting any at this point. (Graft versus host disease is where the new immune system from the donor attacks Laury, thinking her body is foreign.)

Dr. Odenike spent some time going over the various test results from the last few weeks. As Dr. Odenike expected, there is an absence of red blood cells in Laury's blood. There is also an absence of immature red blood cells in the blood called Reticulocytes. Reticulocytes usually mature into red blood cells within twenty four hours after being released from the bone marrow. The fact that her blood shows very low levels of Reticulocytes means that either they are not being produced by the marrow or that they are being killed before they can mature. Dr. Odenike explained that they don't know for sure, but, she suspects that Laury's old antibodies are killing the immature red blood cells before they can leave the bone marrow. We again talked about possible treatments for this but agreed to wait a little longer before taking any action. We are still hopeful that Laury's body will figure it out and we will see healthy red blood cells soon.

Laury and I will be going to the infusion center tomorrow for Laury to get one unit of blood. We talked about Laury not getting blood this week and seeing how she felt. However, Dr. Odenike decided that since the next time Laury could get blood would be next Wednesday it would be too long to go. Laury is also getting a bone marrow aspiration on Tuesday and I felt that she needs to go into that feeling as good as possible.

The best news of all is that Laury was given permission to go to the yoga studio to practice again. Laury will need to be very careful not to pick up any infections, but Dr. Odenike was OK with Laury going back slowly and carefully. Laury said she is willing to wear a mask and gloves to class and bring her own props from home. This is huge for Laury. Reconnecting with her yoga community has been on her mind and she has missed the group practice.

This was definitely a visit where we left saying, "Thank you, thank you!"

All our Love.

Saturday, 12/13/2014 – Six months

"Until I met you," she said, "I never realized how precious each day could be. When I was working, each day was over before I knew it, and then a week just flew by, and then a whole year...What have I been doing all this time? Why didn't I meet you before? If I had to choose a whole year in the past, or a day with you-I'd choose a day with you..." - **Shuichi Yoshida, Villan**

Yesterday was Laury's six month anniversary. We did not have any big plans. The day started with Laury and me wishing each other Happy Anniversary and then off to the infusion center and getting a unit of blood. Afterwards, we came home and I went back upstairs to work. I am not sure what Laury did during the rest of the day until I came down at four. I would occasionally hear her talking on the phone, or to the mailman. But mostly it was quiet.

In the afternoon, Lyndsay came over to pick up some mail and a package. We sat in the living room and talked. When we became hungry we order pizza; each of us getting our own personal pizza. We drank a little wine and laughed and talked about our plans for Christmas day. Lyndsay left around eight to begin her evening, and Laury and I went into our bedroom to watch TV. A short while later we climbed into bed and wished each other Happy Anniversary and went to sleep.

No big celebration, just appreciating the time we have together and the journey we are on.

All our Love.

Tuesday, 12/16/2014 – Rainy day

"Rainy days should be spent at home with a cup of tea and a good book." - Bill Watterson, The Calvin And Hobbes Tenth Anniversary Book

Today was a rainy day, but we did not spend it at home. Laury and I left the house this morning at seven to have Laury's blood checked at the infusion center. After Jessica, our nurse, took Laury's blood and changed her Hiccman line dressing, we drove to the city. Laury's hemoglobin is at 7.7, right in the range where we can get blood or let it go until later in the week. We decided to wait until Friday to get blood. Laury had a nine thirty appointment for a bone marrow aspiration. Leaving the infusion center at seven thirty got us to the U of C right on time. Because of the rain and the rush hour it was a long drive.

After arriving at the U of C, Laury checked in and went to the lab to get her blood checked again. The pathologist needs to have blood to go with the bone marrow aspiration. Laury came out after a very long time in the lab and told me they had taken seventeen vials of blood. After hearing the amount of blood they took, I decide that maybe we would get Laury's transfusion tomorrow instead of Friday. I called Jessica to let her know that Laury and I changed our minds and we would be coming in tomorrow for the transfusion.

Bone marrow aspirations can be very painful. They go through the bone of your hip and take out a small piece of bone marrow. Laury usually goes through the procedure with a local anesthetic, using her meditation to help with the difficult parts. This time Laury had asked Jean, our nurse practitioner, who performs the procedure, to give her something to help. Laury has been very sensitive to pain since her transplant and told Jean she didn't want to feel a thing.

Jean gave her a mix of drugs that pretty much made sure Laury wouldn't feel a thing. After the procedure, Laury said, "That is the way to do it. I will never have a bone marrow aspiration any other way." We will have to wait a few weeks for the results of the aspiration. The doctors are testing the bone marrow DNA and making an assessment of how healthy it is. The good news is that Jean said she was able to get plenty of marrow for the sample.

After the bone marrow aspiration, Laury also had a Pentamidine treatment. Laury has had these treatments every month to help prevent upper respiratory tract infections. Laury was pretty out of it when the second treatment was done, but she still wanted to go visit Robin. Robin had been admitted to the hospital over the weekend and Laury wanted to go up to the tenth floor to see her.

We walked very slowly to the new hospital and to Robin's room. When we entered the ward, once again Laury was greeted by several nurses who remembered her. Laury spent a short time with Robin before she was getting tired and wanted to go home. Laury slept most of the way home. We arrived home around one thirty and after eating some lunch we both jumped in bed for a nap. Laury is still sleeping.

It was a long day. Once again we were reminded of the pain and suffering that goes on at the clinic. There is plenty of hope and joy but you can't miss the sorrow, either. While I was in the reception area waiting for Laury to complete her breathing treatment, I noticed a couple sitting across from me. A nurse came out to answer some questions they had about a trial he had signed up for. The nurse told him that they would give him a CT scan at the beginning of the first week of the trial and then again at week three. The man said to the nurse, "Two CT scans so close together, is that good for me?" He then chuckled and said, "Not that it really matters. I just don't want to increase the speed of this process." The nurse replied, "We won't". The couple thanked the nurse and left. I told Laury the story and she told me she saw two women leaving the room next to hers crying.

I am grateful we are home and have a happy holiday season to look forward to. We witnessed today that some others are not so lucky.

All our Love.

Thursday, 12/18/2014 — Cloudy

"How sweet to be a Cloud Floating in the blue!" - A. A. Hodge

"I feel like I have floated through the last two days," Laury said to me at dinner last night. Laury had spent the afternoon with Kelly doing "Christmas things" and had come home just before I got home from yoga. Laury and I spent the morning at the infusion center where Laury received a unit of blood. It is funny how short two hours feel when Laury only gets one unit of blood. I worked and Laury fell asleep. The nurse came in to check on us a few times and Laury slept through her visits.

I think Laury was still getting rid of the anesthetics from the day before. She had napped for a few hours on Tuesday after we got home and still went to bed at the usual time and slept through the night. Her body is very sensitive to everything right now, everything is magnified.

So, it was natural for Laury to feel cloudy for a day after her receiving such heavy medications. We were talking at dinner and Laury told me something and I looked at her funny. She said to me, "Did you not hear me?" I said, "I heard you but I did not understand a word you said." Laury looked a little befuddled and said, "Let me start over." She was then able to make herself clear. Sometimes the clouds make us feel good and sometimes they confuse us.

All our Love.

Friday, 12/19/2014 – Holiday spirit

"Love, caring, and the spirit of kindness always bring happiness. Our greatest happiness depends on what we love, how we care, and how we share." - Debasish Mridha

Laury loves the holidays. Starting several years ago Laury would have a "woman's" Christmas party. She would invite all her friends and co-workers to a night of food and drink at our house. Some years the party was quite large and noisy and I wondered if we would ever get some people to leave. But mostly the gathering was about celebrating and enjoying each other's company. Since the party was for woman only, the night of the party I would go Christmas shopping. Some years I would go with a friend from work, other times I would have dinner with Laury's dad while he waited for Laury's mom at the party.

The last few years Laury has not had the party. The season just seemed to bring other obligations that made the party impractical. Yesterday, Laury had a small group of women from yoga over for a holiday celebration. It was not the big gathering of thirty or more but four friends enjoying drinks and conversation. While Laury had her gathering I went into town to do some last minute shopping. I went to shops where they know Laury to help me find something special. All of the places I stopped in asked about Laury and seemed to know her so well that they could direct me to things she would love. This helped me find special things, but also to way overspend.

Last night was just like the past years, only on a smaller scale. The ladies left before seven and Laury and I spent the rest of the evening in quiet. The evening did remind me of the reason I enjoyed Laury's parties of the past. It put me in the holiday spirit, reminded me of the joy and excitement of finding just the right gift, and connecting with others who share your spirit and hearing Laury laugh.

All our Love.

Sunday, 12/21/2014 – Hand written

"Whisper to the flashing water your real name, write your signature in the sand, and shout your identity to the sky until it answers to you in thunder." - Christopher John Farley, Kingston By Starlight

Laury has perfect handwriting. I think it has to do with her being a teacher. I, on the underhand, have handwriting that a doctor would be proud of. By the seventh grade my teachers would no longer accept a hand written paper from me; it had to be typed. I think my bad handwriting was to cover up my worse spelling. Handwriting is a personal thing. Even though our handwriting is unique to us it does have influences. I received a Christmas card from my older sister and her handwriting looks a lot like my dad's.

I often ask Laury to write things for me when I want the lettering to be clear. For example, I did a small carving for friend and I asked Laury to write the dedication and title in on the piece, then I signed it.

Today, as Laury was writing a grocery list of things we needed for Christmas day, she said to me, "My handwriting is back." I guess I hadn't noticed the change in her handwriting. Thinking about this change, I was struck by how many things we take for granted that have been changed in Laury during this journey. Her hair, nails, eyesight, and even her handwriting. I think the reason Laury has been able to deal with these changes as well as she has is because she has a very strong sense of who she is.

I am beginning to really understand why this part of the healing is so hard. You are trying to regain yourself, or at least redefine what it means to be you. With all the changes Laury has gone through, she is still the woman I fell in love with and always will be.

All our Love.

Tuesday, 12/23/2014 – Moods

"There are moments, Jeeves, when one asks oneself, 'Do trousers matter?'"

"The mood will pass, sir."

— P.G. Wodehouse, The Code Of The Woosters

I am writing from the infusion center in Naperville. Laury is receiving two units of blood this morning. Yesterday her hemoglobin was 6.3 when taken in Naperville, then 7.1 when taken later in the day at the U of C. Yesterday was a long day. As I said, we had Laury's blood checked in the morning and then we had clinic in the afternoon. Because of the rain, the trip to Chicago took over an hour and a half. Our appointment with Dr. Odenike was at four thirty and we were brought into the room at four ten. The nurse said there were two patients in front of us. I said to Laury after the nurse left, "Let's see. Two patients ahead of us, so we should see Dr. Odenike in about two hours." Laury said. "I hope not." Dr. Odenike came into our room at six.

Laury was not in the mood to wait yesterday. She walked around the room and did yoga stretches like a caged animal. Laury asked me, "I wonder how many hours we have waited here over the past year?" I replied that most of the time we spent at the U of C over the last year has been spent waiting. It is just part of the process.

Dr. Odenike had me give Laury a Neupogen shot last night. Laury's white counts were down again. She is also taking Laury off the Noxafil for a week. Laury's liver enzymes have been up and Dr. Odenike says it shows that something is irritating Laury's liver. She feels it is the Noxafil. If after a week of being off the Noxafil Laury's liver improves, then Dr. Odenike is going to shift her to an antibiotic that we will give Laury through IV at home.

I asked Dr. Odenike if wine could be what is causing the liver enzymes to go up. She looked at Laury and said, "No wine for you!" Laury looked back defiantly and said, "I am not giving up my glass of wine this week." Dr. Odenike looked at me and said, "I am not arguing with those eyes!" Laury was angry with me for having brought up the wine. While driving home I said I was sorry, but I felt Dr. Odenike needed to see the entire picture of what was going on to make the best decision regarding her liver. Laury understood and said she was sorry for getting angry.

To say Laury was in a bad mood yesterday is not fair. What we both felt yesterday was the continued frustration of the roller coaster journey. Laury has maintained such a positive attitude throughout all these months that to say, "Enough" is understandable and human. Today is a different day, however, Laury has already asked me three times to make sure the IV is running at the high rate so we don't have to be here any longer then need be. We will see how the rest of the day goes.

All our Love.

Wednesday, 12/24/2014 – God bless

"You are the best gift that I receive from God,

and you are the Best reason to live in this world.

I love you" - Jervin Balmendiano

Laury started a Christmas Eve tradition several years ago of taking homemade shortbread cookies to friends. The first few years Laury would take Lyndsay with her and I would stay home with baby Keri, and then in later years we all went as a family. The list of people we deliver to has changed over the years: some have passed away, others have moved away. Last year Laury was not up for baking or delivering the cookies. It meant a lot to her to be able to do it again this year. Laury was very excited for today and the delivery of the cookies. I didn't realize how much Laury missed the deliveries last year. Laury was very insistent they she was up for the baking and deliveries this year. The visits energize her and remind us to be grateful for each of our friends. We spent about an hour at each of the three people we delivered to this year. Lyndsay met us and went with us to two of the three friends.

The cookies are an excuse to stop and reconnect with these friends and to share stories of the year and to wish each other a happy Christmas.

Once again, I am grateful for all of the love and support this community has shown Laury and me through this last year. Laury and I look forward to the coming year and to continuing on this journey with all of you. May you all have a wonderful Christmas. God Bless you all.

All our Love.

Sunday, 12/28/2014 – A little order

"He felt a deep urge to put some order in this chaos. Leaning against a large standing-stone by the wayside, he drew out his dreambook and began to write." - Alan McCluskey, The Reaches

Laury and I had a great Christmas Day. It was just the two of us in the morning then Lyndsay came over and Laury's parents joined us in the afternoon. The last couple of years, Laury and I have not bought gifts for each other, choosing to spend the money on the girls and family, instead. This year we both felt the urge to show our appreciation for each other through some gifts. It felt good to be able to buy some special things for Laury that I knew she would not buy for herself.

Friday Laury and I walked in to Naperville to buy a new set of sauce pans for the kitchen. I have wanted a new set for several years and could never justify spending the money. This year I received a generous gift of cash from Laury's parents and the pans were a great way to spend the money.

Laury and I usually have some house projects to work on together while I am off work this week. One of the things we talked about was cleaning and reorganizing the kitchen cabinets. I spent most of Friday on this project. Laury would come in every once in a while and talk but then would disappear. She admitted that she was very tired that day.

It felt good to get the kitchen clean and reorganized. Sometimes it seems easier to live with the chaos then to spend the time to make it right. I think in some ways this year has been one of chaos, and finding small spaces of organization in our lives has made it bearable.

Today I spent most of the day in the shop. I fired up the new table saw and started working on two side tables that I hope to finish tomorrow. Laury rearranged the sun room. She said that she wanted to make the room more functional and livable for what she is doing now.

Laury spoke to her principal on Tuesday and told him she would not be coming back to school this year. She had hoped to be back to work in the spring but she now realizes that isn't going to happen. Laury said she felt like a weight was lifted from her when she finally got it out that she was not going back.

Laury needs to renew her teaching certificate this year. She has been concerned, because she has to make sure she has enough additional education credits to qualify for renewal. Kim, a friend and colleague of

Laury's, helped Laury find all the credits, so Laury is now able to renew her certificate; another weight lifted.

Organizing the kitchen, rearranging the sun room, informing Laury's principal, and getting her credits together are all ways we have created a little order in our chaotic life right now. Tomorrow we get Laury's blood checked and we begin again, going wherever this journey leads us.

All our Love.

Tuesday, 12/30/2014 – Foggy

"Sometimes when you lose your way in the fog, you end up in a beautiful place! Don't be afraid of getting lost!" - Mehmet Murat Idlan

I have heard Laury recently describe where she is in her healing process as, "I have reached the summit, but it is foggy and I can't see where to go next." I think we both felt that at this point we would be "done" with Laury's bone marrow transplant. I can now see why so many people who have gone through a bone marrow transplant describe their life after as "the new normal".

Several years ago Laury and I drove to Boston for a friend's memorial service. On the way we stopped in Syracuse, New York, for Laury's high school reunion. We left the following morning for Boston. We were told that the drive between Syracuse and Boston was wonderful and that there are many beautiful things to see. Laury and I made the drive in a heavy fog, not being able to see much more than a few hundred feet ahead of us. Every once in a while we would rise above the fog and see an incredible landscape of rolling hills and rivers. We then would be thrust back into the fog. We arrived in Boston on time and expressed our disappointment of not having been able to see much on the way there.

This journey seems like that journey to Boston. We can't always see where we are going. We know we are on the right path, and that if we stay on it we will get there. But we don't always know what we are going through or what is just around the bend. I know we will get there, and just like our trip to Boston it will be memorable.

All our Love.

Wednesday, 12/31/2014 – Surprise, surprise

"Ha, Eleanor thought, you'd be surprised what could be a surprise at this point." - Rainbow Rowell, Eleanor & Park

Yesterday turned out to be a surprising day. Laury received a unit of blood in the morning. Either the bag was small or Laury and I have gotten so used to sitting and waiting that two hours no longer seems like a long time. We were both surprised at how fast the time went by and how quickly we were back home.

Later in the afternoon Laury had an appointment with her therapist, Pat. On the way to the appointment Laury and I were talking about how Laury has been feeling lately. I said that I had done some research on her anemia caused by her antibodies attacking the red blood cells and I found out that one of the symptoms is being grumpy. Laury exclaimed, "I have been saying that! When my blood gets low I get in a bad mood." It is understandable that Laury would be in a bad mood with the numbers when they are down, but to find out that her bad mood may actually be caused by the low numbers was a surprise.

Later in the evening I took Laury to get her eyes checked. Laury has had trouble seeing since her transplant. Every time we mentioned the poor eyesight to the doctor she would remind us to wait, and that the eyesight should improve with time. The last time we saw Dr. Odenike, we asked about Laury's eyes again. This time she suggested we go ahead and have Laury's vision checked. During the exam the doctor discovered Laury's eyes have improved since the last exam in March. The reason Laury couldn't see clearly with her glasses is that they are now too strong. Needless to say, this surprised not only us, but the doctor as well. The doctor said she has never seen that happen with chemo patients.

Yesterday I wrote about sometimes feeling like we are in a fog and not sure where we are going. Like driving in the fog, sometimes it opens up and we see surprising things. And now Laury can see them even clearer! (Once she gets her new glasses.)

All our Love.

CHAPTER TWELVE

January

Friday, 1/2/2015 – Blood loss

"Listen to me. Someday you're gonna look back on this moment of your life as such a sweet time of grieving. You'll see that you were in mourning and your heart was broken, but your life was changing." - Elizabeth Gilbert, Eat, Pray, Love

I took Laury to a yoga class this morning. It was a gentle class which is perfect for Laury right now. Laury admitted she was a little scared to go back and was not sure what she could do and how it would go. When we got to the studio, Laury became, as she says, "weepy". It was hard for her to talk to others and she asked me to not say anything to her, and to be her "silent" partner at the class. She did really well and said the class was perfect and it met her and she met it. It was a big step in her healing.

Laury has been a little weepy lately. She has had a couple of good cries over the last few days. Laury says that part of what she is crying about is the loss of part of herself due to the transplant. I asked her what she meant and she said that the blood her parents gave her is no longer part of her- it doesn't contain hers or her parents' DNA anymore. Laury said she knows that she needed new blood, but she never thought about having to lose her old blood, and the impact this would have on her. I guess I never thought of her grieving over the loss of this part of her. I always have concentrated on getting rid of the disease, but that, too, was part of her. Maybe Laury's being able to grieve the loss of her blood is the last thing standing in the way of her body accepting the new blood. There are so many things that impact our healing that it would make sense that if Laury has been holding on to her old blood, that her body would attack the new blood. I can't find any medical research that says Laury has this kind of power over her body, but it doesn't mean it isn't happening.

Laury says that cries have been good and that she feels that she is moving on now. This journey has touched every part of her and us. As Laury has said to me several times during this journey, "If you don't know yourself going into this, you certainly will know it when you are done." It is time to say good-bye and thank you to Laury's old blood. It served her well and gave all it could. In with the new.

All our Love.

Tuesday, 1/6/2015- A complication

"When you walk to the edge of all the light you have and take that first step into the darkness of the unknown, you must believe that one of two things will happen. There will be something solid for you to stand upon or you will be taught to fly." - Patrick Overton, The Leaning Tree

Laury has been very tired for the last several days. We both felt that she needed blood and I even thought that we should have gone to the ER over the weekend to have her blood checked to make sure it wasn't too low. Yesterday I called and got Laury into the infusion center to have

Laury's blood checked. To our surprise, her numbers looked really good. So why is Laury so tired? We decided to call and make an appointment with Dr. Odenike for later in the week. We thought we had an appointment for Thursday, but we wanted to make sure. Laury called and found out we had an appointment already scheduled for yesterday, so we decided to keep it and try to find out what was going on.

We left the house around twelve thirty and arrived back home at seven last night. Our appointment with Dr. Odenike was at two thirty she finally saw us at four thirty.

Laury explained to Dr. Odenike how she has been feeling and we looked at Laury's blood numbers. Laury's liver enzymes are up. We have been watching them go slowly up over the last few weeks and Dr. Odenike took Laury off the Noxafil to see if that was causing the rise in the liver numbers. Yesterday, the liver numbers were way up. Dr. Odenike and her Fellow, Dr. Pettit, were looking at the numbers and discussing between themselves what the numbers could mean. Laury said to them, "You guys are scaring me." Dr. Odenike said to Laury, "I am sorry. We get excited when we talk and I sometimes forget that everything we talk about might not helpful for you to hear." Dr. Odenike ordered a bunch more blood tests and an ultrasound of Laury's liver. Dr. Odenike also wants Laury to see the liver specialist this week and she said he will probably order a liver biopsy.

Laury was overwhelmed by all this. She asked Dr. Odenike if this meant things were going bad. Dr. Odenike said no, that this was just a complication and she doesn't like complications. Dr. Odenike went on to say, "What you see in me is that I don't like not knowing. We, as doctors, are supposed to have answers for you. If it were up to me I would do all the tests right now to get to the bottom of this and be able to give you answers. It doesn't mean that there is necessarily anything major wrong, it just means I don't know and I want to find out as soon as possible." Dr. Odenike went on to say that most times when a person shows high liver enzymes, if the doctors can't find any reason for the numbers they will just monitor the numbers for a while. The numbers usually spike then go down as the liver recovers from whatever was going on. But since Laury has recently had a bone marrow transplant, they can't treat her the same way.

When we left the hospital this summer after Laury's transplant, they gave Laury a card to keep with her that has some critical medical information on it. The doctors instructed us that if Laury ever had to go to the hospital to make sure she showed the card to the doctors. On the way home yesterday Laury and I were talking about all the tests, and Laury asked me if this was the new normal. I said I think this is why they gave us the card. Something that might seem small if it happened to me is potentially a bigger deal to Laury, since she has recently had a bone marrow transplant. Thursday Laury and I head back to the U of C for a long day of an appointment with the liver specialist, the ultrasound, more blood work and an appointment with Dr. Odenike. I think the thing that is most trying of all this is the unknown. But Laury has done so well we both feel that this is another hiccup and we will get beyond this one, as well.

All our Love.

Wednesday, 1/7/2015 – Back again

"With a certain frustration I knew I spoke too soon, too urgently. I wanted to get out of the way the things I knew to say, wanted to say, the things I'd been thinking, all in the hope of moving into the unforeseen." - Denis Johnson, The Name Of The World

Yesterday there were so many change of plans that Laury and I weren't sure where and when we were supposed to be this morning. The doctors have been trying to rearrange and pull up some of the tests to get them done sooner. Laury and I headed down to the U of C this morning at seven for Laury's liver ultrasound. We checked in at the clinic and found out that the ultrasound was going to be done in the old hospital. Laury was too tired to walk that far so the receptionist found us a wheel chair and we headed over to the radiology department. The test took about twenty minutes and then Laury and I headed back to the clinic. We were taken back into the room to meet Jean at about ten. Laury received another shot in her series of pneumonia vaccinations. Laury also received a breathing treatment. Neither of these treatments was scheduled, so we had to wait a little extra to get them completed.

While we were waiting, Jean said that Laury was going to need blood; her hemoglobin was down to 6.6. Paula, our nurse, was going to call the infusion center in Naperville to schedule the transfusion for tomorrow, so we didn't have to come back downtown.

Jean came back into the room a few minutes later while we were still waiting for the respiratory therapist to show up, and told us that after talking with Dr. Odenike they were admitting Laury to the hospital. Initially, Laury said no, and was angry and frustrated. Jean sat with her and explained that Laury's liver enzymes were higher today than on Monday and by admitting Laury they could do more tests and get them done sooner to find out what was going on. Jean said to Laury, "Don't not do this. If you go home and this gets worse, then we will have a real emergency on our hands." Laury agreed, but said she was still frustrated at having to go back into the hospital.

After Laury completed the breathing treatment we went up to the seventh floor of the new hospital to wait for a room to open. I left Laury in the sky lounge and went home to pack some things and show our kind neighbor how to take care of the cats while we are gone. When I got back to the hospital Paula had moved Laury to the 10th floor into an outpatient room so they could start giving her blood. The nurse just came in and started the blood. The nurse told us that they have a room for Laury and we should be moved over there in about an hour.

The concern the doctors have is that Laury has graft versus host disease.

This can be treated, but is dangerous, Laury's new immune system is attacking her liver, and if left untreated it could kill the liver. The doctors are not completely sure that Laury has GVH, but all of the tests over the next two days will tell them what is going on. The sooner the doctors find out for sure, the sooner they can start treatment. So here we stay.

At least this time I knew what to pack, except I forgot the toilet paper. The stuff here is really bad. I will keep you all informed as the test results come in. For now, Laury will be getting a lot of rest- now that she is done venting.

All our Love.

Thursday, 1/8/2015 — Wait

"Time crawled past on leaden hands and knees." Sonya Hartnett, Surrender

Thank you all for your prayers and uplifting comments. Laury and I have forgotten how much of your day in the hospital is spent waiting. Laury was scheduled for her liver biopsy at eight this morning. At nine we asked the nurse if she could check to see when they would be coming for Laury. At ten our nurse told us Laury was now scheduled for twelve thirty. At twelve thirty they came and got Laury and we went to the prep area and waited until one thirty before they took Laury in. The procedure involves going into a vein in Laury's neck and following that vein into the liver to retrieve a small piece of the liver. The procedure takes about thirty minutes, so I went back to our room to wait for them to bring Laury back up. Laury arrived back in our room at three thirty. The nurses finally brought her back after waiting forty-five minutes for hospital transport. Laury is doing fine, and she has a large pressure bandage on her neck. Other than that she said she didn't feel a thing.

Laury was hungry but we had to wait to hear from the doctor to tell us it is OK for Laury to eat. We are now waiting for the hospital to send up a new IV pump so Laury can get her second bag of potassium. Laury offered the nurse to have me go back down to the procedure area and retrieve the pump she went down there with. The nurse said to Laury, "Did you hear what you just said to me? I can get another pump." Laury replied, "But it was such a nice pump." We all chuckled.

We are not sure how long we will have to wait for the results of the biopsy. I think I remember the doctor saying it takes a day or two. We hope we don't have to wait that long.

Laury and I have no idea what tomorrow will bring. We will just have to wait and see.

All our Love.

Friday, 1/9/2015 – Improvement

"Small steps may appear unimpressive, but don't be deceived. They are the means by which perspectives are subtly altered, mountains are gradually scaled, and lives are drastically changed." - Richelle E. Goodrich

Laury has made some progress today. The doctor came in with the preliminary results of the liver biopsy. It looks like Laury has Graft versus Host disease. This is what they suspected, and last night Dr. Bishop started Laury on a high dosage of steroids. The steroids suppress the new immune system and allow the body to adjust. The doctor said that this is not uncommon and eventually the new immune system will figure out that Laury's body is not foreign and will start protecting it as its own. Already this morning the most important liver number has started to go down. The other numbers went up a little more but Dr. Bishop said that was to be expected because of the biopsy. As he put it, "We poked around in there and made it unhappy."

The doctors will continue the steroids until they see the numbers all improving, and then they will taper down the dosage. The dosage Laury is on right now is too high for her to go home. The steroids can affect her blood sugar level, so the nurses have been checking her sugar regularly. Today Laury did receive one unit of insulin. The hope is that Laury's liver will respond quickly, and we might still get home by the end of the weekend.

Most importantly, Laury is feeling better, both physically and emotionally. Dr. Bishop came in last night and asked Laury how she was doing. Laury replied, "I am discouraged." Dr. Bishop asked her why and Laury replied, "I was doing so well and now look where I am." Dr. Bishop told her, "You are still doing really well." That seemed to pick Laury up a bit. Today when Dr. Bishop made his rounds, two of the nurse practitioners Laury had during the transplant were with him. After Dr. Bishop left the nurses stayed and talked and caught up with Laury. This really made her feel good. Laury heard about weddings, promotions, and family, all things that didn't include Laury's current condition. It took her mind off of things and recharged her extrovert energies.

Later this afternoon one of the nurse practitioners came back to give Laury the results of the biopsy. She talked with Laury a little about her journey. The nurse has a friend who was just diagnosed with Leukemia back in Michigan and she is very concerned for him. Laury gave her some really good advice on how to reach out to him. It was good to see Laury being Laury, concerned more about others than herself. That is the surest sign of improvement there is for me.

All our Love.

Sunday, 1/11/2015 – Brothers

"The world is so empty if one thinks only of mountains, rivers & cities; but to know someone who thinks & feels with us, & who, though distant, is close to us in spirit, this makes the earth for us an inhabited garden." - Johann Wolfgang von Goethe

Laury continues to slowly improve. Yesterday Laury started out feeling very tired again, but after our walk and the visit from the doctor she began to feel stronger. I asked the doctor if this is how this part of her healing was going to go. He replied, "Yes, up and down for a little while more and then she should begin to feel good again." On Friday night the liver specialist came in to see Laury. The doctor confirmed that what she was seeing in the biopsy was GVH. Laury asked the doctor to help visualize what Laury's liver needed to heal. The doctor said that the cells that make up the lining of the bile ducts in the liver are the ones that GVH attacks. The doctor said if you look at these bile ducts under a microscope they look like an old fashion well. The ducts are round but lined with square cells that look like bricks. The doctor went on to say that if you look at Laury's bile ducts right now there are many bricks out of place or broken. The doctor said the broken ones need to be replaced and the ones out of place need to be moved back into place so the walls of the well become smooth again.

The last few days we have gotten to know our nurse, Tina. She came to the US in 1999 as a war refugee from Albania. Tina told us stories about herself as a 15 year old, living in an open field waiting for the Red Cross to bring tents. Then, waiting to see which country was going to take them in. Tina said many days they would sit and wonder if anyone in the world cared about what was happening in their country. Eventually her family was taken to Salt Lake City. She said they have never met a nicer group of people and will be forever grateful for the love and compassion they were shown.

Yesterday, Lyndsay and Kelly came to visit. My brother, Kurt, from Australia came too. He is in the US for some training in California, but decided to come early to spend the weekend with us. Since Laury and I were at the hospital, Kurt has been staying at our house with the cats. It was so good to see him. We hugged and cried. Kurt and I went to the Sky Lobby on the 7th floor and got some lunch and sat and talked. We shared stories about our Mom and Dad and caught each other up on our families. The visit was short but fulfilling. We hadn't seen each other for a few years and we talk maybe two times a year over Skype. When we are together it is like Kurt said, "We are back in our shared bedroom."

The doctor said yesterday that Laury should be ready to go home today, but he doubted that all of the medication logistics could be worked out on Sunday, so it would probably be Monday when she gets released. We are both ready to go home. Thank you again for all your prayers and kind thoughts. And thank you, Kurt, for being my brother and coming all the way across the country to spend a few hours with me. Yesterday you were my keeper.

All our Love.

Sunday, 1/11/2015 – Home again

Just a quick update. Laury was released from the hospital today and we are home. Back down to U of C tomorrow.

Tuesday, 1/13/2015 – Battle hardened

"May we each find in ourselves the courage we forgot we have, to see the beauty we forgot is inside us, while battling the demons we forgot we can slay, on a battlefield we forgot we can win." - Agnostic Zetetic

The last two days have been filled with new information, new directions and rebuilding. After arriving home on Sunday afternoon, we spent the rest of the day quietly trying to make sense of all that had happened during the week. Yesterday we headed back to clinic. Laury and I went to the new infusion center on the 10th floor of the hospital for Laury to get her anti-fungal infusion. The nurse took blood and we sat for about an hour while the medication dripped into Laury. After the infusion, Laury and I went back down to the clinic to meet with Dr. Odenike. Laury's liver numbers were down yesterday. We hope that means that they have peaked and the steroids are working. Dr. Bishop said he hoped to see the liver numbers peak by Wednesday. Dr. Odenike said that just because the numbers were down it doesn't necessarily mean they have peaked. She said they can continue to go up and down for a while before actually peaking. Laury had a blood draw this morning and we will see if the numbers are still down. If they are, then we can say they have peaked. Interestingly, Laury's other blood numbers have been going up, including her hemoglobin. What we think is happening is the steroids are not only suppressing Laury's new immune system, but her old one as well. Laury has been fighting an internal battle on two fronts. Laury's old immune system has been attacking her new red blood cells and her new immune system has been attacking her liver cells. The steroids appear to be having a positive effect on both battle fronts.

Today the home care nurse is stopping by to re-teach me how to hook Laury up to the anti-fungal IV at home. Laury is back on the Prograf, and for now we are just watching her blood sugar and she does not require any insulin. The doctors are going to keep a close watch on Laury and we have to go back to clinic on Thursday and Saturday.

Yesterday, while we were driving down to the hospital, Laury and I talked about the last few days. Laury apologized for treating me the way she had in the hospital the first few days. She said she was angry and confused and needed to vent. Laury said, "There is no metaphor for what I am going through right now. Journey, summit, path, none of these worked last week." I agreed that she needs to be able to vent when she feels angry and that I can't take it personally. We both thought the worst was over, but we now realize that this is how it is going to be for a while. Laury and I have to pay attention to every little thing, because something small can turn into something big really really fast. Before leaving the house to go to clinic, Laury asked me if she should pack a bag to take with us in case her numbers were still up. Laury said that she knew if the numbers were still going up that there was a good chance that Dr. Odenike would want to admit her to the hospital again and she was OK with that.

It is hard to say where we have been the last few days. Are we still on the path, where is the path, is this the path? Laury said part of what made her so angry was that once again her health had kept me from my family. She said to me, "I kept you from attending your Mom and Dad's funerals and now I kept you from spending more time with Kurt." Laury went on to say that she is amazed that I am still sitting in the chair next to her. I said, "Where else would I be? This is what we committed to thirty two years ago." She squeezed my hand and smiled.

All our Love.

Wednesday, 1/14/2015 — New normal

"We may run, walk, stumble. drive, or fly, but let us never lose sight of the reason for the journey, or miss a chance to see a rainbow on the way." - Gloria Gaither

The results of Laury's blood work yesterday show that her liver numbers are going down. We are not sure this means they have peaked, but it is good news either way. After we arrived back home from the blood work, Laury went back to bed. She had trouble getting to sleep the night before and was really tired. The home-care nurse rang the doorbell around ten thirty and I went downstairs to answer the door and wake Laury. I opened the front door and saw that our nurse was covered with snow on his legs and back. I said to him, "Please tell me you didn't fall on the ice in the driveway." He said he had but he was alright. I felt terrible, and I couldn't apologize enough. I went into the bedroom to wake Laury and she said she didn't want to get up and that the nurse didn't need to see her.

I came back into the living room and told the nurse that Laury was sleeping and that I thought it was best not to wake her. He said that was fine and we talked for a few minutes and he showed me again how to work the anti-fungal IV. I kept telling the nurse how sorry I was he fell and he kept saying it was OK and he was fine. The nurse left after about twenty minutes and I went back up to work.

Laury got out of bed around noon and she said she felt much better. Laury said she wasn't sure if she slept, but it felt so good to be in bed. It felt so warm and soft that she thought, "This is where I need to be right now." I know the feeling. Sometimes a nap is the best medicine.

Laury and I have been replaying the events of last week in our heads and in our discussions. We both know we didn't handle the situation as well as we would have liked. I guess that I was tired of having to always be "on" as the caregiver and Laury was tired of being the patient. We both wanted the journey to be over. We fell into the trap of wanting things to be "normal". Laury and I embarked on this journey to give Laury back her life. We know that what happens after this transplant will never be the same as before. In many of the survivor videos we watched before the transplant, people talked about the "new normal" of their lives.

I remember several years ago while battling a lengthy illness, I said to my doctor, "I just want to go back to normal" and he replied, "Normal is what got you here. We need to define a new normal for you." I think this is what has been so hard about this journey: there is no finish line. Laury and I are on a journey of our lives, and the goal is to make it as long and as happy as we can. No matter what "normal" looks like.

All our Love.

Friday, 1/16/2015 – Expectations

"You can't always get what you want

But if you try sometimes you just might find

You just might find

You get what you need" - **Rolling Stones**

Laury and I went to clinic yesterday. Laury's liver numbers continue to come down. Her bilirubin number is coming down, but very slowly. This is to be expected, according to Dr. Odenike. She said even though it was the last number to go up, it usually is the last to come down. Dr. Odenike is going to have Laury continue the high dose of steroids until the bilirubin number is back in the normal range.

Laury's other blood numbers have continued to improve, as well. Her hemoglobin was up to 8.9, her white blood count is 5.3 (solidly within the normal range), and her platelets were up to 110,000. It appears that the steroid suppression is working and allowing the new marrow to get stronger.

I asked Dr. Odenike if when we start tapering off the steroids we would see Laury's blood numbers start to drop again, or, did she think that the marrow might now be strong enough to overcome Laury's old antibodies. Dr. Odenike said that sometimes they see the numbers go back down, other times they seem to have reached a turning point and continue on. Dr. Odenike also said that sometimes when the steroids are reduced, the GVH can flare back up. Dr. Odenike went on to say, "Any of these things happening are not unreasonable expectations." I guess this means that it is anyone's guess at this point what is going to happen.

Laury and I can visualize her getting stronger and her blood numbers to continue to improve. We just can't expect it. Laury says she had expected to be farther along on her healing path by now. If I am honest with myself, I shared that expectation as well. These expectations are what lead to such great disappointment last week. Instead of being disappointed we should be thankful that we found the GVH early and Laury is healing. The treatment for GVH might just be the thing that causes her bone marrow to turn the corner and overcome its last hurdle to become A positive. Neither Laury nor I could have expected that.

All our Love.

Sunday, 1/18/2015 – Clinic time

"To live is to travel, on a voyage more epic than the odysseys of myth - not from place to place, but through the poignant strangeness of time." - T. L. Rese

Yesterday Laury and I headed down to the U of C for clinic. The clinic we usually go to is closed on Saturdays, so we went to the new infusion center in the hospital. It was strange to get a close-in parking spot and to see the campus so quiet. We passed no one but the security guard on our way up to the tenth floor. Laury had her blood drawn and her numbers continue to improve. Her liver numbers are still coming down and her other blood number continue to rise.

We waited for about an hour for the blood chemistry results and found out that Laury needed Magnesium. This meant staying for another two hours while they ran an IV unit into Laury.

We arrived at the clinic around eight thirty and left around twelve thirty. We stopped and got a sandwich before we left the hospital and ate in the car on the way home. It was the shortest commute time we have ever had. Thursday night when we went home the sign said ninety minutes from downtown to I294, and the entire trip home took two hours. Yesterday we were home in thirty-five minutes.

Once again, time takes on a different personality when we are at the hospital. You simply cannot be in a hurry. When the nurse came in and said that Laury needed Magnesium she said we could go home with pills or Laury could stay and get the IV. The pills can sometimes cause upset stomach and diarrhea. We decided that we were not in a hurry and it would be better for Laury to get the IV. The strange thing was that we weren't in a hurry. I think that the events of the last two weeks have reminded us that doing what is best for Laury is what matters most and that we can't measure her progress by time. Letting go of watching the time makes spending four hours in the clinic almost enjoyable. We are together surrounded by people who want Laury to be healed as much as we do. It actually is a nice feeling.

All our Love.

Tuesday, 1/20/2015 – Welcomed healing

"Sometimes we must yield control to others and accept our vulnerability so we can be healed." - Kathy Magilato, Healing Hearts: A Memoir Of A Female Heart Surgeon

Yesterday Laury and I went to clinic at the U of C. We met with Dr. Pettit, a Fellow of Dr. Odenike's, and with Dr. Liew. Dr. Odenike was out of town. The clinic was quiet and Laury was taken into the lab right away and we only had to wait a few minutes to see Dr. Pettit. The lab was running slow yesterday, so we had to wait for Laury's blood results. We left before all of the blood chemistry results were in but Laury's white blood, red blood and platelets all continue to rise. Laury's hemoglobin was at 9.3. We are trying to remember the last time it was above 9. We are pretty sure that the liver numbers and Bilirubin are continuing their downward trend. Laury's eyes are clear of all the yellow, and she has no other symptoms.

Dr. Liew examined Laury and said, "After looking at your liver numbers, I didn't expect you to look so good." I think this was his way of saying Laury is doing great. Laury said after the visit that she knew what he was trying to say, but how he said it was not as helpful as she would have liked. We are continuing the large dosage of steroids for now. Dr. Liew reminded Laury to stay active because the steroids attack the large muscles. He told Laury that even when she is sitting she should continue to lift her legs occasionally. Laury and I are going to try to get a walk in every day and Laury is going to walk up and down the stairs a few times a day.

Laury feels she has her new sailing orders and can work at what she is supposed to do to continue healing. We have no expectations or goals related to this healing- just welcoming.

All our Love.

Friday, 1/23/2015 – Disappearing act

"For your every tear, know that I'll always be here. To bare one pain we both will share, know I'll never disappear." - Anthony Liccione

Yesterday when Laury and I checked in at the clinic they gave us a pager and said that is would beep when it was our turn to be seen. This was new. When our pager went off the nurse came out and showed us into our room. We asked the nurse why they started using pagers instead of the usual process of just calling our name. The nurse replied that a "high profile" patient had gone to the president of the clinic to complain that their name was being called out in public. The clinic decided that the pager system would be more private. The pagers are loud and just add more confusion to the waiting area. Laury said that the person who complained needs to get over the embarrassment of being sick.

 Laury's blood numbers are stable. We were a little concerned because her hemoglobin, white and platelet counts were down a little from Monday. Dr. Odenike pointed out that Laury's numbers yesterday were almost identical to her numbers from the last two weeks, and Monday's high numbers were the ones that were unusual.

Laury's liver enzymes are continuing down, and her bilirubin was down as well. Because of the downward trend, Dr. Odenike decided to begin to taper off the steroids. Laury has been on a very high dose of 100 mg per day of steroids. Today Laury will start taking 80 mg. The hope is that the graft versus host will not return and we can keep dropping the dosage. This is really good news. The steroids have really taken a toll on Laury's muscles.

Dr. Odenike said that once the steroids are reduced, the muscle should start coming back, but it was important for Laury to stay active. Dr. Odenike signed the paperwork for Laury to get some in-home physical therapy to help rebuild her muscles. We hope that the therapy can start next week.

Yesterday, Laury's temperature and her weight were the same number. I said to Laury, "I don't want to watch you disappear." Laury replied, "I am not going to disappear, at least I don't think so." We chuckled. On the way home we stopped and bought more coffee ice cream.

All our Love.

Saturday, 1/24/2015 – Bricks and mortar

"Your heart is able to see things that your eyes aren't able to." - Kholoud Yasser

Laury and I had clinic this morning at the U of C. One of the nice things about Saturday clinic is the light traffic down and back. Another nice thing is that we get to see people we haven't seen since July, and who have been so important to Laury's care. When we walked into 10 Central we were greeted by Jillian. Jillian was Laury's nurse on the last few days before we went home in July. Laury was excited to see her and they both hugged for a long time. Jillian lead us to our room and stayed to get caught up with Laury on everything that has happened since we last saw her. We saw two other nurses today that Laury had back in June. They both were glad to see Laury. You get the sense that these nurses are proud of, and grateful for their successful patients.

Laury's liver numbers continue to improve. Her bilirubin is almost back to the normal range. We hope that we will be able to continue to decrease the steroids more when we see Dr. Odenike on Monday. Laury's face has been puffy the last two days, which is an expected side effect of the steroids.

After Dr. Cline read Laury her liver numbers, Laury he told him about the visualization she has been using to help heal her liver. She told Dr. Cline that all her family, friends and past relatives have been coming to her in her visualizations with bricks to help rebuild the walls of her well (If you remember the doctor gave Laury the image of a brick lined well for her bile ducts). Laury told me that even my parents and her grandparents have come bearing bricks and a helping hand. She says it has been very comforting to think of all these people helping her.

Dr. Cline agreed that having a positive image of the healing helps. He said they are not sure how it helps, but they know it does. I want to thank everyone who brought a brick and helped place it into Laury's healing liver. We never stop believing that you all matter in helping us on this journey.

All our Love.

Tuesday, 1/27/2015 – More adventures

"Make everything an adventure. Otherwise, it will suck." - Nita Morgan

The last two days have been quite an adventure, but when I think about it, probably not more so than the last year. Sunday Laury met with the physical therapy nurse for her evaluation. Laury is beginning in-home physical therapy to help rebuild all the muscle she has lost due to the steroids. Near the end of the meeting the nurse brought out a scale and placed it on the living room floor. Laury stepped on the scale and said, "Yes!" The scale read 105.5lbs. I said to Laury, "Do you really think you have put on seven pounds since yesterday?" The nurse said it was probably her scale. At least Laury's weight is no longer the same number as her temperature.

Sunday we also had a nice visit from our friends, Becky and John. Becky made a nice kale and cheese casserole that we had for dinner.

Yesterday, Laury had her first in-home physical therapy session. She really likes the therapist and Laury says the exercises are simple but effective. In the afternoon, we went down to the U of C for clinic. Laury and I drove down in snow showers that turned into a snow squall closer to the lake. The way the snow was coming down caused the sky and the lake to become one. Driving along Lake Shore Drive felt like we were in the mountains and the lake shore was a cliff, and if we would have walked to where the beach should be, we would have seen a thousand foot drop into nothing.

Laury's blood numbers continue to improve. Her bilirubin is 1.1 which is almost normal. Her other liver numbers have come down, as well, and are approaching the normal range again. Dr. Odenike decided to again reduce the steroid dosage. Laury is now down to 60mg a day. Dr. Odenike expects to reduce it again on Thursday. Dr. Odenike explained that they have to taper Laury off the steroids and it will probably take a couple of weeks to get her completely off them.

The steroids are having another side effect, besides attacking Laury's muscles, they are causing her to have high blood sugar. Yesterday Laury had to get a shot of insulin and I got to give it to her. The nurse came in to show us how to draw the correct amount of insulin out of the vile and how to give the shot. Laury was not comfortable giving herself the shot so I said I would. The nurse was impressed with my shot-giving skills. We stopped on the way home to pick up the insulin and supplies to continue to test Laury's blood sugar and give her insulin, as needed. This morning we wasted three test strips before we got enough blood and an accurate reading. I then had to strain my eyes to measure out one unit of insulin. Hardly seemed worth it (I could almost hear my sister Kim laughing at us).

Last night as we were driving home, we hit a stretch of I355 that was black ice. I was driving around 65 when I felt the car lose traction. I backed off the gas and let the car slow down on its own. Thankfully, we only had about two more miles to go before we could get off the toll way. The experience caused my heart rate to go up and it suddenly got warmer in the car. We made it home safely. Just another adventure. One of many lately.

All our Love.

Wednesday, 1/28/2015 – Eating right

"If you are not feeling well, if you have not slept, chocolate will revive you. But you have no chocolate! I think of that again and again! My dear, how will you ever manage?" - Madame de Sevigne

Dr. Odenike told Laury that she needs to restrict her intake of sweets while on the steroids. Ordinarily, this is not a problem. Laury has honed her diet over the years and eats very healthy. Most times she will not eat a lot of sweets, not because she doesn't like them, but because they are "not good for you." When we were sitting in the examination room with Dr. Odenike and she was reviewing Laury's blood numbers and noticed that Laury's sugar was in the 400's, Dr. Odenike asked Laury if she had eaten any sweets before coming to clinic that morning.

Laury replied that she may have had some but she usually eats really well, but had been eating more to try to keep her weight up. Dr. Odenike asked Laury what sweets she had eaten that morning. Laury replied sheepishly, "Well, I had some raisin bran cereal, maybe some coffee ice cream, and, oh yeah, I had a piece of bunt cake, a piece of English toffee, and I had a couple of dunker cookies with my tea." Dr. Odenike stood up and laughed, "I didn't put you on a restricted diet with the steroids, but it sounds like I should have." Laury replied with a half-smile, "I don't usually eat this way. Everyone keeps telling me I need to eat to keep my weight up and I just try to eat what sounds good. I will be more careful."

As we were driving home, Laury and I were talking about what Dr. Odenike had said and Laury replied, "I am glad I forgot to tell her about the caramel corn!"

All our Love.

Friday, 1/30/2015 – From this side

"I feel really blessed for the journey, all that I have learnt & the enormity of emotions that exist because of the presence of you." - Truth Devour, Wantin

We had a great clinic visit yesterday. Laury's liver numbers continue to improve and her Bilirubin is now in the normal range. Dr. Odenike reduced the dosage of steroids again to 40mg a day; she also dropped our Saturday appointment. The whole visit went smoothly. Laury got her blood draw right away. Laury and I then went over to the infusion center to have her line dressing changed. They took Laury back after only waiting about five minutes. While I was waiting for Laury, the pager went off saying they were ready for us to see Dr. Odenike. Our appointment was at four thirty and we saw Dr. Odenike at four forty-five. Pretty amazing.

Driving home last night along Lake Shore Drive Laury turned to me and said, "I am sorry, sweetie, that you have to go through this." I said it was nothing compared to what she was going through. Laury replied, "I sometimes think it is easier for me to sit here on my side and have everyone take care of me than it is to sit on your side." I am sure there is some truth to that. Laury said to me, "They saved my life, didn't they?" I said, "Yes, and they saved mine too."

Last night I had a dream that Laury and I split up. Laury has had similar dreams a few times and always tells me about them through tears the next morning. I now understand the devastation of those dreams. I don't remember the details except as I was driving away from Laury someone sitting next to me asked, "What are you going to do?" My crying woke me up. I wanted to reach for Laury but at 3:00am her sleep trumped my need for a hug.

It is hard to watch Laury go through this. To look at her skinny body and puffy face that as Laury says doesn't even look like her to her, is tough. I watch Laury walk up the stairs as if her boots are full of lead and I want to carry her the rest of the way. When we reach the top of the stairs Laury turns and smiles at me, "The stairs are good for me," she says. I know it is true, but it doesn't make it any easier to watch.

But, she is still Laury, and I love her with all my heart. I am happy to be at her side and to be going through this with her.

All our Love.

CHAPTER THIRTEEN

February

Tuesday, 2/3/2015 – Driving home

"Living is like driving," my grandmother used to say. "You have to pick a lane." Have I chosen the right lane? It feels like this place, this moment in time, lies exactly halfway between my past and my future." - Kathleen Flinn, The Sharper Your Knife, The Less You Cry: Love, Laughter, And Tears At The World's Most Famous Cooking School

Laury and I went to clinic yesterday. Laury's liver numbers continue to improve. Her Bilirubin is still in the normal range and the other numbers are approaching normal, as well. Dr. Odenike reduced Laury's dosage of steroids to 20mgs per day. This is especially nice because Laury can take all 20mg at once so she doesn't have to take any before bed. The steroids had been making it hard to get to sleep, so now Laury can take them in the morning.

As a result of reducing the steroids, Laury's other blood numbers have been dropping a little. Her white counts and platelets have dropped. But this is nothing that concerns Dr. Odenike. Laury's hemoglobin is staying up, which is really good, because this means that she will not need a transfusion this week. It seems like there are always tradeoffs: to get some positive effect in one area you have to take a little negative effect in another. But, we all agree that Laury is feeling better, gaining strength, and healing. Dr. Odenike said yesterday that Laury has improved faster than she thought she would and she is amazed and pleased at Laury's progress.

The journey continues. Yesterday Laury and I left the house early for our appointment since we were not sure what the roads would be like. The drive down to the U of C was clear and quick. We had expected to run into traffic or bad roads, and neither was there. Coming home after dark was a little slower, but still not a lot of traffic, and we moved right along. We reached one point and all of a sudden the traffic came to a stop. I could see up ahead there was a car up against the wall in the median and there were a couple of people pushing another car out of the left lane. We slowly moved through the section and we notice that under the over-pass there was about a foot of snow and ice on the road. Up to this point the road had been clear, and after we got past the over-pass, the road was clear again. Laury said to me, "How would you know that was there? You are going right along and then you hit the mess. That could have been us." That is our journey right now. Sometimes the sailing is clear and other times we have to be careful in the dangerous sections, but we still make it home.

All our Love.

Wednesday, 2/4/2015 – Career Change

"A career is wonderful, but you can't curl up with it on a cold night - Marilyn Monroe

Ever since Laury left work last March she has been on paid medical leave. Last Monday Laury informed her school that she would not be able to return to her job on March 12th when her leave runs out. Yesterday, the school called to tell Laury that she will have to resign as of March 13th. Laury does not have enough years with the district to retire, although we are looking into if she has enough to retire with the Teacher Retirement System. Either way, we will lose Laury's health care coverage. I can get coverage through my job, but we need to find out what will be covered and how much it will cost. We may have to pay the deductibles again with the new company.

This journey that we are on has been one of healing, but also life examination. Back when we first knew Laury would someday need a bone marrow transplant, I changed jobs and took one for a lot less pay but which gave me the flexibility I knew I would need to work from home and take care of Laury. It was a big financial adjustment, but we are really happy now that I did it. Laury has been spending a lot of her time thinking about what to do with her career moving forward. Should she go back to teaching? Is there something else that she would rather do? Laury and I have also examined what is really important to us as a couple. I am glad Laury is not going back to teaching. I think it would be dangerous to her health both physically and mentally. I know how much Laury loves teaching and I am sure she will find something that feeds that part of her. Giving up her job is another loss- one of many that we have had to deal with on this journey. But it is also freeing. Laury and I can look at all possibilities and define a new future.

Laury and I know that the jobs, the house, the cars are all things we could give up if we had to. The one thing that we won't give up is each other.

All our Love.

Friday, 2/6/2015 – Not in a hurry

"One of the great disadvantages of hurry is that it takes such a long time." - G. K. Chesterton, All Things Considered

Yesterday Laury and I went to clinic. Laury's liver numbers continue to improve with all the numbers normal or just above normal. However, Laury's white counts and platelets have dropped a little more and I had to give Laury a Neupogen shot last night to stimulate more white cell growth. Dr. Odenike cut back the steroids again. Laury is now taking 20mg on one day and 10mg on the next. Dr. Odenike is very pleased with Laury's progress and told her to keep doing what she is doing.

Laury's weight was above 100lbs yesterday- the first time this year. Laury's reaction to her weight was to raise her arms and shout, "Yes!" Laury then went on to ask me if I notice that she has a little tummy. I said, "I don't think you have a tummy, I think that everything else is so small right now it only looks that way."

When we drive home, right as you get on to the freeway there is a sign that shows the current travel time to I294. Every day Laury asks me what the sign said, she always forgets to look. The time can vary from thirty minutes to ninety minutes depending on the time of day and traffic. Yesterday the sign said sixty minutes and it took ninety. What Laury and I have noticed is that like yesterday, when things go quickly at the clinic and we get out in a reasonable time, we run into more traffic. Pretty much we get home around seven at night no matter if we left at four forty- five like last night or at six on Monday. No matter how much of a hurry we are in we always arrive home at the same time. I guess this is just another reminder of the healing journey we are on - we will get there when it is time, no matter if we hurry or not.

All our Love.

Monday, 2/9/2015 – What to eat?

"To eat is a necessity, but to eat intelligently is an art." - Francois de La Rochefoucauld

Over the last few days Laury has had some heartburn, nausea, and a little vomiting. Amazing what we have to keep track of these days. Everything matters. Laury and I need to pay attention to all of these things and make sure we mention them to the doctor today. We can never be sure if they are just something Laury ate or something more serious. Now Laury has to watch her sugar intake, pay attention to things she eats to see if they are what are causing the heartburn. She also still needs to eat to put on muscle.

It would be much easier if taste didn't play a part. Food is not like all the medications- you can't just take what you need when.

I grocery shop on Saturdays and Laury and I always talk about what we might like to eat during the upcoming week. It is hard to shop right now. Laury is never sure what is going to sound or taste good or what she will be in the mood to eat. Sometimes, like last night, when I do make something Laury enjoys, she has heartburn after dinner and we are left with questions. Should Laury eat the left-overs, was it the food or the time she took her medicine, what in the meal caused her sugar to go up?

Thinking so much about food can take the fun out of eating. Our meals together are together time, sacred. I will be glad when Laury is off the steroids and her system has a chance to recover.

All our Love.

Tuesday, 2/10/2015 – Always learning

"Life is made of connections. Who knows why fate throws things in our direction, but one thing's for sure, new things are there to offer value to our lives and teach us something new about ourselves. It's what makes life exciting." - Serina Hartwell

Laury and I went to clinic yesterday. Dr. Odenike was out of town so we met with Dr. Liew. It was a good visit. Laury's liver numbers are almost back to normal. Two of the three key numbers are actually in the high-normal range now. Dr. Liew said that they will probably continue the low dosage of steroids for a while to make sure the GVH doesn't come back. We hope that we can get Laury off all the steroids very soon, so we are eager to talk with Dr. Odenike on Thursday to see how long she thinks Laury will need to stay on them.

Laury's other blood numbers have dropped a little. This could be caused by the Bactrim she is taking on the weekends to prevent respiratory infections. Dr. Liew said that the Bactrim can cause the blood numbers to drop. Since Laury is only taking it on the weekends, we should see a rise in the numbers on Thursday. Laury and I had hoped the numbers would stay up but it looks like since we have dropped the dosage of the steroids they are going back to what they were before. This might mean that Laury will need transfusions again, but for now we are hopeful that her hemoglobin will stay up.

Laury also needs to get magnesium this week. The Prograf Laury is taking removes magnesium from her system. The home care nurse is coming over this morning to show me how to hook Laury up to a gravity fed IV. In the past, we have used a pump, but for some reason this time the doctor want us to use an IV pole, and so Laury gets to walk around the house trailing a pole. Always something new. I learn how to do something and they change the procedure on me.

Yesterday, after Dr. Liew left the room, Laury said, "I feel really good about this visit." I said, "Why?" and Laury replied, "I feel like Dr. Liew is the hard professor and when you get a compliment from him it really means something." All and all, Laury is doing really well, and her strength continues to improve. Me, I get to add another skill to my caregiver resume: gravity fed IV hookup. Part of me would like to not have to ever use these new skills again, but I am glad I know how to do them and it is fun to learn new things.

All our Love.

Wednesday, 2/11/2015 – Honestly

"This is a difficult balance, telling the truth: how much to share, how much to keep, which truths will wound but not ruin, which will cut too deep to heal." - Ally Condie, Matched

Yesterday the home care nurse stopped by and showed me how to hook up the gravity fed IV. It is really easy- much easier than the pump. Laury did notice that it ran too fast set at wide open like the nurse recommended. Today I asked the nurse at the infusion center about how fast the IV should run and she showed me how to set the roller clamp to slow it down. The nurse said that running Magnesium too fast is not good for the heart. Great, that's all I need to do, give Laury a heart attack.

Laury and I met with Pat, Laury's therapist, last night. It was a good visit. I usually don't go in with Laury but she asked me to join her this time. Both Laury and I admitted that this last hospital stay took a lot out of us and we had not handled it as well as we would have liked. Pat told us not to be too hard on ourselves, this is a long journey.

I also admitted that I am tired. My brain is full. I need a day off. This is hard for me to say. I love taking care of Laury, but between working full time, and taking care of Laury I never have a day off. Mostly, I feel it in my head. I need to find ways to clear things out that don't need to be there and are just taking up space. I am going to try meditating. At least while I am doing it my mind will be clear - that is the hope anyway.

Later in the evening while watching TV I asked Laury if it was hard for her to hear me say I was tired and needed a day off. She said no, and thanked me for being honest.

This morning on the way to the infusion center to have Laury's blood checked, Laury asked me, "Do you ever resent me?" I said, "What do you mean?" Laury replied, "I have this really easy life right now. I get up when I want, eat when I want, have friends over, do what I want." I said that she has that life because she is sick and trying to recover. I told her it reminded me of a story I heard about Alvah Curtis Roebuck, who had sold out to his partner Richard Sears and had lived most of his life poor instead of wealthy like Sears. Sears died at 51, and later, when Alyah was in his eighties, the Sears Company brought him back as a figure head for store openings and events. At one of these events a young reporter asked Alvah if he ever wished he could have traded places with Sears. Alvah looked at the young reporter and replied, "Son, he has been dead for thirty years. No."

I don't resent Laury trying to do everything she is doing to get healthy. How could I? Getting healthy is what this journey is all about. For Laury and for me, too.

All our Love.

Friday, 2/13/2015 – Comparison

"Comparison is the death of joy." - Mark Twain

I am writing today from the infusion center in Naperville. Laury is receiving a unit of blood this morning because her hemoglobin is down to 7.0. We went to clinic yesterday and we went up to 10 Central to have Laury's blood drawn and dressing changed. It was good to see the nurses again and to not stick a needle in Laury's arm to get blood. Earlier in the week we got Laury's blood typed and cross matched in case she needed a transfusion. Laury's numbers have been dropping since we reduced the steroids.

It is hard not to be disappointed about the numbers, but Laury and I knew it was a possibility that once the steroids left the system, Laury's numbers would go back to where they were before. Dr. Odenike said, "I know I am not supposed to say this, but I was hoping we turned the corner with your numbers. I am a little disappointed."

Once we confirm that Laury is going to need blood, usually Paula will call the order into Jessica, our nurse at the infusion center. Jessica texted Laury yesterday at five and said she had not gotten an order yet and she needed to place the order for blood if we were coming in this morning. We tried to find Paula but we later found out she had left the clinic and her phone was not working. We managed to find Dr. Odenike and she agreed that Laury needed a unit of blood. Jessica told us this morning that Paula did finally call her, but she placed the order based on our direction. Jessica said, "I wouldn't ordinarily do that but you guys are so on top of things that I knew it would work out and I wanted to make sure you would get your blood."

Earlier this week I had a blood draw for my annual physical today. It was strange being in the lab and having the technician ask me my name and birthday and I almost replied, "Laureen Hartman, 11/9/57." Later that day when I was talking with Paula about the results of Laury's tests she kept saying, "You this and you that" and she finally said, "I mean Laury, not you." I told Paula the story about almost saying Laury's name and birthday instead of mine at the lab and she laughed, "Yes it is hard to separate yourself, sometimes."

Yesterday at the clinic Laury and I ran into a woman we had met a few weeks ago who is just over a month out of her transplant. She and Laury have been talking and exchanging notes about their experiences. After talking with her yesterday, Laury said to me, "I know I am not supposed to compare myself to her, but she seems to be doing so much better than me." I said to Laury that she looked and felt that good when she was at that stage of her transplant as well, but she was right, she is different and it doesn't do any good to compare. I told Laury that I had looked at all my blood test results. I have gotten much better at understanding what they are telling me and my numbers all look good. I said, "My hemoglobin is 16.4." Laury replied looking sad, "Why would you tell me that? There is no comparison between you and me right now!" I said, "Exactly!"

All our Love.

Saturday, 2/14/2015 – Slippery

"He awaits himself while walking, out of the icy circle to escape." - Dejan Stojanovic, Circling: 1978-1987

I had my annual physical yesterday afternoon. Our family doctor is in Glen Ellyn, so Laury went with me and I dropped her off at her parents while I went to my exam. Dr. Lobue has known us a long time; he is Laury's doctor, too. He asked how Laury was doing and I brought him up to speed on her health. I described our journey to Dr. Lobue in this way. "It is like we are walking together across a frozen parking lot to get to our car. We can't see the car so we don't know how far we have to go. We have to walk very carefully for fear of falling and getting hurt. The walking is slow and sometimes we fall and when we get back up we find we have moved back several steps and have to start over. We know we are making progress and the car may appear anytime but we just don't know right now when that will happen."

Dr. Lobue said it was a good visualization. We recognize we are making progress but we also understand the reality of the situation.

When I arrived back at Laury's parents, we sat in the sun room and talked. Laury went down to their basement to look at a chair. Laury's parents and I heard a funny noise and Laury's Mom called out, "Laury, are you OK?" Laury replied back that she was OK but had fallen down the stairs. I ran to the stairs to make sure she was OK. Laury was at the bottom of the stairs laughing. She showed me her back that had a roughed-up spot, and her finger was bleeding. I said we needed to wash the finger and get a Band-Aid on it. Laury started laughing again. She tried to tell me through her laughing that she thought she saw herself sliding down the stairs in the mirror at the bottom of the stairs. She said it looked funny. Laury's Dad took her into the bathroom and cut a Band-Aid to fit her finger and put it on for her. Laury told me it was a very tender moment.

Perhaps if I hadn't picked an icy parking lot as the metaphor for our journey Laury wouldn't have slipped on the stairs. Who knows?

All our Love.

Sunday, 2/15/2015 – A clean break

"I will continue my path, but I will keep a memory always." - Rosie Thomas, Iris and Ruby

Yesterday, Laury and I met Laury's co-teacher, John, at her school and we cleaned out her desk. Laury and I knew we had to go to the school to do this and we had to pick a time when there wouldn't be anybody at the school. There wasn't much to bring home: one box, a couple of lamps and a desk organizer I had built. I wondered how Laury would feel about cleaning out her space. The act had finality about it. We are not sure if she will ever be back to teaching.

Laury said she had prepared herself for cleaning out and it wasn't as hard as she thought it would be. Laury said that it still feels the right thing to do. That might be, but I am sure that just because it the right thing to do, it didn't make the hurt any less.

This is like any journey; to make progress you have to leave something behind.

All our Love.

Tuesday, 2/17/2015 – Beautiful

"Beauty is not caused. It is." - Emily Dickinson

Yesterday was a clinic day. The drive down was quick. Being a holiday, traffic was light. When we arrived at the clinic, the place was a zoo. Every seat in the waiting area was full and people were standing around outside the area near the elevators. When we view a scene like that we know it is going to be a long wait. Laury and I went over to the infusion center to have her blood drawn. As busy as the doctor's area was, the infusion center was quiet. They took Laury back after only a short wait and we headed back to the doctors' waiting area.

We found a couple of chairs outside of the area and settled in for a long wait. Slowly they took patients in, and after about two hours we were the only ones left. Laury and I were finally called back to our room, and waited there as well. Dr. Pettit came in and talked with us. Laury's blood numbers rebounded nicely since Thursday. Laury's White and Platelet numbers went up and her hemoglobin is at 8.9. All of her liver numbers are normal or high normal. Dr. Odenike came in after another short wait and she reduced Laury's steroid dosage again: down to 10mg every other day. Dr. Odenike explained to us that the reason she has Laury taking the steroids every other day, instead of just reducing the daily dose, is that while on steroids her body can stop making its own steroids. By taking the external steroids every other day, the hope is that her body will start to produce its own on the off days, so that once Laury is completely off the external steroids, her body will be producing them on its own. Another balancing act.

Laury had some red spots on her face and she told Dr. Odenike she thought it was from a facial mask she used over the weekend. Laury also asked Dr. Odenike when she could color her hair. Dr. Odenike said that she should not be using any kind of skin peel right now because the steroids can thin her skin. Dr. Odenike also said that coloring Laury's hair would not be a good idea right now either. Dr. Odenike asked Laury, "Why do you want to color your hair? It looks wonderful, the grey and black looks very sharp." Laury replied, "I am not feeling very pretty right now. I know it is an ego moment, and I am trying to get over it." Both Dr. Pettit and Dr. Odenike told Laury how good she looked and they gave her an assignment to watch the Oscars and to notice how many stars now have grey hair and look fabulous. Laury agreed to do it.

I know it must be hard to look in the mirror and see how much she has changed. Laury is still beautiful and always will be. Her beauty goes way deeper than her skin.

All our Love.

Friday, 2/20/2015 – Dancing days

"David tells me that fairies never say 'We feel happy': what they say is, 'We feel dancey'." - J. M. Barrie, Peter Pan In Kensington Gardens

Yesterday was a good clinic day. The traffic was light going down to the city. Laury and I were greeted with smiles and welcomes at 10 Central where we got Laury's blood drawn and her dressing changed. After talking with one of the nurses while waiting for the blood results, we found out that her husband used to work for me at Motorola. Small world.

Laury's blood numbers took a nice jump from Monday. Her white cells were up enough that I didn't need to give her a Neupogen shot last night. Laury's platelets are up to over sixty thousand and her hemoglobin was the same as Monday. These numbers made us very happy. It means that things are improving again, not just maintaining, and Laury did not need a transfusion this week.

Laury's liver numbers continue their downward trend and Dr. Odenike decided to keep Laury on the low dosage of steroids until Monday. If the numbers remain down she will take Laury off the steroids all together. Another piece of good news.

The traffic was light going home and we had a nice dinner before watching a little TV and going to bed. A "dancey" day, indeed.

All our Love.

Tuesday, 2/24/2015 – Wrong answer

"In the past, I always used to be looking for answers. Today, I know there are only questions. So I just live." - Sarah Brightman

Yesterday Laury and I went to clinic. Laury's blood numbers are still looking good. Her white counts are stable and her platelets continue to go up. Laury's hemoglobin was down a bit, but not enough for us to think she will need a transfusion any time soon. The doctors are still trying to balance the magnesium. Last Thursday Laury's magnesium was too high, so they stopped giving Laury the IV and she was just taking one tablet a day. Yesterday Laury's magnesium was too low so we are going to start the IV's again, only this time with two grams, versus the four, previously. Hopefully, we can get this balanced.

There are two events coming up that Laury really wants to attend. The first is a workshop by the author of a book that Laury has been reading about the journey the soul goes through when battling cancer. It is written by a local woman who is speaking at the Wellness House in Hinsdale this weekend. Laury wanted to go with her friend Robin; it is something they could share. The second event is that our yoga studio is offering a class for cancer survivors and their caregivers. Laury did her homework on the work shop to find out if there was a place she could sit away from others and if she could come late to avoid the continental breakfast.

Laury carefully explained all of this to Dr. Pettit, whom we saw first, and she said she would talk with Dr. Odenike and see what she said. Laury asked Dr. Pettit, "It is the Prograf and the steroids, isn't it?" Dr. Pettit replied, "Yes, they are both suppressing your immune system, so we have to be careful." Laury replied with tears in her eyes, "I was on this "f***ing Prograf for seven months and was off it for two weeks and attended one yoga class and then got GVHD and wound up in the hospital. I can't think about how much longer I have to be on it."

When Dr. Odenike and Dr. Pettit came back into the room, Dr. Odenike said that Laury's liver enzymes had gone up a little since Thursday. Laury asked if this meant that the Graft Versus Host disease had come back, and Dr. Odenike said, yes, this means it is still active. Dr. Odenike said that she was going to increase the steroids back to twenty milligrams every other day to see if the numbers go back down. Dr. Odenike said that she will increase the steroids until the numbers come down and then begin reducing them again. Dr. Odenike said it is a balancing act: enough steroids to keep the GVHD away but not more.

Dr. Odenike had to leave to handle a family issue, so she left Dr. Pettit to answer Laury's questions about the two events. As soon as Dr. Odenike left the room Dr. Pettit's face turned red and Laury said to me later that she knew what the answer was going to be. Dr. Pettit explained that there is a new respiratory virus going around and it has hit their transplant population hard, sending many to the hospital. Dr. Pettit said that she and Dr. Odenike felt that it would not be a good idea for Laury to go to the workshop. Laury asked, "What about the yoga?" and Dr. Pettit replied, "No yoga either." Laury began to cry, and so did Dr. Pettit. Dr. Pettit replied, "I know it is hard. This time is so long, but you have done so well and we just don't want you to have a setback right now." Laury said she understood and she didn't want a setback, either. Laury thanked Dr. Pettit and said, "Thank you for crying with me, too."

On the way home, Laury called Robin to tell her she would not be able to go to the workshop this weekend. Laury cried and said that Robin cried too. Laury said it was to be their special time together. When we got home Laury was telling Kelly about the events and said, "I don't know if Dr. Odenike really had to leave early or if she wanted Dr. Pettit to give me the bad news, but, it was good for Dr. Pettit to have to give me the news. She will have to learn how to give bad news to her patients and it was good that she cried with me." I knew from that exchange that Laury had already begun to move on, to take yet another disappointment in stride, to make the best of it, and to look for today to be better.

All our Love.

Friday, 2/27/2015 – Affirmed

"Affirmations are our mental vitamins, providing the supplementary positive thoughts we need to balance the barrage of negative events and thoughts we experience daily." - Tia Walker, The Inspired Caregiver: Finding Joy While Caring For Those You Love

Laury and I braved the snow and went to clinic yesterday. The drive down took about thirty minutes longer due to traffic and the snow. We first went to 10 Central to have Laury's blood drawn and have her line dressing changed. Using the 10 Central facility to draw Laury's blood from her Hiccman line instead of her veins is much nicer. Laury was sitting in the chair and looked down at her arms and said, "My veins are almost healed."

Laury's blood numbers were up. Her hemoglobin went up, as well, so no transfusion this week. We did find out from Dr. Brewer that one of the reasons the blood numbers go up when you are on steroids is that they force the new cells out of the marrow. Dr. Brewer said that not all the new cells leave the marrow right away. They tend to hang around in the marrow for a while, but the steroids force them from the marrow, and therefore, the numbers measured in the blood become higher. It was interesting to learn yet more about how this amazing marrow works.

Laury's liver enzymes were mixed; one went down a little and the other two went up a little. Dr. Odenike was happy with the numbers and is leaving Laury on the 20mg of steroids every-other day dosage for now. Dr. Odenike said that she wants to see all the numbers come down and stay in the normal range before she will start tapering the steroids down again. She said it is trial and error right now.

It was a good visit. We teased Dr. Odenike that she left early Monday to have Dr. Pettit give Laury the bad news. She laughed and said she really did have to leave, but it was good for Dr. Pettit. Dr. Odenike reiterated that she supports everything that Laury is doing to become healthy. She said she is amazed and grateful for all that Laury does to stay healthy. It was uplifting to hear, and the affirmation was much needed. We continue on.

All our Love.

CHAPTER FOURTEEN

March

Sunday, 3/1/2015 – Goodbye, friend

"Piglet sidled up to Pooh from behind. "Pooh?" he whispered.

"Yes, Piglet?"

"Nothing," said Piglet, taking Pooh's hand. "I just wanted to be sure of you." - A. A. Milne, Winnie-The-Pooh

Friends have played an important role in our journey. Laury has reconnected with old friends she has not seen for years. Laury and I have grown closer to some friends. We have made new friends. We have said good-bye to old friends. Laury and I both know that this journey has been made better by our friends. Laury taught me to tell my friends I love them. It surprises some of them, but everyone seems to like to be told they are loved as a friend.

Kelly has been a good friend of Laury's for years. They met when our girls were babies and have stayed connected through moves and life transitions. Kelly was there for us many times over the last year; bringing Lyndsay to visit us in the hospital, washing our cloths, helping keep the house clean. But of all those things Kelly has been Laury's "play buddy", someone she could call to just have fun with.

Kelly is moving to Atlanta and yesterday she stopped by to do some laundry and say goodbye to Laury. I know they will remain friends. Laury will miss having someone to "play" with at a moment's notice. I will miss the joy that Kelly brought to Laury's life over the last several months.

Thank you, Kelly, for being such a good friend to Laury and to me. We both will miss you very much. I love you.

All our Love.

Tuesday, 3/3/2015 – One year

"You can't know what an experience will mean to future-you until you are future-you. You need millions of seconds of perspective, which ultimately, only time can buy." - John Green

Yesterday Laury and I went to clinic and as we had hoped, Laury's liver numbers continue to improve. Dr. Odenike wants to keep Laury on the higher dose of steroids until all the liver numbers are in the normal range and stay there. Laury's blood numbers were really good as well. Her hemoglobin is at 9.1, so no transfusion, again, this week. It was a good visit.

Today marks a year since I started this journal. Neither Laury nor I thought that we would still be writing to you all at this point. The past year has been one of great discovery, loss, joy, love and change. We couldn't have gotten this far without all of your help, prayers and love. If I am honest, as prepared as Laury and I thought we were for this journey, we were not prepared for its length. I am no longer sure that this journey has an end. Not in the sense that Laury is cured and back to "normal". This is the model of healing that we have all been conditioned with. We get sick, we get better and we go back to being who we were. Nothing could be farther from the truth with this journey. Laury and I will never go back to normal. We have been changed forever. We are not the same as we were a year ago.

Laury has gone from being a cancer patient to being a transplant patient. Yes there will be a time when Laury's health doesn't dominate our every moment, and my role as caregiver will be greatly diminished. This doesn't mean the journey has ended. I fully intend to be on this journey with Laury until the day I die. The last year has been one of many journeys we have shared together, so far. But like our parenting journey, it doesn't just stop, it changes.

I have thought of when would be the right time to end this journal. But, I no longer can think of a single event that would signal that it is a good time to stop. When I first thought about stopping the writing I thought the 100 day mark would be a good point, but clearly we were not ready. I had hoped to end with the announcement that Laury's blood type had changed - but we now know that it could take much longer than we thought. At what point in the journey are we far enough along to no longer need all of your support? Maybe never. Maybe that is the point of all this. We discover that this journey we are on is one of community. Laury and I gain support from you all and hopefully we are able to support you all, as well. That is what communities do.

Should I continue this journal? I don't know at this point. I guess we will see what tomorrow brings.

All our Love.

Friday, 3/6/2015 — The journey continues

"Not all those who wander are lost." - J. R. R. Tolkien, The Fellowship Of The Ring

And so our journey continues. Yesterday Laury and I went to clinic. We first stopped at 10 Central to have Laury's blood drawn. There we were taken to the sun and warmth of Florida through our nurse Jillian's sun-tanned face as she told us about her long weekend of beaches and deep-sea fishing. Jillian changed Laury's line dressing and we quickly headed down to the clinic for our appointment. Our appointments are usually at four thirty, but yesterday it was scheduled for three thirty. I had asked Dr. Odenike on Monday if we really needed to be here that early, and she replied, "Yes, I have a new patient coming in and I wanted to make sure I saw you guys before them. If you get in after the new patient you will be waiting a long time." Dr. Odenike is not kidding when she says we would wait - she usually spends at least an hour and a half with new patients, so we wanted to get to the clinic on time.

While we were waiting to be taken back, we saw AJ. AJ manages all the administration staff and she came around from behind the desk to talk with us. AJ told us that Dr. Odenike is changing her office hours beginning in April. Dr. Odenike will no longer have afternoon hours and will have morning clinic on Tuesdays and Thursdays, only. This means my current work schedule will have to change. Right now I work from seven to two on Monday and Thursday, our clinic days, every other day I work seven to four. This way I can take Laury to clinic and not have to take any time off work. However, with morning clinic it means that I will have to take the time off or work from noon to seven on clinic days. Hopefully, by April we will only be going to clinic once a week. Another change for this introvert to absorb.

Laury's blood numbers continue to improve. Her hemoglobin was 9.2 and her platelets were eighty thousand. Laury's liver numbers did not change. We hoped they would continue down, but Dr. Odenike was happy with them so we are not concerned. Laury has some swelling on each shoulder near her neck. She kept forgetting to tell Dr. Odenike and finally remembered yesterday. Dr. Odenike thinks it is probably nothing, most likely puffiness caused by the steroids, but as with everything, Dr. Odenike is being very cautious and ordered an ultra-sound for our Monday visit.

I thank you all for your comments on my last post. It is nice to know that you all are still with us on this wandering journey. We may not be sure where we are going but we are in very good company.

All our Love.

Monday, 3/9/2015 – Projects

"She was full of some strange energy that morning. Her every movement had purpose and life and she seemed to find satisfaction in every little thing." - Anna Godbersen, Envy

Laury and I love to do projects together. We are always looking for things around the house that we can work on together. Over the last year the projects have been smaller, and have been more one-sided, with me doing most of the work. However, the last two weekends I have begun to see a change. Last weekend we decided to finally refinish the study and north bedroom hardwood floors. I refinished the hallway floor years ago and the floor in the south bedroom a few years ago. I wanted to tackle the floors before Laury went in for her transplant, but I ran out of time.

Laury and I began the process by removing all the furniture from the rooms and setting up a temporary office for me in the south bedroom.

This is where I first noticed the change in Laury. Like I said, lately these types of projects would be me moving all of the stuff and Laury watching, helping a little and keeping me company. This time, however, Laury worked side-by-side with me, and when she disappeared it was not to sit and rest but to gather some beads she found in the bedroom. Laury went up and down the stairs with stuff for the basement almost as many times as I did.

I know that some of this energy is due to her hemoglobin being higher, but I can also see renewed mental energy. Laury wants to do things around the house and is excited by being able to do some of them again. Laury has begun talking about what she can do to make money while not being able to work. This too, is new. Only a few weeks ago Laury was wondering if she would ever have her energy back.

The projects Laury and I work on together are an important part of our relationship. We have missed doing projects together over the last year. It was nice to have my work buddy back at my side.

All our Love.

Tuesday, 3/10/2015 — Giving

"For it is in giving that we receive." - Francis of Assisi

Our visit to clinic yesterday was a bit of a roller coaster ride. The drive down was beautiful. We finally had some spring weather, and we drove with the sun roof open all the way. Laury and I did our usual routine of going to 10 Central to have Laury's blood drawn. We didn't stick around to wait for the results because we had another appointment for Laury's ultrasound. We went to the 5th floor and checked in for the procedure. After a few minutes we were taken into the ultrasound room. The technician took the ultrasound of Laury's neck and arms tracing her arteries and veins checking for clots. After the technician had completed the test she said that she wanted to call our doctor and she wanted us to wait until she heard back from her.

Laury came and sat next to me and said that she didn't like how much time the technician spent on her left side. Laury said she was a little concerned. A few minutes later the technician came back in and said that she hadn't called the doctor because she wanted her colleague to check something first. Laury asked her if everything was OK and the technician replied that she thought she saw some reverse flow. Laury looked at me with concern and I said I have no idea what that means.

After a minute or two another technician came in to the room and Laury got back on the table for him to check her left side again. The technician spent a few minutes going over the area and talking with the first technician. After he was done Laury came back over and sat with me while they went to call Dr. Odenike. Laury said to me she was scared. Laury said that she started to think about what could be wrong and if she needed surgery, and how she couldn't handle another setback. Laury asked me, "Are you worried?" I said to her, "I do not have the energy to worry about things until they need to be worried about. Right now we have no idea what is going on and until we are told it is something we need to be concerned about, I am not worried." Laury said to me, "That is good, you are living in the moment, I need to do that, too."

The technician came back in the room after a few minutes and said we could go. Laury asked her if everything was OK and the technician said we could talk with our doctor about the results. We headed upstairs for our appointment with Dr. Odenike. After being placed in our examination room, Dr. Pettit stopped by and she said the results of the ultrasound were in and everything was fine. We told Dr. Pettit about what had happened and she just shook her head and said, "I don't know what that was all about, but there are no clots and everything looks good." I could see Laury relax a little at the news.

Dr. Odenike then came into the room and we went over Laury's blood numbers. Her liver enzymes are stable and one went down a little more. Laury's other blood numbers are stable, as well, so no transfusion this week. We were all happy with the blood numbers. While Laury was sitting on the examination table, both Dr. Pettit and Dr. Odenike complemented Laury on her necklace. Laury said that she made it and they both replied that she should be selling her creations. Laury took off the necklace and said to Dr. Odenike, "Here I want you to have it." Dr. Odenike replied that she couldn't take it. Laury got down off the table and tried to hand it to Dr. Odenike. Dr. Odenike then tried to hide behind the table to keep Laury from giving her the necklace. The way Dr. Odenike moved, you would have thought Laury had taken a live snake from around her neck. Finally, Dr. Odenike said OK, and let Laury place the necklace around her neck. Dr. Odenike then said that it was her birthday and somehow Laury must have known it.

Laury told both Dr. Odenike and Dr. Pettit how grateful she is for their care. Dr. Odenike replied, "It is amazing how grateful you are for someone who is just doing their job." Laury replied, "It is how you do your job that I am grateful for." Laury went on, "See, it is not always easy to receive. That is all I have been doing is receiving, now it is your turn."

We drove home with the sunroof open and talked about the events of the visit. Laury said that she still can become so afraid of bad news and can snowball. We agreed that we both can do that at times and we depend on each other for strength. After everything, we agreed it was a good visit. We learned, gave, and received love.

All our Love.

Wednesday, 3/11/2015 – Dr. Odenike

"When angels visit us, we do not hear the rustle of wings, nor feel the feathery touch of the breast of a dove; but we know their presence by the love they create in our hearts." - Mary Baker Eddy, Poems By Mary Baker Eddy

Laury and I have encountered many angels on our journey. Sometimes we seemed to know right away they are angels and other times we were not aware they were angels until much later.

We first met Dr. Odenike in 2008. Laury and I had gone to MD Anderson in Houston to get a second opinion on her Myelofibrosis. Laury's blood numbers had begun to change and the doctors who had been treating Laury at the U of C had begun talking with us about having Laury go through the bone marrow transplant. The doctor we met at MD Anderson told us he would not transplant Laury and said that we had one of the world's best experts on Myelofibrosis right here in Chicago, and her name was Dr. Odenike.

After coming back to Chicago we made an appointment with Dr. Odenike. At our first meeting Dr. Odenike spent over an hour with us, talking about the disease and the possible treatments. She also explained why the doctors at U of C talked about transplant when the doctor at MD Anderson said not now. She said that there were several things that they look at to determine when it is right to transplant, and the last few blood tests Laury had had at U of C showed these indicators. However, when Laury's blood was tested again, the numbers had changed.

Laury left the meeting with Dr. Odenike not really liking her. Laury had only heard Dr. Odenike tell us that people with Myelofibrosis had an average life span of ten years. Laury kept saying, "She told me that I am going to die in ten years."

When it became obvious that Laury needed the bone marrow transplant,

Laury and I went back to see Dr. Odenike. Laury and I were in a different place for this meeting. We knew much more about what was happening to Laury and we knew the transplant was the right thing to do. Laury and Dr. Odenike formed a new relationship. Laury now loves her.

Laury now recognizes that Dr. Odenike was an angel all along- it was just hard to see at our first meeting.

We have met other angles and we will meet more I am sure.

All our Love.

Friday, 3/13/2015 – Young at heart

"The older I grow, the more I distrust the familiar doctrine that age brings wisdom." - H.L. Mencken

Yesterday was a clinic day. Another beautiful spring day driving with the sun roof open all the way down to Chicago. Laury's liver numbers have stabilized- still not quite in the normal range, but good enough that Dr. Odenike is reducing the steroid dose. Laury had been taking 20mg of steroids every other day, now she will be taking 15mg every other day. It is a small decrease, but Dr. Odenike wants to go slower this time to make sure the GVHD doesn't come back. Dr. Odenike is also reducing the magnesium to every other day.

Laury's blood numbers are holding steady, as well. Her hemoglobin was 9.8. Laury has not been above hemoglobin of ten for almost a year.

All the extra hemoglobin is giving Laury tons of energy.

I took the day off today to work on refinishing the wood floors in my office upstairs and Keri's old bedroom. I rented a sander from Home Depot and got started at eight this morning. The floors proved to be in worse shape than I thought, and the job became much bigger than I had planned. After finally finishing the small study I took a break and sat in the living room with Laury while she beaded. I said to Laury, "Why do I do these big projects that wipe me out?" Laury said that perhaps my next project should be more "age appropriate". Ouch!

All our Love.

Tuesday, 3/17/2015 – Yes, Yes!

"To get the full value of joy you must have someone to divide it with." - Mark Twain

Yesterday Laury and I went to clinic at the U of C. Laury's blood numbers are doing great. The last time we reduced the steroid dose her blood numbers dropped and she needed a transfusion. This time Laury's numbers continue to improve. Her white count is solid and her platelets are over 100,000. Laury's hemoglobin is 10.3! When Dr. Pettit told us the hemoglobin number Laury jumped up and down and clapped her hands, "Yes, Yes!" she said.

Laury and I were talking on the way home trying to remember when the last time her hemoglobin was over 10. We think it has been at least a year. Having a higher hemoglobin means more oxygen is being carried by the blood and Laury has much more energy- enough to jump up and down several times!

Laury's liver enzymes are stable with one exception, her ALT. ALT is released into the blood when there is liver damage. In Laury's case the liver damage is being caused by some lingering Graft Versus Host Disease. Dr. Odenike is not concerned with the slight uptick in the ALT.

She left Laury on the same dosage of steroids and we will see what the numbers look like on Thursday. Overall, Dr. Odenike feels Laury is doing really well and beginning in April, if the numbers stay the same or go down, we can cut back to once a week clinic. This is great news, because in April Laury and I have to start going down in the morning for clinic. To make it to an 8:00am appointment, we need to be at the clinic by seven to get blood drawn. This means we have to leave the house at 5:30am because of morning rush hour traffic. Laury and I are hoping we only have to do that once a week. Laury will still get her blood checked a second time during the week but we can have that done out here in Naperville.

A few weeks ago when we were with Dr. Pettit, Laury talked about getting her hair colored. Dr. Pettit and Dr. Odenike both told Laury she could not get her hair colored right now and that they liked her grey hair and thought she looked really good. Last week Dr. Pettit told Laury that there was a colleague who had just gotten her hair done and she thought Laury would love it and it would show Laury how good grey hair can look. Yesterday, Dr. Pettit brought the colleague in to show Laury her hair. Laury, Dr. Pettit and her colleague (I can't remember her name.) stood and talked about hair, hair color, hair styles, where to find cool hair styles, hair products, etc. I just sat there and thought, "I need a haircut."

Laury felt so good after the visit that we drove home with the sun roof open, not listening to our book-on-tape, but just talking and enjoying the good news.

All our Love.

Wednesday, 3/18/2015 – Farewell to a dear friend

"To part is the lot of all mankind. The world is a scene of constant leave-taking, and the hands that grasp in cordial greeting today, are doomed ere long to unite for the last time, when the quivering lips pronounce the word - 'Farewell" - R. M. Ballantyne

I took Laury to see her dear friend, Joan, yesterday. Joan is dying. Joan has stopped seeing people as the end of her journey nears, but she agreed to see Laury. We sat with Joan and Clyde in their living room. Joan was having trouble staying awake but was able to recognize Laury and was happy to see her.

Laury and Joan became prayer partners in 1996. Even with the difference in their ages, Laury and Joan are close. Laury says that Joan was her "great encourager". Laury had wanted to go to Africa on a mission trip and Joan helped her figure it out and make it come true. Clyde told us that one of the young women Joan encouraged to go into nursing was Joan's nurse the first night she was in the hospital here in Naperville.

As we were getting ready to leave, Laury quietly told Clyde that she would not be able to attend Joan's funeral and Clyde said he understood and that Joan would, too.

It wasn't a long stay. Our visit was to say farewell to a good friend. Farewell Joan. God bless you and Clyde.

All our Love.

Friday, 3/20/2015 – Not lost

"We make a lot of detours, but we're always heading for the same destination" - Paulo Coelho

We had another great clinic visit yesterday. Laury and I arrived a little late (more about that below) but we were taken right away into our room at 10 Central and Laury had her blood drawn and her line dressing changed. We then went down to the clinic and had a short wait to see Dr. Odenike. Laury's blood numbers are still looking great- virtually unchanged from Monday. We got in to see Dr. Odenike so quickly that the rest of the lab numbers were not yet available. Dr. Odenike decided to leave everything as we have it, and if the liver numbers changed she would call us. We were out of the clinic before five and home around six thirty. Another really nice visit.

On our way to clinic, yesterday, I noticed a message on one of the overhead signs said something about an incident that had closed all northbound lanes of the freeway. Unfortunately, the closure was right before we get off I55 on to Lake Shore Drive. I am not very familiar with this part of Chicago, since we always take the same route to the clinic. We slowly exited and after a few turns I felt we were headed in the right direction. It helps to know that if the lake is in front of you, you are heading east and if the city is in your rear view mirror you are heading south. We needed to go south from where we were to the clinic. Laury was trying to get her iPhone to give us directions but her phone wanted to send us back to the freeway. We figured out the route and were only about ten minutes late at the clinic.

I can't say we enjoyed the new route or saw something interesting that we wouldn't have seen if we had not gotten off our normal path. It is not a great part of Chicago. But it did remind me that just like this journey we are on there are times when we find ourselves having to get off our normal path. It helps to have a destination in mind and a little understanding of your surroundings. It builds enough confidence to know that despite not really knowing where we are that we are heading in the right direction and that we will eventually get there.

All our Love.

Sunday, 3/22/2015 – Spring

"It is spring again. The earth is like a child that knows poems by heart." - Rainer Maria Rilke

Yesterday was a beautiful spring day. Even though they are predicting snow tomorrow, spring is finally here. I was thinking about last spring and the thing that struck me most is that I can't remember the feeling of spring last year. Yes, there were times when it felt good to open the sun roof of the car and drive with the windows rolled down, but it seems like spring never really existed last year. Perhaps the reason for these feelings is because last spring we were in the midst of planning for Laury's transplant.

Spring around our house always has a sense of energy with the coming of warm weather. The plans of our spring usually revolve around outside living spaces and gardens. Last year was different. In some ways we missed spring. Not this year. Even though Laury will not be able to get into her gardens this year, she has the energy of spring in her again.

Yesterday, Laury and I went into the city to get our hair cut. Afterwards, we went across the street to a big salvage warehouse and looked for nothing in particular. Laury kept saying how fun it was to just go through all the stuff at the warehouse and think about what we could do with some of the more unique items. Laury bought an old piece of planking and we brought it home in the Mini. Laury rearranged the sun room to make a space for this new find. She was like a little puppy; she has tons of energy, then when I left to go grocery shopping she crashed and slept while I was gone.

It is good to notice spring again. I saw the chipmunks and rabbits chasing each other around the yard across the street. When you walk outside, the first thing you hear is the cardinal calling. It is not that those things were not there last spring, it is that we were not there. I think one of the greatest gifts of healing is to be able to notice spring again.

All our Love.

Tuesday, 3/24/2015 – More change

"Love the moment for its simplicity, it may give or take nothing from you, but in the blinking of an eye it will have change so many things forever." - Steven Redhead, The Solution

Laury and I watched the snow come down heavily yesterday morning and I thought, "Great. I write about spring and this will be the first time that the weather has kept us from going to clinic." The snow stopped around noon and we decided to leave early, anticipating heavy traffic. We left the house at one and got to the clinic a little after two. We hit almost no traffic. We were so early that 10 Central was not ready for us. We offered to come back, but the nurse said they would squeeze us in and do a quick blood draw. The nurse took Laury's blood and we went down to the clinic to wait for Dr. Odenike. We had a normal wait and saw Dr. Pettit first. Dr. Pettit relayed that Laury's blood numbers are still looking really good. Her hemoglobin was up again to 10.6. Her platelets and white counts were down a little but not enough to be concerned.

We waited a little while longer and Dr. Odenike came in the room. Laury's liver numbers are about the same. The ALT which had been going up came down and the AST which had been coming down went up a little. Dr. Odenike was pleased with the results and decided to leave the steroid dosage the same. Laury's magnesium level was also good, so we are sticking with the everyday routine.

Next week, Dr. Odenike is out on spring vacation. We will see Dr. Pettit on Monday and then have Laury's blood checked on Thursday out here in Naperville. The following week we start seeing Dr. Odenike on Tuesday mornings, and will do the second blood draw, if necessary, in Naperville. It will be a nice change to only have to go downtown once a week.

We left the clinic at four forty- five and headed home. Usually, when Laury and I leave before five, the drive home takes two hours. Yesterday we were home in less than an hour. Sometimes the bad weather can work in your favor.

This morning Laury just learned that Joan passed away last night. We are saddened by the news. Please keep Clyde and the rest of Joan's family in your prayers.

All our Love.

Thursday, 3/26/2015 – True strength

"Discipline is strength to the muscles your heels will need to climb up the hills of greatness" - **Constance Chuks Friday**

Laury was released from physical therapy yesterday. The nurse showed up and spent some time with Laury talking and observing how much Laury had progressed since the first time they met. I have not talked much about how much discipline Laury has applied to her healing. She has always done what is asked of her by the doctors and therapists. It is hard to be home on your own and follow these routines; it takes discipline.

I have not been able to go to my yoga classes for a long time. I have not developed my own home practice like Laury has. I said to Laury the other night how much I admire her strength in doing the yoga and exercises every day on her own. It is a strength I don't think I possess.

Laury is getting physically stronger every day. I can see some definition in her arms and she can go upstairs better than I. Laury is able to lift and move things that just a few weeks ago she was not able to. This renewed strength is good to see, however, Laury's true strength lies in her ability and discipline to keep doing what needs to be done to get healthy.

All our Love.

Friday, 3/27/2015 – Sense of freedom

"There is freedom waiting for you,

On the breezes of the sky,

And you ask "What if I fall?"

Oh but my darling,

What if you fly?" — Erin Hanson

Laury and I had a busy day yesterday. Laury had an eye appointment at noon. I was on a senior staff meeting conference call. The meeting was from eleven thirty to one. I was on the call for a few minutes before I had to run downstairs to take Laury to her appointment. I left the call on and told Autumn, our cat, on the chair next to me, "Pay attention to the call and let me know if anything important happens." I drove Laury to the eye doctor about five minutes from our home. I dropped Laury off and watched her walk in to the office with some of the same feeling as watching our girls walk into their first day of school. I then drove back home and found Autumn sound asleep where I left her. Funny, but this is what usually happens to me during these staff meetings, too.

Laury texted me a short while later and said she was done at the doctor's and was walking to Starbucks for a coffee. My meeting was almost done so I hung up and drove back to town to pick Laury up. Laury said it was nice to walk around by herself. She said she felt a sense of freedom. I guess I never thought of that, but for the last several months Laury has not gone anywhere by herself- there is always someone with her.

Later in the afternoon Laury and I drove down to clinic. We had Laury's blood drawn and her dressing changed at 10 Central and then went down to clinic. After a short wait Dr. Odenike came into the room. Almost before she finished saying hi to us she said, "Your liver numbers look wonderful! I can go on vacation without having to worry about you." Dr. Odenike said that after she saw the numbers she couldn't wait to come tell us. All of Laury's liver numbers came down. Dr. Odenike said that she hopes this means that we have turned the corner and the GVHD is going away. All Laury could say was, "Yes, Yes!" Laury's other blood numbers went up, as well. Her hemoglobin is at 11.1 and her platelets are over 110,000. The numbers could not be better. After checking Laury's spleen, lungs and heart, Dr. Odenike said we were free to go. We wished her a safe and fun vacation.

Laury and I walked to the elevators and then back to the car. I must have heard Laury say "Wow, wow, my liver numbers went down" at least fifteen times on the short walk. We hope we have turned the corner. It might be a little too early to tell, but yesterday gave Laury and me a sense of the freedom that comes from healing.

All our Love.

Monday, 3/30/2015 – Risks

"Love has no demand of us but to keep practicing, to do the next hard thing. Love says, Come dear. Take the next step." - Anna White, Mended: Thoughts On Life, Love And Leaps Of Faith

Our daughter, Lyndsay, is looking for a new (used) car. She doesn't have a lot of money to spend and has asked me for my help in finding a car within her budget. The process of buying a used car is fraught with risk. You are never sure you are getting a good car or that you are not getting taken advantage of, etc. There is also the risk that you will pick a car that you like and not one that your daughter wants. Saturday Laury, Lyndsay, Bryan and I went looking at used cars. There are not many to look at in Lyndsay's price range and the ones we found I felt were not a good buy. After several hours of driving and looking, Lyndsay was frustrated that the process had been taken out of her hands. Lyndsay feels like she doesn't have the knowledge to know a good car when she see it and that perhaps I have taken too much control over the decision making.

I have decided to step back and let Lyndsay find her own car. It is a risk I know, but I also know that it has to be Lyndsay's car and her decision.

On Friday, Laury's mom was admitted to the hospital with pneumonia. Laury, of course, was very concerned and talked with her dad to see how things were going. I asked Laury if she wanted to go see her mom and she said, "I don't know if I can risk going to the hospital." While we were out looking at cars, Laury's mom called Laury. They talked for a few minutes and afterwards Laury said to me, "OK, I now understand why it was so important for my parents to hear my voice when I was in the hospital." I asked Laury again if she want to go see her mom, and again she replied, "I don't think I can risk it."

Sunday morning Laury was sitting drinking her tea and she said to me, "I think I want to go see my mom." I said, "OK, let's go." Laury replied, "Do you think it is crazy for me to be going into a hospital?" I said that no, we would be careful, and if it was important to see her mom, it was worth the risk. So we got ready and we drove to the hospital. Laury wore her mask the entire time we were there and washed her hands twice. Laury also got to spend some great time with her mom and to see that she is on the mend. Later in the day we delivered some chicken soup and a roast chicken dinner I made for Laury's dad. We spent a few minutes getting caught up on Laury's mom, and Laury's dad again said how glad Laury's mom was to see us and how much it meant to her.

Were there risks in Laury going into the hospital? Yes, but there is no such thing as risk-free love.

All our Love.

Tuesday, 3/31/2015 – The time is right

"He nods, as if to acknowledge that endings are almost always a little sad, even when there is something to look forward to on the other side."
- Emily Giffin, Love The One You're With

Yesterday was our last afternoon visit to the clinic. Starting next week Laury and I will be going once a week on Tuesday mornings. We will be swapping an easy drive in and a long drive home for a long drive in and an easy drive home. We met with Dr. Pettit and Dr. Liew yesterday. Laury's blood numbers continue to be great; with her hemoglobin still above 11. We did not get the liver results before we left, but Dr. Pettit promised to call us with the results today. We all feel the numbers will be the same or better than last week.

Yesterday was also our last official meeting with Dr. Pettit. She is not shifting her hours to the morning with Dr. Odenike. It is a little sad to know we won't see her on our visits. Dr. Pettit always brought a smile and compassion to the room. On Thursday we will have Laury's blood checked here in Naperville, this is also part of our new routine.

Laury seems to have turned a corner- her energy is good, her blood numbers are strong, she looks and feels great. Laury and I are excited not to have to go to clinic twice a week. We will not miss the drive or time these visits take, because our clinic days are long. However, with any change there is a little sadness, like not seeing Dr. Pettit and perhaps some of the other staff that will not be there in the morning.

Last time we cut back to once a week visits we were glad that things were going as well as they were. Now we look back and realize that Laury is in so much better shape now then back then that we feel this time it is right. We don't need to be going twice a week. This is a really good feeling.

All our Love.

CHAPTER FIFTEEN

April

Monday, 4/6/2015 – Easter to Easter

"Awareness born of love is the only force that can bring healing and renewal. Out of our love for another person, we become more willing to let our old identities wither and fall away, and enter a dark night of the soul, so that we may stand naked once more in the presence of the great mystery that lies at the core of our being. This is how love ripens us -- by warming us from within, inspiring us to break out of our shell, and lighting our way through the dark passage to new birth." - John Welwood

I took Thursday and Friday off work last week to try to get caught up on some projects around the house. On Thursday I rented an edge sander to sand the floors upstairs. As the name implies, the edge sander sands the floor close to the baseboard where the big sander can't reach. I spent a couple of hours working on the floors before we had to go and get Laury's blood checked. We had Laury's blood drawn in Naperville on Thursday, and Jessica was very glad to see us. Jessica said that sometimes when you don't see a patient for a long time it is a good thing. After drawing Laury's blood, Jessica sat down in her chair and said, "So tell me what is going on." This was not just a medical question, but also a personal one. Laury brought Jessica up to date on all the happenings in our lives and Jessica shared some of hers as well. Jessica called us later in the afternoon with the blood results and Laury's blood numbers were unchanged. Things are still looking really good.

Friday morning Lyndsay came by and Laury, Lyndsay and I went to look at a car for Lyndsay. I found the car at a dealership about twenty miles away and Lyndsay had confirmed a time with the agent to come see it. The car turned out to be really nice and we got it for a good price. Lyndsay is happy and I am happy to have removed another item from my "list".

Saturday morning Laury and I got up early and went to Chicago to get our hair cut. It was good to see Magen again and Laury's hair now has a style not just "grow back". After getting home from Chicago, I rented the big floor sander, and with the help of Pete, got the thing upstairs and finished sanding the floors. After about four hours of sanding I was finally done, and again with Pete's help, brought the sander downstairs and returned it to Home Depot. After a shower I went grocery shopping.

Yesterday Laury and I went to see Laury's parents. Laury's mom came home from the hospital on Saturday and is on the mend. Laury made her parents some cookies and we made them a ham dinner. Later in the afternoon Lyndsay and Bryan stopped by.

It was a very full few days off. As usual, I never get done all the things I want to get done. Yesterday I sat at the computer to begin working on our taxes. I thought about last Easter. The day before Easter last year Magen taught Laury how to wrap scarfs around her head in anticipation of Laury losing her hair. The day after Easter, Craig came and cleaned out the gardens. A lot has changed since then. Laury recently told me that she feels ready for the healing now more than she did before her last hospital stay. Laury said the last hospital stay changed her outlook. Laury said it was almost like she had something left that she needed to let go of before the complete healing could take place. Easter is all about rebirth. But to have rebirth you have to have death. Laury and I have died to many things over the last year: giving up things that we thought were important, giving over control to others, excepting limitations. All of these "deaths" gave us room for rebirths. Easter reminded Laury and me that we have seen lots of rebirth in the time since our last Easter.

All our Love.

Tuesday, 4/7/2015 – Early Morning

"Morning drew on apace. The air became more sharp and piercing, as its first dull hue: the death of night, rather than the birth of day: glimmered faintly in the sky. The objects which had looked dim and terrible in the darkness, grew more and more defined, and gradually resolved into their familiar shapes. The rain came down, thick and fast; and pattered, noisily, among the leafless bushes." - **Charles Dickens**

So maybe the morning wasn't as gloomy as what Charles Dickens described, but it was raining and really dark when Laury and I left the house at five thirty this morning. Today was our first morning clinic visit with Dr. Odenike. We really had no idea how long it was going to take to get to the U of C at this time of the morning so we gave ourselves plenty of time. The drive down wasn't too bad and we arrived a little before seven. Ten Central, where we get Laury's blood drawn, doesn't officially open until 8:00am, but they told us we could come as early as seven and someone would be there to do the draw. We stopped on the 7th floor and Laury got a cup of coffee and we sat in the lounge area until a few minutes after seven. Laury wanted to give the nurses a chance to set up so she didn't want to go up right at seven.

Laury got her blood drawn and her line dressing changed and we headed down to the clinic at seven thirty. We checked in and hoped the wait wouldn't be long. Laury and I were scheduled as Dr. Odenike's first appointment. After about ten minutes we were taken back to our room and about ten minutes later Dr. Odenike came in. The visit was short because most of Laury's blood numbers were not back from the lab yet. Laury's hemoglobin is now up to 12.0 and her platelets and white counts are stable. We hope to hear later today on the rest of the numbers, especially the liver functions.

We left the clinic around eight forty-five and were home before nine thirty. I am a little tired from getting up early but it is nice to know that once we are home Laury and I don't have to go back out after work. I think this new time is going to work. Hopefully the traffic will be this good every time and everything will run smoothly. We will see how next Tuesday, goes.

All our Love.

Wednesday, 4/8/2015 – Water

"Water - a thoroughly underrated drink." - Wayne Gerard Trotman

Yesterday we once again learned the importance of drinking enough water. Paula, Dr. Odenike's nurse, called yesterday to inform us of a new hydration routine. Laury's kidney numbers have been slowly going up over the last few weeks. The numbers are still well within the normal range but the fact they are going up means we have to act now before the numbers get into the high range. The kidney numbers reflect the stress the medications - particularly Prograf, puts on Laury's system. When Laury went back on the Prograf to help fight the Graft versus Host Disease, the doctors put her on a fairly high dosage. Each time they do a blood draw on Laury the doctors check the Prograf level to make sure it is in the proper range - not too low to work but not too high to do damage.

The Prograf levels have been inching up at the same time as the kidney numbers. So we are reducing the Prograf starting today. Also, to help the kidneys, the doctors are increasing the amount of intravenous fluids Laury will be getting. Right now Laury receives her Magnesium every other day in a 250ml bag of fluids. Starting tomorrow I will be giving Laury the magnesium in a 500ml bag. In addition, the days when Laury doesn't get the magnesium, she will get a 500ml bag of plain saline. Today Paula wants Laury to get an entire liter of plain saline to help jump start the process of flushing her kidneys.

Laury's liver numbers have come down a little again and the last one that is still out of the normal range is now very close to normal. We hope we haven't traded a liver problem for a kidney problem. Paula says we haven't, that we just need to keep the kidneys flushed to prevent a problem. Last time Laury got a liter of fluid her feet looked like water balloons when it was done. I am running the fluids very slowly this time and we hope that Laury will be able to get rid of the fluids as fast as it is going in.

Laury admitted that she hasn't been drinking as much fluids as she did before- partly because she is trying to stay away from sugar and she used to drink a lot of juice. So now we are looking for teas or other drinks that don't include sugar to help Laury get enough fluids.

Sometimes it feels like we plug one hole and another one appears.

All our Love.

Wednesday, 4/8/2015 – They Won!

"To subdue the enemy without fighting is the acme of skill" - Sun Tzu, The Art Of War

A few months ago I talked about how Laury's blood type is B positive and her donor's blood type is A positive, and at some point Laury's blood type would change over to A positive. I used the image of a war going on between the old antibodies, that were in greater number but did not have any re-enforcements, and Laury's new antibodies that were outnumbered but producing re-enforcements and would eventually win the war.

I had a feeling with Laury's increasing hemoglobin number that the battle had been won and this change over had happened. To confirm my suspicions I asked to have Laury's blood typed and cross matched as part of her last blood check on Tuesday. Dr. Odenike asked me why I wanted the test because they usually only order it if it looks like Laury would need blood. I told Dr. Odenike that I wanted to know, and the change is a big milestone. This afternoon Dr. Odenike called and told us that Laury's blood type is now A positive!

Laury has talked about how the last hospital stay caused a shift in her. She says it forced her to go deeper emotionally and to give up more physically. Maybe these had to happen for the shift to finally take place. Laury becoming A positive is a huge physical and emotional milestone. Physically it means that Laury's new bone marrow is firmly in control of her blood antibodies and her old antibodies are no longer needed to protect her. It also means no more low hemoglobin and transfusions. Emotionally, it means we are over the worry and stress of wondering if the transplant was successful. There is no going back now.

We won!

All our Love.

Thursday, 4/9/2015 – Giving thanks

"Cultivate the habit of being grateful for every good thing that comes to you, and to give thanks continuously. And because all things have contributed to your advancement, you should include all things in your gratitude." - Ralph Waldo Emerson

Thank you all for your wonderful comments on our happy news.

I was on a conference call yesterday when I heard Laury talking excitedly on the phone while coming up the stairs with her IV pole in tow. I quickly put the speaker phone on mute and turned to tell Laury I was on a call. She was so excited when she saw me she said, "It is Dr. Odenike. My blood type is A positive!" I turned back to my conference call and told them I had to step away for a couple of minutes to talk with my wife's doctor. I put the phone on mute again and went back to Laury. Laury put her phone on speaker and we heard Dr. Odenike explain why when the initial blood results came back the report said Laury was still B positive. This is what Paula had reported to us yesterday morning when she called. Dr. Odenike explained that after she saw the results, she called the doctor in charge of the blood bank to confirm the results. Dr. Odenike said that the blood bank will not change a blood type until all the antibody tests are completed, and will sometimes ask for additional test to make sure they are correct. Dr. Odenike asked the doctor if Laury's blood is in fact A positive and he answered, "Yes".

After hearing this Dr. Odenike congratulated Laury and Laury congratulated her. I went back to my conference call and tried to pay attention to what was being said. After my call was completed I sat for a few minutes to absorb the news from Dr. Odenike. I was very excited and for a second I reached for the phone to call my mom. Reality hit me and I began to cry. I went downstairs and saw Laury in the kitchen. I told her what had happened and she hugged me and said, "She knows." I said, "Yeah she probably knew before we did."

Laury called her parents to give them the news but they were at the doctor's office and her dad said he would call back when they got home. Laury and I were sitting in our bedroom watching TV when her dad called back. We first heard the good news of Laury's mom continued healing, and then Laury shouted into the phone, "My blood type is now A positive!" Her yelling scared both cats and they ran from the room.

Laury and I tried to decide what to do to celebrate. Laury can't have alcohol or sweets right now so that removed a lot of things from the list. We decided to have a nice dinner. After dinner we sat quietly watching TV. I frequently would look over at Laury and most times she was looking back at me. We would smile at each other and say in a soft voice, "Thank you".

All our Love.

Monday, 4/13/2015 – Thirty again

"Pan, who and what art thou?" he cried huskily.

"I'm youth, I'm joy," Peter answered at a venture, "I'm a little bird that has broken out of the egg." - J.M. Barrie, Peter Pan

I had trouble keeping up with Laury this weekend. At times I felt like we are on two different life trajectories: Laury getting younger and me getting older. I must have heard Laury say, "I feel like I am thirty again!" at least twenty times over the weekend. Laury and I have laughed and joked about what she was going to be like with normal hemoglobin. Laury's hemoglobin is at 12.1 right now- still low by normal standards but her energy is amazing. This weekend we moved furniture around the dining room so Laury could strip the old wallpaper border. She spent several hours on the step ladder steaming and cleaning the walls. One thing we did find out was that while hooked up to a gravity fed IV you can't have your heart above the IV bag or the whole system works backwards. Laury called me while I was at the grocery store to say that there was blood in her IV line. I told her to come down off the ladder and the flow would return to normal. It did and Laury was fine, but she was not happy that she had to wait for the IV to finish before she could resume stripping the wall paper.

On Saturday I attended Joan's memorial service. The service had been planned by Joan and it was a true reflection of her spirit and personality. There were laughs, tears, and even a Dixieland band playing a New Orleans funeral march. I kept saying to Marty sitting next to me, "This is so Joan." Laury was not able to attend but was there in spirit.

I finished sanding the floors upstairs and managed to get two coats of varnish on the floors. I also started installing the bookshelves in the dining room on Sunday. Laury kept me hopping. I told Laury last night that I am going to have to start running again to build up my stamina to keep up with her. I don't think either one of us realized how much Laury's energy had dropped over the last few years. Now that is it coming back I am going to have my hands full. I love it.

All our Love.

Tuesday, 4/14/2015 – Excitement and freedom

"I sat down and tried to rest. I could not; though I had been on foot all day, I could not now repose an instant; I was too much excited. A phase of my life was closing tonight, a new one opening tomorrow: impossible to slumber in the interval; I must watch feverishly while the change was being accomplished." - Charlotte Bronte, Jane Eyre

Laury and I just got back from our morning appointment with Dr. Odenike. Once again everything ran smoothly and the lab even had Laury's blood chemistry numbers ready when we met with Dr. Odenike. Laury's hemoglobin is now up to 12.5, which Dr. Odenike said she believed was higher than her own. Laury's kidney function numbers were back down into the normal range so we can quit the extra fluids. Laury's liver numbers are still stable so Dr. Odenike is reducing the steroid dosage. Laury also told Dr. Odenike that she could no longer feel her spleen. If you remember, a year ago Laury's' spleen was so large that Laury looked six months pregnant. Dr. Odenike today said that Laury's spleen is the smallest she has ever seen it. Everything looks really good.

Laury had a bunch of things to ask Dr. Odenike about this visit, mostly having to do with removing some restrictions now that Laury is doing so well. Laury asked Dr. Odenike about attending a yoga class at our studio for cancer survivors. Dr. Odenike was reluctant the first time Laury asked to sign the approval form but today she signed it and Laury can now go to the class. Laury asked about driving, and Dr. Odenike said it was fine for Laury to begin driving again. It has been almost a year since Laury last drove and so today, after we stopped at the grocery store, Laury drove home. As we turned into our driveway was saw our neighbor, Mary Ann, and Laury yelled to her, "I'm driving! The first time in a year!" Mary Ann yelled back her congratulations. Laury is going to drive herself to an appointment with her energy healer later today. I am nervous and excited for Laury to have this new freedom.

I asked if Laury could be cleared for travel. Dr. Odenike said, yes that Laury can now travel- no planes but we can drive to Michigan and see my Mom's house once more before it is sold. We hope to get up there in the next three weeks.

Laury still needs to avoid crowds and people who are sick. Unfortunately, that means Laury can't visit her mother right now, who is still recovering from pneumonia.

The visit was full of newfound freedom, excitement and celebration. When we got home I had to go upstairs to work, and Laury wanted to go out and play and celebrate. I told Laury on the way home, "You have to promise me that with this newfound energy and freedom you will go easy on me." She laughed and said that yes she will try to remember that I don't have thirty year old blood like she does.

All our Love.

Friday, 4/17/2015 – Jessica

"Kindness is a calling. Caring about people is powerful. Love changes lives." - Rachel Hamilton

Yesterday Laury and I went to the cancer center here in Naperville to have Laury's blood checked. Laury's blood numbers are really good and basically unchanged from Tuesday.

When Jessica, our nurse, saw us she quickly came up to Laury and hugged her saying, "Congratulations on your blood changing. That is really great news!" We had told Jessica several months ago that we wanted her to be the one who called us with the news. Jessica would always check after the blood results were back and text Laury with the results. When we heard that Laury's blood had changed I said we should text Jessica with the news. Laury sent a text to Jessica with the news of her blood the morning after we heard from Dr. Odenike.

We were sitting talking to Jessica as she took Laury's blood, Jessica told us that she was the charge nurse the morning Laury texted her. Jessica said she was in the middle of handing out assignments when she got Laury's text. Jessica said when she read it she yelled out, "People, stop what you are doing. Laury Hartman just texted me that her blood changed over to A positive!" Jessica said that all the nurses gave a cheer: she said they were truly excited and happy for Laury.

These nurses are special people. It is nice to know that they care so much and that we were able to give them some good news to make their day better.

All our Love.

Monday, 4/20/2015 – Perspective

"Each of us sees things not as they are but as we are." - Jack Provonsha

Before Laury went in for her transplant she had some friends over to help her "undecorate" the house. All of the live plants had to be removed. All of the tree branches, moss and other outside things Laury had brought in needed to be taken out. Laury gave away the house plants her friends took some of her favorite stumps for safe keeping until they are allowed back in. The friends also helped remove some of the items on shelves and the walls to make cleaning easier. The house looked bare, or less cluttered, depending on your point of view.

Laury has been redecorating some of the rooms in the last few weeks. The live plants and stumps are still not allowed, but some of the other "clutter" has found its way back. This weekend I started the installation of the new bookcases that are going on the end wall of our dining room. I got the basic boxes and the track lighting installed. As we were sitting looking at the new bookcases, Laury said she couldn't wait to decorate them.

Laury said to me, "Do you remember when my friends helped me "undecorate" the house?" I said I did, and Laury went on, "They kept telling me while we were doing the work, 'Just think of how much fun you will have redecorating it after', I kept saying to them, 'But my house is done, I don't want to redecorate it'. I guess I was just too tired to think about redecorating." Laury then said to me, "Doing these projects is like when we were first married and before kids. It is fun to do them again and they don't seem overwhelming at all, just exciting."

Laury's perspective has changed with her increase in energy. Never once did I think Laury would not redecorate; it is in her nature. Laury once called me at work and said, "What would you think if I painted the living room green?" I said I was OK if it was a nice green. Laury replied, "Oh good, I think you will like it." I said, "You already have it painted don't you?" and Laury replied, "Yup!" I fully expect to see the stumps, branches and moss appearing any day.

All our Love.

Thursday, 4/23/2015 – Happy

"When I was 5 years old, my mother always told me that happiness was the key to life. When I went to school, they asked me what I wanted to be when I grew up. I wrote down 'happy'. They told me I didn't understand the assignment, and I told them they didn't understand life."
- John Lennon

The last few days have been full. Monday, Laury's new garden helper, Kirk, came over and spent the day with Laury working in the garden. Kirk is doing the garden work that I would do, but the difference is Kirk knows what he is doing. For most of the day Laury was out watching Kirk and doing small jobs that didn't involve digging. I went outside at one point to check on their progress and Laury came up to me smiling through her mask, and said, "I am so happy!" The only thing that would make it better is if Laury could get her hands dirty.

Tuesday we went to our morning clinic visit. Laury's hemoglobin is now 12.8. Dr. Odenike jokingly said, "You have so much now you might have to give some away." Laury's liver numbers went up a little. We are watching them this week without changing any medications to see if it is a trend. I really see how balancing the medications is an art. Lowering the Prograf helped Laury's kidney numbers come back to normal but without the extra Prograf her Graft Versus Host disease might not be as well controlled. Raising the Prograf might help control the GVHD but it puts pressure on the liver. Everything is connected and the art is to get them all in balance and to keep them there. It is always a moving target.

Laury asked Dr. Odenike if she could prune the bushes and water the plants. Dr. Odenike said no to both and then Laury said, "What if I water using a long wand?" Dr. Odenike turned to me and said, "Your wife knows how to negotiate the littlest things out of me!" Dr. Odenike then agreed that Laury can water with a long wand. Laury clapped her hands and said, "Yeah I can water!" Laury told me how happy she is to be able to water the plants. Another small step towards full gardening privileges.

Yesterday, Laury and I attended her first Yoga class this year. The studio we go to offers a free class for cancer survivors and their caregivers. As we were driving to the studio Laury said, "I feel like this is my first day at school. I am excited and happy and nervous all at the same time." The class was nice, and even though I didn't check on Laury every minute, it was nice to have her by my side. We both were happy she was there.

When I thought about what to say regarding the last few days, the first word that came to mind was "busy". But the more I thought about our days, the word "happy" seems to be a better descriptor. I can see how happy Laury is and she tells me she is happy all the time. Happy is a good place to be.

All our Love.

Tuesday, 4/28/2015 – Simple things

"The simplest things are sometimes more powerful than you can possibly imagine." - Steeven Shaw

"Those blood numbers are the best I have seen in a post-transplant, Myelofibrosis patient in a very long time!" Dr. Odenike told Laury as she turned the computer screen to show us Laury's latest results. Laury's White counts are stable and her hemoglobin is now at 12.9 and her platelets have climbed to 120,000. When you view the test results on the computer screen, numbers that are high or low are marked with a red up or down arrow. Dr. Odenike used to laugh when the lab would call her to tell her that Laury's hemoglobin was below normal. She said, "I would tell the lab technician, 'I am an oncologist. All my patients' blood numbers are abnormal'. What did they expect?" Laury's report has fewer red arrows then I can ever remember seeing before. So many of the numbers listed are now in the normal range- it is amazing.

For the first time today we talked with Dr. Odenike about a plan to get Laury off the IV's and remove her central line. Laury's Hiccman line was put in on June 4th of last year during her first day in the hospital. We asked the nurses then how long the central line can stay in. The nurses told us that the lines are usually good for six to eight months. Laury's line has been in eleven months. Dr. Odenike says that if Laury's numbers are as good next week then she will take Laury off the IV anti-fungal medication and the IV magnesium and if everything remains stable Dr. Odenike will remove the central line.

Laury has not been able to take a bath or normal shower since the central line was placed, because she can't risk getting the area wet. For the last year Laury has been showering with the hand-held shower head on the floor of the shower and bending over to wash her hair. The bottom half of Laury gets the shower, the top half gets a wash cloth. Laury says the first thing she wants to do when the line is removed is to take a long bath. Of course, once the line is removed it means Laury will go back to getting her arm stuck to get her blood checked. Laury says it will be worth it.

Dr. Odenike decided to make no changes in Laury's medications this week. Dr. Odenike wished us a safe trip and told us to enjoy our time together and with family this weekend as we head to Michigan. Small freedoms that we all take for granted- a shower, a road trip, seeing friends and family- are coming back into Laury's life.

All our Love.

Wednesday, 4/29/2015 – Memory

"If you wish to forget anything on the spot, make a note that this thing is to be remembered." - Edgar Allan Poe

Laury asked me yesterday if I thought her short term memory would come back. To tell the truth, I don't remember what we were talking about, but Laury asked me the same question she had asked earlier in the day. At first when Laury was home after the transplant she had a difficult time keeping some things straight. We called it "Chemo Brain". The effects of chemotherapy are known to affect memory, and mostly the short term memory.

I have noticed that Laury's memory has improved greatly and she manages to keep her memories straight most of the time. Yesterday, I got a reminder call from the dentist office for my upcoming cleaning. Since the appointment is at 7:00am I was concerned that I wouldn't remember it. I asked Laury to remind me so I wouldn't forget. Last night I left a note on the refrigerator to remind me.

As I was getting out of bed this morning Laury said to me, "Don't forget the dentist appointment." I was impressed that she remembered and I took a shower and got ready to leave for the dentist. I left the house at six forty- five and arrived at the dentist at six fifty- five. The door to the office was open and I sat down to wait. The office was really quiet but it wasn't until the dentist came out and looked at me funny and asked me what time my appointment was that we both realized that my appointment is tomorrow.

I drove back home laughing. I can't blame Laury. She remembered the dentist appointment. I just got the day wrong. I wonder if chemo brain is contagious.

All our Love.

CHAPTER SIXTEEN

May

Monday, 5/4/2015 – Road home

"...what happens when you return

and find nothing

but a hollowed shell,

shingles and floor,

walls and echoes

and the light that lead you here

has now burned out

and the ones who built it

have traveled afar

and you can't go to them,

no matter what shoes you wear." - Kellie Elmore, Magic in the Backyard

This past weekend Laury and I went to Michigan. It was our first road trip in almost two years. As we were packing the suitcase Thursday night I said to Laury, "This feels strange. I packed this suitcase four times in the last year, but this is the first time we are not taking it to the hospital." The trip was freeing is so many ways. We left early Friday morning, and as we got on I355 heading south I said to Laury, "When we get to the I55 exit to Chicago make sure I am in the left hand lane I am afraid out of habit I might just take the wrong exit and find ourselves heading to U of C instead of Michigan." Everything beyond I55 on I355 felt new and wonderful, even though we have been this way many times. Just to be on the road to somewhere different was nice.

Laury and I always stop at the first rest stop in Michigan. It is an hour and half from home and the first real opportunity to go to the bathroom. At the rest stop I hooked Laury up to her magnesium IV by hooking the bag to the clothes hook in the back window. It worked to keep the bag up high and it meant we didn't have to bring the IV pole. Laury figured out a routine for using the public rest rooms with a combination of mask, gloves and wipes so we were pretty confident of staying away from germs. The hotel we stayed at is located where Lake Huron empties into the St. Clair river, dividing the US and Canada. I asked for a river view room and we were able to sit on our balcony and watch the lake freighters go under the bridge. After we unpacked I called my sister and arranged a time to meet up, and then Laury and I went for a walk along the river. The breeze was off the lake, so it was cool, and the walk back to the hotel was into the wind, but it still felt good to stretch our legs after six hours in the car. After a short nap Laury and I got ready to go to my sister's.

It was good to see my sister, Kim. When we walked up to the front door, Kim met us. She couldn't hug Laury, so she gave me a hug for the both of us. I thought she would never let me go - we get our hugging from our Dad who could hug the stuffing out of us. Kim had collected a few boxes of things from my parents' house for me and we brought the boxes up from their basement and briefly went through the items. Laury and I then got into the car with Kim and her husband, Barry, and we headed down to see my Mom's house. I wasn't sure what I was feeling. Part of me thought I should be feeling sad, but I think what I was feeling was strange. I have no better way to describe it. When we arrived at the house, I didn't expect my Mom or Dad to be there to meet us. There wasn't a great feeling of loss walking around the outside of the house. Maybe I had already dealt with those emotions. The feeling walking around the empty house was surreal. I have never seen the house empty. I remember the how house looked when my grandparents lived in it and when we lived in it and when just my Mom lived there, but not empty. The house was empty the memories are not in the house.

We stopped at the grave yard and saw the freshly seeded area where my parents' graves are next to my Mom's parents. The headstone will be set later this summer.

We stopped at a local restaurant and had a nice dinner on the way back to Kim and Barry's. Laury and I then went back to our hotel and sat for a few minutes on the balcony and watched the nearly full moon rise over the river.

The next morning Laury and I ate breakfast at the hotel restaurant and talked about the previous day's events. I think it was the first time we were able to talk about the entire past year. There were tears and a feeling of loss and amazement of what we have been through. I said that the saying goes, "Don't sweat the small stuff" but this journey has been all about sweating the small things. When we looked at the journey as a whole it was almost overwhelming. I think both Laury and I sitting there got a feeling of what all of you must have been seeing - the big picture. We lived it one day, one small event at a time. The big picture was too scary - it still is.

Later that morning Laury and I went back to Kim and Barry's and met up with my sister, Lee, and her husband, Ron, and my younger sister, Jann. It was good to get caught up and hear another side to some of the stories of the last year. Laury and I went back to the hotel around two and took a two and half hour nap. We both agreed that we have been living such a quiet life that just the activity of engaging in group conversation for several hours took a lot out of us. I felt bad that I didn't get more time with

Jann- it is hard to pay attention to multiple conversations at once.

Later that evening Kim and Barry met us at the hotel restaurant for dinner. Laury was pretty tired and her stomach was not used to two days of restaurant food. After Kim and Barry left we went to bed. Sunday morning Kim and Barry stopped at the hotel on their way to church to bring the boxes of stuff from my parents' house, and we loaded up the car, said our goodbyes and headed home. We were ready to be home.

It was a good trip. I am still sorting through my emotions, I can't say what I am feeling about my parents, and I think it is going to take more time to process it all. I do know that I have never felt better sitting next to Laury blasting down the freeway. In some ways we were able to put a lot of last year in our past with this trip. We know we still have a ways to go, but seeing Laury, smiling, with the sun on her face, and feeding me pretzels is the best memory from the entire weekend.

All our Love.

Tuesday, 5/5/2015 - Traffic

"The enormous energy of the twentieth century, enough to drive the planet into a new orbit around a happier star, was being expended to maintain this immense motionless pause." - J. G. Ballard, Crash

It rained this morning probably because we had hooked up the sprinkler system and watered last night. We needed the rain. The gardens were very dry, and cracked looking, more like August than May. Most mornings the rain would have been welcome, however, this morning we had to drive to clinic. The rain acts on the traffic like a big anchor tied to each car, causing it to slow down, and frustrating all of the drivers. Our normal forty-five minute drive turned into an hour and a half of stop-and-go fun.

Once we finally got to clinic Laury had her blood drawn and dressing changed. Due to a miscommunication we were not on the schedule for 10 Central, but as usual, they took Laury in and were happy to see us.

We usually stop on the way to 10 Central and get Laury a coffee. Since we were late, Laury got her cup of coffee on our way from 10 Central to the clinic. Somehow, the rain had affected the computers at the coffee shop and the girl behind the counter was at a loss as what to do. She couldn't make Laury's Latte without first entering the sale into the computer. Finally, after waiting, about ten minutes Laury said to the girl, "We can pay cash and you could write down the sale and enter it later when the computer is back up." The girl agreed and we left with our small Latte. Laury was not leaving without her morning coffee.

The visit with Dr. Odenike was good. Laury's blood numbers remain stable and her hemoglobin is now 13. Laury's liver enzymes are almost back to the normal range, and there is only one that is about ten points out of normal. Dr. Odenike decided to reduce the dosage of steroids slightly and see what happens to the numbers. If the numbers remain stable or go down then Dr. Odenike will reduce the steroids again next Tuesday. Once Laury is at a dosage of 10mg every other day, Dr. Odenike is going to take Laury off the IV anti-fungal and the Hiccman line can come out. Laury received her final shot in the pneumonia vaccine series- another milestone.

Other than the long commute, the morning was full of continued good news.

All our Love.

Sunday, 5/10/2015 – Pain

"Another secret of the universe: Sometimes pain was like a storm that came out of nowhere. The clearest summer could end in a downpour. Could end in lightning and thunder." - Benjamin Alire Saenz, Aristotle And Dante Discover The Secrets Of The Universe

Today is Mother's Day. It is the first Mother's Day that I won't be calling my Mom. I had been preparing for the emotions of the day for a week. Last weekend when we went through her house the final time I thought again what it would be like not to call her on Mother's Day. My sister, Kim, sent me an email on Friday saying the closing on the house went off without a hitch on Thursday. The work of selling the house is done. The pain of my mom's passing is getting better.

Last night I experienced a different kind of pain; one like the storm described in the quote above. At midnight I woke up with severe lower back pain, and even though my mind wanted to believe it was something I had eaten, I knew right away it was a kidney stone. I had a kidney stone about five years ago and the pain was very familiar. I woke Laury to ask her if she could drive me to the emergency room. I knew she would not be able to come in with me, but I couldn't drive there on my own. The treatment for the pain has improved since the last time I had a kidney stone. Last time they gave me a pain pill and waited to see if it would help. So for what seemed like an eternity, I was in excruciating pain until they finally gave me a shot. Last night the nurse went right to the shots and within twenty minutes I was pretty much pain free.

I was not prepared for a kidney stone, or my Mother's death. The pain of these events took me by surprise.

This morning I am feeling the effects of the pain medication and I am able to move around, but I won't be driving to Laury's Mom today to celebrate her. The medication has made it possible to carry on, and this, coupled with drinking as much water as I can, should take care of the kidney stone. The selling of my Mother's house and getting through this first Mother's Day without her will also help in getting through the pain of her being gone.

All our Love.

Wednesday, 5/13/2015 – Patience

"A waiting person is a patient person. The word patience means the willingness to stay where we are and live the situation out to the full in the belief that something hidden there will manifest itself to us." - Henri J.M. Nouwen

I managed to feel good enough to drive Laury to her clinic visit yesterday. The last few days have not been fun, as kidney stones never are. Once the pain is managed you spend every two hours going to the bathroom hoping you have passed the thing. I have not, as of this writing. Sorry if this is too much information. I am glad this didn't happen anytime over the last year when Laury would not have been able to drive me to the emergency room or help out at home. Laury said to me yesterday, "It is a good thing our roles were not reversed and you went through the bone marrow transplant. I would have had to learn how to cook, or all our friends would have disappeared from getting asked to bring dinner every night."

We all have roles we play, and cooking is not one that Laury plays too often.

Laury's numbers are stable, and after the visit with Dr. Odenike yesterday, she is leaving all the medications the same for another week. The game plan is that if the numbers remain stable another week, Dr. Odenike is going to reduce the steroids again, and then if they still remain stable, she is going to take Laury off the IV anti-fungal and magnesium and remove the Hiccman line. If everything goes well, Laury should have the Hiccman line removed in early June.

Laury has been spending a lot of time in her gardens. Sometimes I see Laury out there with her gloves and mask on cutting a plant, and I will knock on the window and tell her she is not supposed to be doing that, and she will show me her gloves and mask. It is a fine line between her following the rules and having so much good energy spent in the garden. Both are good for Laury's healing. I love seeing Laury in her garden. She is so happy and full of energy moving from one garden to the next and spending the entire day with nature.

On Monday, Kirk Laury's garden helper, did not come because of the rain. I was off work and sleeping most of the day because of the pain medication, but Laury was like a kid stuck in the house on a rainy day. She wanted to be out in the garden. She kept saying to me, "I think we could have worked outside, it is not raining that hard." As it was, Laury spent a few hours out in the rain marking plants she wants Kirk to move when he comes on Thursday.

I am so grateful that Laury is doing so well. I wanted to so bad to finish the bookshelves in the dining room, but I was not able to because of the pain. I knew I could get to them this weekend, so it wasn't the end of the world. I can't imagine what Laury went through last summer watching her gardens and knowing she had to wait at least a year to get back into them. We have said that patience and waiting is such a large part of this journey, and I was reminded of that this weekend. Sometimes the hardest thing to do is to allow ourselves to be sick and simply wait to get better.

All our Love.

Monday, 5/18/2015 – Masks

"If we're wrapping ourselves up to conceal any vulnerability, whatever happens to us has to go through all those extra layers. Sometimes love doesn't even reach where we truly live." - Alexandra Katehakis

When I work in my shop I wear a mask to keep the dust out of my nose and lungs. It is sometimes a pain to have to take the mask off and on. It can slow me down. The past two weekends I have been working on the final trim for the bookcases in the dining room. I measure the piece of wood and then go out into my shop and put on my mask, and ear protection and measure and make the cut. Then I remove the ear protection and mask and come back in to see how well the piece fits. It would be a lot easier if I didn't have to wear the mask. But I have learned over the years that breathing the dust used to give me sinus headaches and sometimes even sinus infections. So the little extra time I have to take to put on the mask is worth it. I also find that sometimes putting on the mask slows me down in a good way. I can get in a hurry to finish a project and make a mistake. The little extra time it takes to put on the mask gives me time to slow down and think about what I doing.

Laury has been wearing a mask a lot the last year. At first for her it was a pain and a source of some arguments. Now wearing the mask out in public has become so natural for Laury she sometimes forgets she is wearing it. On Friday night we went to a local home improvement center to pick some crown molding for the bookcases. While we were walking into the store Laury said she wished she hadn't worn the t-shirt from the high school she worked at. I was about to ask her why and she said to me, "See there are a couple of people looking at me." Then she said, "Oh wait, they are probably looking at me because I am wearing a mask!" We both laughed, and I said, "Yeah I am sure it is the t-shirt."

The mask Laury wears is for protection, just like the one I wear in the shop. However, Laury and I have talked about the other masks we have worn over the last two years. Laury used a wagon that I bought for her last week. The wagon has a feature that it can dump the load by pulling a lever, making it easier to unload. I bought it for Laury because I saw she was having difficulty emptying the old wheel barrow. When I bought it Laury said she thought to herself, "I don't know why he bought that, I am done with gardening." Both of us were masking our true feelings but were afraid to admit them to each other. On Saturday we were driving in the Mini and Laury asked me, "Did you buy the Mini because you thought I was dying?" I said that I knew that she had always wanted one and yes, the thought had occurred to me. Again the masks.

I think some of the healing Laury and I have gone through in the last year has been due to removing masks. We thought the masks were necessary to protect ourselves, and the other person but they needed to be removed to get to the real issues and to help heal.

People have asked us if this disease and going through a bone marrow transplant has gotten in the way of our life together. The answer is yes and no. Of course, I am glad Laury no longer has cancer and is getting her energy back. But our life has always been about each other. The last few years we have been in some sense forced back together. We had to take our masks off and deal with each other unprotected. Fortunately, what we found when the masks came off, was the person we fell in love with. Laury keeps saying being together now feels like "our first marriage", she then says, "I mean when we were first married."

We can never know if we had to go through this to regain this closeness, but it is nice to have it again either way.

All our Love.

Wednesday, 5/20/2015 — Why?

"Understanding is the first step to acceptance, and only with acceptance can there be recovery." - J.K. Rowling, Harry Potter And The Goblet Of Fire

Laury and I got up early yesterday to head down to the U of C for clinic. We arrived a little ahead of schedule so we walked over to Starbucks to get Laury a Latte. After checking in at the clinic we waited a few minutes before Laury was taken back to get her blood drawn and dressing changed. I stayed in the waiting area because I found out last week that there is no place for me to sit in the small room where they take Laury. After several minutes Laury reappeared. She explained that the reason it took so long was that the nurse this week was Helena and she hadn't seen her in a while and they had a lot to catch up on.

Laury and I waited a few more minutes in the waiting area and then we were taken back to the exam room. Dr. Odenike came in shortly after that and immediately told Laury her blood numbers were looking great. Laury's White, Red, Hemoglobin and Platelets were virtually unchanged from last week. The blood chemistry results were not back but Dr. Odenike expected them to be stable, as well, so she reduced Laury's steroid dose to 10mg every other day. Dr. Odenike went on to say that next week, if everything remained stable, she will take Laury off the IV magnesium and anti-fungal and remove the Hiccman line. If the Hiccman line is removed next Tuesday it will be one week short of being in a year. Dr. Odenike also said that starting in June we can come to clinic every other week instead of once a week. Dr. Odenike says everything is looking great and she is pleased with where Laury is in the process.

Laury asked Dr. Odenike if she could, while wearing gloves and a mask, weed her gardens. Dr. Odenike got very serious and sat down next to Laury and said, "I know you are feeling better. It is hard to understand when things have gone so well how things can go so bad. I see the other side all the time." Dr. Odenike went on to explain to Laury why working in the dirt is not good for her right now. Even though Laury has a normal number of white blood cells in her system these cells are not strong enough to fight infections. Dr. Odenike said that Laury is similar to someone who has AIDS. The white blood cells have a protein called CD4+ T that fights infections. The AIDS virus strips this protein and makes the patient vulnerable to every virus and bacteria found in our environment. Dr. Odenike said that all of the immune suppression drugs Laury is on, plus the steroids, has lowered her CD4+ T number. The normal measurement for the CD4+ T is around 2,000. The last time Laury's level was checked was in December and her level was 120. A reading under a level of 200 is considered to be severe immune suppressed and in danger. This is why Laury has to wear the mask and is not allowed to dig in the dirt. Any small bacteria in the dirt could cause Laury great harm. Normally these bacteria would not bother us because our bodies can naturally repel them, but with the low CD4+ T, Laury cannot.

Laury said afterwards that she knew that Dr. Odenike would say no to the weeding but it was good to be reminded why. Dr. Odenike ordered the blood test to check the CD4+ T level to see where Laury is at for next week. Once Laury is off the Prograf, her numbers should start to come up, but she will still have to be careful. Dr. Odenike said maybe by the end of summer Laury will be able to dig in the garden.

Sometimes we need to know the why to make the directions easier to follow.

All our Love.

Tuesday, 5/26/2015 – Forgetting how to wait

"Waiting is one of the things that human beings cannot do well, though it is one of the essential things we must do successfully if we are to know happiness. We are impatient for the future and try to craft it with our own powers, but the future will come as it comes and will not be hurried." - Dean Koontz, Odd Interlude: A Special Odd Thomas Adventure

Today was a clinic day. Laury and I left the house at 5:30am and the traffic moved along quickly enough to get us to the U of C a little after six thirty. After parking we walked over to Starbucks and got Laury a Latte. Latte in hand we walked to the clinic and checked in. There was only one other person in the waiting area and we figured this would mean Laury would be taken back shortly for her blood draw and dressing change. After an hour and half waiting we realized that this was not going to be a good morning for getting in and out in a hurry. The long wait for the blood draw dropped us out of Dr. Odenike's queue for our eight thirty appointment. The room was available for us at eight thirty, but Laury was still getting her blood drawn so the technician took the next patient and we had to get back in line.

The wait seemed more arduous this morning. Laury said to me, "It is like we have forgotten how to wait." We finally saw Dr. Odenike a little after ten.

Laury's numbers continue to be stable or improving. Dr. Odenike left the steroid dose the same but took Laury off the IV anti-fungal and is putting her back on the oral version.

If Laury's liver numbers are not negatively impacted by the oral anti-fungal they are going to remove the Hiccman line at our visit next week. Laury will also start getting her immunizations at the next visit. The first of these is her Tetanus shot; we don't have the schedule for the remaining immunizations yet.

We are also moving to every other week clinic visits after June 2nd. On June 16th the doctors are going to do the one year bone marrow biopsy. Both of these next two visits will mean a lot of waiting. I hope Laury and I haven't forgotten how to sit patiently and enjoy being together and noticing the special happenings around us.

All our Love.

CHAPTER SEVENTEEN

June

Monday, 6/1/2015 – Anniversaries

"The question is not what you look at, but what you see." - Henry David Thoreau

A wise friend once told me that anniversaries of events are significant. Our mind attaches something important to the event and even if we don't recognize it our subconscious will. Over the last few months there have been many anniversaries of significant events. Yesterday was my birthday. I am not saying that in of itself that my birthday is a significant event, but it did force me to think about all that has happened since my last birthday.

My brother and a few friends called to wish me a happy birthday. Each of them commented on what a year it had been since last time they wished me happy birthday. Each of these calls made me stop and think. How did I feel a year ago? We were days away from Laury entering the hospital, busy with working out all the last minute details for a month away from home. Was this last year the worst year of our lives or perhaps the best? It is hard to have a definite answer.

I would not wish anyone to have to go through what Laury went through last year. It was not fun. There were times when Laury and I wished things were different and we didn't have to live this way. However, in many ways it was the best year of our lives. Laury is now cancer free. The shadow that was over us for the last nineteen years is gone. Removing that threat from our lives has to make the previous year one of our best ever.

This is the way my mind goes when I look back at the last year. Days of hardship, pain, worry, suffering and great loss. Yet, I also remember excitement, closeness, joy, love. The truth is that the past year was both: our best and our worst. I don't know how long these anniversaries will elicit deep pondering. I know that I view life differently now than I did last year. Some thoughts are practical, like washing my hands. Others are emotional, like always taking time to be grateful. I know that Laury and I have never been closer. I hope that my next birthday will find us as in love as we are now. I think it will.

All our Love.

Wednesday, 6/3/2015 – Emotional journey

"Man himself is a great deep, whose very hairs Thou numberest, O Lord, and they fall not to the ground without Thee. And yet are the hairs of his head easier to be numbered than his feelings, and the beatings of his heart." - Augustine of Hippo

Yesterday was a day of many emotions. The first emotion encountered was frustration at the traffic; it took an hour and a half to get to clinic. The second was impatience while waiting to get a package of parking passes. It seemed like from the very start the day was going to be one of many differing emotions. We arrived at the clinic a little after seven and checked in. The woman behind the counter told us we were second in line to be taken back to have Laury's blood drawn. When we sat down to wait I looked over at the woman who was ahead of us and noticed she was the same woman who had been ahead of us last week and had taken so long that it threw our schedule off. I could tell Laury was a little uptight so I mentioned to her it was the same woman in front of us as last week and Laury said, "Maybe I should just go to the lab and have them take the blood from my arm." Laury walked up to the desk and told the woman we were going to go to the lab instead of waiting for someone to take her blood from her main line.

We walked over to the lab and after a short wait they took Laury back. When we arrived back at the doctor's waiting area, Pam, the nurse, was waiting for us. Pam said she had been looking for us because she wanted to make sure she got Laury back to get her blood drawn right away so we didn't go through what happened last week. Laury thanked Pam and said she had already gotten her blood draw. Laury then asked Pam about the removal of her Hiccman line. Dr. Odenike told Laury last week that they would take the line out at today's visit. There had been some confusion over where and when the removal would take place, but the last thing Laury was told was that it would be handled by one of the nurses in the clinic. Laury told this to Pam and she said she would check and get back to us. Pam came back a few minutes later and told us that they couldn't take the line out in the clinic because it was minor surgery.

Laury and I became frustrated and Laury said she wanted the line out today. Shortly after that our pager went off and we went back to the room to meet with Dr. Odenike. When Dr. Odenike came in, Laury asked Dr. Odenike about having her line removed and Laury told her about the confusion over where the procedure would take place. Dr. Odenike said, "Oh man, I am going to have a cow! Nobody paged me. They could have simply asked me." Dr. Odenike left the room to page Paula, her nurse, to find out if the procedure had been scheduled. A few minutes later Paula came in and said yes, the procedure had been scheduled and we simply had to go to the seventh floor of the hospital after our visit with Dr.

Odenike and check in. After receiving this news we all were able to calm down and focus on the rest of our visit with Dr. Odenike.

Dr. Odenike went over Laury's blood numbers. A couple of the numbers dropped a bit from last week. Dr. Odenike was not concerned, she said it could be the reduction in the steroids. Steroids can give a bit of a bump up in the numbers and when you drop the steroids the numbers may take a few weeks to return to normal. Dr. Odenike does want Laury to have her blood checked next week to see if everything comes back up.

I asked Dr. Odenike if the Lymphocyte Panel test results were back. She pulled up the results on the screen and showed them to us. Laury's CD4+ level is 164. The normal range is between 550 and 1,200. Dr. Odenike said that anything below 200 is considered severely immune deficient. What this means is that Laury is still at great risk of catching what Dr. Odenike called an "opportunistic infection". These are caused by bacteria and fungus in the environment that our body fights off every day. But because Laury's system is so weak, hers cannot fight back. Once again Dr. Odenike got very serious when she said to Laury that she understands the importance of gardening to Laury's emotional and spiritual and physical healing but she could not approve of Laury being in the garden right now. It is simply too risky.

After we left Dr. Odenike's office we got on the elevator to go to the hospital. I asked Laury how she was feeling, thinking perhaps she was getting nervous about the procedure to pull her Hiccman line. Instead Laury said to me, "What Dr. Odenike told me about gardening right now scared me. I guess I need to buy some more beads." I could tell she was sad. The best analogy I can imagine for what Laury is feeling is if a doctor told me I couldn't work in my shop. It is one thing to have someone come over and do something for you; the job gets done. It is another thing not to be able to participate in the activity. For me working in the shop is not just about the end result, the process is as important. I am sure gardening for Laury is the same way.

After Laury and I checked in at the hospital and were given our pager we sat in the waiting room overlooking the city. The view hadn't changed much since we were here a year ago. The same Purple Martins I used to watch were chasing bugs around the hot air exhaust of the power plant next to the hospital. The parking garage was completed, and the workers and construction cranes gone, but for the most part nothing had changed. Laury and I sat there for a while in silence then I finally said, "It feels strange to be sitting here again." Laury agreed and we both admitted that we were not sure what emotions we were feeling. I think it will be awhile before Laury and I have the emotions sorted out.

After a short wait our pager went off and we were escorted down to the procedure room. The nurse told us that the procedure would take place right in the room and the doctor would be in shortly. Laury was concerned that it might be painful to have the Hiccman line removed because it had been in so long. When he came in the doctor said that no, Laury shouldn't feel a thing other than some tugging. I sat next to the bed while the doctor worked away. It wasn't the most comfortable situation for me and I couldn't watch the entire process. The doctor did have some trouble getting the line out and Laury ended up with two stitches. After the procedure was complete Laury said to the doctor, "I think this was harder for you than it was for me." The doctor asked us if we wanted to see the line one more time before he disposed of it. We said yes and I was amazed at how much of the line had been inside Laury. Earlier in the week Laury said to me as I was flushing her lines, "I bet you won't miss having to do this every day." I said I wouldn't but there was something sacred and intimate about the process that I would miss.

We drove home in silence and Laury went straight to the couch to take a nap when we got home. It was an emotional day. I think that some of what we have gone through is just now hitting us and the emotions don't always make sense. I think it is good that Laury and I recognize this and are willing to voice what we are feeling. It might take us a while to sort it all out but we will get there. It is just another part of this journey.

All our Love.

Monday, 6/8/2105 – Knowing and understanding

"You think you want to know something, and then once you do, all you can think about is erasing it from your mind." - Sue Monk Kidd, The Secret Life Of Bees

Laury and I have eagerly watched Laury's blood numbers for over a year now. Sometimes they brought good news, and sometimes disappointment. We were never sure what to expect or how we would react to a particular set of blood numbers, or if I would react the same way as Laury.

Laury admitted over the weekend that her latest numbers had bothered her. She knew something was bugging her since our last visit with Dr. Odenike but she couldn't put her finger on it. On Saturday after we got back from getting our hair cut Laury said to me, "I know now what has been bothering me." Laury went on to tell me that seeing her CD4+ number so low really scared her. She said her mind immediately went to "Here I am a year out from transplant and I am still really low and at risk. What if I still have Graph versus Host disease?" I reminded her that the main reason this number is so low is because of the medications she is on and they don't have anything to do with GVHD.

Laury then said, "That is why I hate seeing my numbers sometimes, I never know where the numbers are going to take my head."

I understand this completely. There were times when I would view the numbers and feel fear or disappointment and I would be concerned about how to talk to Laury about it. We are always reminded by Dr. Odenike that the numbers are only part of the story. How Laury looks and feels is another part of the story, too. We really want all the parts of the story to be saying the same thing, but sometimes they disagree. It is then, when this mismatch of information occurs we can take ourselves into different places emotionally.

I was glad Laury got to what was bothering her and shared it with me. When we are on the same page emotionally this journey is a lot easier.

All our Love.

Tuesday, 6/9/2015 – Here we are again

"I know enough of the world now to have almost lost the capacity of being much surprised by anything" - Charles Dickens, David Copperfield

I am writing this post from room 10052 of the University of Chicago Hospital. Laury was admitted this afternoon. Laury and I had gone to the clinic in Naperville to have Laury's blood checked. Dr. Odenike wanted to check Laury's blood to make sure the dip last week was only that - a blip. We waited for the results of the CBC and the numbers were really good. Laury's white count was back up and her platelets were back to 120,000 and her hemoglobin remained at 13. These are very good numbers and we were happy and headed home. As part of the blood tests they do a blood chemistry to look at the liver and kidney functions. After being home about an hour Paula, Dr. Odenike's nurse called to say that Laury's kidney function numbers were high and they wanted Laury to get a bag of fluids. We called the infusion center in Naperville and they got us in right away. Laury received a liter of fluids and we went back home. About an hour later Paula called again to say that Jean, the nurse practitioner, wanted to have Laury admitted to the hospital.

I asked Paula why and she said that Laury's Prograf level was very high and they wanted to make sure her kidneys were functioning properly. Paula went on to say that they wanted to do some additional tests and keep an eye Laury for a few days. Paula said the hospital would call when they had a room ready for us. I had to break the news to Laury, and as you can imagine she was very angry. She feels like someone dropped the ball and should have told us her Prograf numbers were high last week. She did not want to go back to the hospital, but here we are.

The doctors are going to do some more blood tests and a kidney ultrasound tonight to make sure everything is OK. It could be something as simple as Laury has not been drinking enough fluids.

I will post more as I know more. Right now Laury is trying to deal with her anger and I am trying to figure out what to say to her. I don't think either one of us is succeeding right now.

All our Love.

Wednesday, 6/10/2015 – Go with the flow

"The only way to make sense out of change is to plunge into it, move with it, and join the dance." - Alan W. Watts

Last night ended on a much better note. Dr. Pettit was the on-call doctor last night and came in to see Laury. Laury was glad to see her and was able to be honest with Dr. Pettit and vent and listen. Dr. Pettit assured Laury that this was nothing bad, but because her numbers were out of whack, the doctors wanted her in the hospital to make it right. Dr. Pettit said that most likely the re-introduction of the Noxafil put some stress on Laury's kidneys and caused them not to process the Prograf as effectively as they had. This caused the Prograf in her system to go up, which in turn messed up her Potassium. Dr. Pettit went on to say all of this is easily fixed by flushing the kidneys and reducing the amount of Prograf Laury is taking.

Laury's Prograf level was high last week and the dosage should have been reduced. No one called us to give Laury a new prescription so the Prograf had been building up. Laury was initially upset that someone dropped the ball. However, at around 8:00pm, Laury got a call on her cell phone from Dr. Odenike. It was 2:00am in Nigeria where she was and Dr. Odenike got an email that Laury had been admitted. She emailed back to find out why and when Dr. Odenike discovered the cause she realized that she had missed checking Laury's chemistry before she left. Dr. Odenike felt so bad she called Laury to apologize. After hearing Dr. Odenike's voice Laury cried and said that she could no longer be angry and couldn't believe Dr. Odenike called her.

Later in the evening we watched the fireworks show from Navy Pier out our window.

This morning a technician came in and gave Laury an ultrasound of her kidneys and bladder. The results show that everything is normal. The doctors stopped by later and told Laury and me that they are going to keep her here one more day to make sure everything comes back down to normal. The doctor said that all the numbers were already recovering and he had no reason to believe that she will not be going home tomorrow.

Laury admitted that some of her anger was fear. It is hard not to be afraid when you get admitted to the hospital. We have been here so many times that I sometimes forget it is still a big deal. Laury and I talked this morning about how we each could have handled the situation better. We are not perfect but we are getting better.

Thank you all for your wonderful thoughts and prayers. Once again you made this journey so much easier for us.

All our Love.

Thursday, 6/11/2015 – Balance and direction

"Any order is a balancing act of extreme precariousness." - Walter Benjamin, Illuminations: Essays and Reflections

Laury and I are home. Laury's numbers continued to improve and after a second bag of magnesium the hospital sent us on our way. We need to go back to 10 Central on Saturday to have Laury's blood checked to make sure everything is still moving in the right direction.

What we learned again, that balancing Laury's blood is very difficult and more of an art than science. Today, again the doctor reiterated that the Noxafil caused the Prograf to go up and the Prograf caused the potassium to go high. Today Laury's blood numbers were down - her white count was below 2, so the nurse gave her a shot of Neupogen, something Laury hasn't needed for a few months. The doctor said her blood counts are down because of all the fluids they were pushing.

Sometimes I think the doctors must feel like the little boy with his finger in the dike; every time they get one thing fixed it breaks something else. So to some extent we start again. The doctor took Laury off several medications and they are going to re-introduce them as Laury's kidney numbers improve. I think it will be a few weeks before everything is back to "normal".

Once again we were taught to pay attention to any little detail or change in how Laury is feeling. Looking back Laury had some signs that things weren't right: a shaky hand, more tired, looking like she had lost weight. All of these were pointing to her blood being out of order. This morning I read to Laury the Caring Bridge Journal from this time last year. We have come so far but we are not there yet. The journey continues as we try to balance out Laury's medications and blood again. But we are still all together and heading in the right direction.

All our Love.

Friday, 6/12/2015 — A day of birth

"He allowed himself to be swayed by his conviction that human beings are not born once and for all on the day their mothers give birth to them, but that life obliges them over and over again to give birth to themselves." - Gabriel Garcia Marquez, Love in the Time of Cholera

A year ago tonight Laury received her new chance at life in the form of a small bag of donated stem cells. Laury and I talked about how we wanted to mark this anniversary. Many people who have bone marrow transplants call this day their second birthday. It certainly makes sense, but Laury's life didn't begin again a year ago. Every day for the last year I have been thankful for that small bag of life that was given by a stranger. Every day I look at Laury and I am filled with love and gratitude that she is still here with me.

Today is another one of those days. I spent the day at home. I called in sick, really worn out from this last hospital stay. I think that I just wanted to be with Laury all day all to myself.

Laury and I didn't do anything special but just spent time together and took a long nap. No special dinner or party- just the two of us doing what we like most in the world, spending time together. Maybe some year Laury and I will take a trip or have a party but this year we are content to just rest and be together. I know that I have been reborn over the last year. I look at things differently than before the transplant. I know Laury is still trying to fully come to grips with what she has been through.

This has been a remarkable journey; one that we have shared with all of you. Laury and I wanted to make sure that today of all days we remembered to thank all of you. You all have been with us on this journey our strength and our support. We could not have gotten this far without all of your help. So thank you all again, on this Laury's first birthday.

All our Love.

CHAPTER EIGHTEEN

The Final Post

Friday, 7/17/2015 – The final post

"In normal life we hardly realize how much more we receive than we give, and life cannot be rich without such gratitude. It is so easy to overestimate the importance of our own achievements compared with what we owe to the help of others." - Dietrich Bonhoeffer, Letters and Papers from Prison

I have decided that today will be my final post. I arrived at the decision watching Laury drive away this morning. Laury is off to yoga, something she is now doing five times a week, and then after yoga off to her Mom's. Laury is feeling and looking great- gaining more muscle and emotional strength every day.

While Laury and I both know that she is not completely out of the woods we also realize that most of great dangers are now in our past. The journey doesn't end it just changes. Laury and I will continue on this journey until the day we die. I look forward to every step.

This last year and half has been a painful and wonderful experience. There were times of great loss and great happiness. Things will never be the same. We are living in a "new normal". One thing has remained constant through it all– love. The love I have for Laury has only increased and the love this community has showed us has been amazing.

When I started the posts they were to help cut down on the number of phone calls to bring family up to date on Laury's condition. The posts then grew into a community and a way to communicate Laury's progress to our friends and family. But the community grew to become much more; a family of love. I wanted to post to let you all know what was going on, but I also wanted to know what you thought. We gained so much strength and comfort from your responses. We grew to depend on them.

Laury and I know that we can never thank you all enough for your love and support throughout the last year. Over the last month Laury has asked me to read to her some of the posts and your responses. She doesn't remember everything that happened and it is still too hard for her to read the posts herself. Laury and I often cry not only at what I wrote but also how you all responded. We were always held in love, we knew it then and we know it now.

I have found the posts to be at times a lot of work. Finding the right quote sometimes took longer than writing the words. I tried explaining as much as I understood about what we were going through, but also how we felt about it. It was important to Laury from the beginning that we were honest in our feelings with you. I have never been as open with my feelings as I have been with this community. I wrote from my heart. It was sometimes very scary to share. You all made me realize that there are many more benefits from taking the risk and sharing than holding it in. I will miss posting and reading your comments. This part of the journey is ending.

Laury and I want to thank you again from the bottom of our hearts. This community carried us; we could not have done it without you. I hope you all know how much Laury and I love all of you.

Thank you.

All our Love.

EPILOGUE

Our journey continues. Even though I am not posting every day, Laury and I try to maintain a connection with our Caring Bridge friends and family.

I know that the journey Laury and I are on will not end until we die. The experience of the transplant will be with us forever.

The doctors, nurses, and technicians of University of Chicago and Northwestern Cancer Center are some of the most amazing people we have ever met. To go through a transplant you have to have the upmost faith in your doctors. But it also really helps if you like them and can connect on a personal level. Every person we met seemed to be truly concerned about Laury. We could not have asked for better care. It is a tough job. Laury and I know that not every story these doctors deal with has a happy ending. I think that is why when they do have a success like Laury they want to celebrate with us.

Laury and I were constantly surprised at the outpouring of love showed us by our Caring Bridge community. They carried us. The comments showed such concern and love it was amazing to hear what the community had to say. I wanted to share our wins but I was also not afraid to show our defeats. Every time Laury and I needed the right words to lift us they would appear from someone on the site. Sometimes it was comforting to just see someone was still reading and aware of what we were going through. Laury and I never felt alone. I cannot thank our community enough – it saved our lives.

So much of the healing process is physical, but as we knew going in and were constantly reminded, healing involves the body, mind and soul. The journey tested me an all fronts. There were times when I was exhausted, frustrated and angry. But I kept looking at Laury and her presence and love kept me going.

I thank God every day that Laury is still with me.

About the Author

Dan Hartman resides in Naperville, Illinois with his wife, Laury where they enjoy practicing yoga, taking walks and spending time together. His job as an Information Architect requires Dan to carefully observe and understand how people interact with technology. Dan's daily writings on Caring Bridge, detailing his observations and experiences as his wife's full-time caregiver during her 2014 bone marrow transplant, are the basis for this book. Dan's writings are an honest journal of their life before, during and after the transplant. He hopes you find inspiration in Laury's story.

Made in the USA
Columbia, SC
27 September 2021